THE
COMEDIAN
AS
CONFIDENCE
MAN

Humor in Life and Letters Series

*A complete listing of the books in this series
can be found at the back of this volume.*

General Editor

SARAH BLACHER COHEN
State University of New York, Albany

Advisory Editors

JOSEPH BOSKIN
Boston University

ALAN DUNDES
University of California, Berkeley

WILLIAM F. FRY, JR.
Stanford University Medical School

DON L. F. NILSEN
Arizona State University

JUNE SOCHEN
Northeastern Illinois University

THE
COMEDIAN
AS
CONFIDENCE
MAN

Studies in Irony Fatigue

Will Kaufman

WAYNE STATE UNIVERSITY PRESS DETROIT

00   99   98   97   5   4   3   2   1

Library of Congress Cataloging-in-Publication Data

Kaufman, Will.
    The comedian as confidence man : studies in irony fatigue / Will
Kaufman.
        p.   cm. — (Humor in life and letters series)
    Includes bibliographical references and index.
    ISBN 0-8143-2657-9 (alk. paper)
    1. Irony in literature. 2. Comic, The, in literature. I. Title.
II. Series: Humor in life and letters.
PN56.I65K38 1997
809'.918—dc20   96-20848

FOR SARAH AND REUBEN

Well, against a joke there's no argument,
and so I came to you with the proposal.

FRANZ KAFKA, *The Castle*

Laughing at evil means not preparing oneself to
combat it, and laughing at good means denying the power
through which good is self-propagating.

UMBERTO ECO, *The Name of the Rose*

I'm not a comedian.

LENNY BRUCE

Smile when you say that.

GARY COOPER, in Lewis Lighton's film of
Owen Wister's *The Virginian*

Contents

Acknowledgments 9

Introduction 11

1
Sinclair Lewis, Garrison Keillor, and the Dangers of Grumbling through Minnesota 19

2
Ben Franklin and Herman Melville: The Comedian as Confidence Man 41

3
Lenny Bruce: "I'm not a comedian" 70

4
Bill Hicks: "Bob, they're just jokes" 113

5
Kurt Vonnegut: "I had to laugh like hell" 147

6
Mark Twain: "My hated nom de plume*"* 187

7
Conclusion: A Bad Case of Irony Fatigue 232

Notes 243

List of Sources 259

Acknowledgments

I wish to thank Clive Meachen at the University College of Wales, Aberystwyth, who supervised the earliest versions of this study as a doctoral thesis; also A. Robert Lee at the University of Kent at Canterbury, Sanford Pinsker at Franklin and Marshall College, and Thomas Grant at the University of Hartford, who in their readings of the thesis and its later versions, respectively, provided me with invaluable guidance. Sarah Keates at the British Library was a true wizard in conjuring up of all sorts of source material for me, while Wilf Hunter at the University of Central Lancashire redefined the word *patience* in his laborious transcriptions of American video material into British format. My former student Mat Tate introduced me to the comedy of Bill Hicks before it was too late; and I must thank him for that pleasure, along with the following people who either provided me with, or directed me to, information about Hicks's life and work: Charles Brand, Seamus Cassidy, William Cook, Paul Dawson, Lucy Eagle, Rupert Edwards, John Lahr, Duncan Strauss, and—especially—Colleen McGarr and Kevin Booth. I am likewise grateful to Mary Reese Hicks and the Estate of Bill Hicks, for permission to quote from unpublished material. My thanks go to Elizabeth Burns for the indexing, and finally to my colleagues in the Department of Cultural Studies, University of Central Lancashire, whose willingness to shoulder an increased workload released me to complete this book on sabbatical. Portions of this work have appeared in *Thalia: Studies in Literary Humor* and in *Revista de Estudios Norteamericanos*.

Introduction

In Kurt Vonnegut's *Breakfast of Champions*, the comic writer Kilgore Trout finds himself in a situation perhaps familiar to many comedians: "After Trout became famous, of course, one of the biggest mysteries about him was whether he was kidding or not." His response to the endless questioning as to whether he could be trusted—"whether he was kidding or not"—is the work of a trickster determined to preserve the inscrutability of his confidence game at all costs:

> He told one persistent questioner that he always crossed his fingers when he was kidding.
> "And please note," he went on, "that when I gave you that priceless piece of information, my fingers were crossed."
> And so on.
> He was a pain in the neck in a lot of ways.[1]

It is fitting that Wayne C. Booth should have used this passage as one of the many chapter epigraphs in his study, *The Rhetoric of Irony*, which explores the strategies of ironic play in literature—grossly put, the strategies of saying one thing and meaning another—for purposes of persuasion and self-defense. My intention in this book is to focus on the consequences of that play for the comedian who, while absolutely committed to the impression of play, at the same time wishes to be taken seriously as a social critic. His entire state is an ironic one, inescapable as long as he wishes to maintain the dual role of the critic at warning and the comedian at play. The "pain in the neck," however, is not reserved solely for the audience who might drive themselves crazy in attempting to grasp "the truth" or "the meaning" or "the message" behind the mask of play (assuming they can in the first place confidently identify an utterance *as* playful); there is a pain in the neck for the comedian as well. After all, he has a necessary masquerade to keep up with, his requisite confidence game: "Only kidding, folks." The consequences of his failure are easy to imagine. As George Bernard Shaw said of Samuel Clemens, "He has to put things in such a way as to make people who would otherwise hang him believe he is joking."[2]

But what might be the wages of the comedian's effort to succeed, let alone the success itself? Samuel Clemens had no choice but to become the fiction, Mark Twain, at great cost to his everyday and historical identity, as his biography shows. His overtly dual persona, and the legendary crisis it caused in him, is perhaps the starkest example imaginable of the conflict between the serious-minded critic and the necessarily playful comedian. Of all the figures studied in this book, Clemens/Twain most readily represents not merely any old ironic state, but the particular ironic *identity* of the critic-as-comedian. It is almost palpable in the image of the two conflicting personae in one shared body—hence the title of Justin Kaplan's dual biography of this single figure, *Mr. Clemens and Mark Twain*. Few comedians have possessed such a well-defined alter ego as Clemens had in Twain; but, as I intend to show, it is likely that many will have embodied a similar conflict. As long as social critics aim to be identified as comedians (or vice versa), their very identities are ironic. They have little choice but to become ultimately untrustworthy tricksters—in Johan Huizinga's words, necessary "false players" or "cheats" in the game of public relations and communication—for the alternative would be to face the noose that awaits the earnest iconoclast, what Huizinga calls the "spoil-sport": ostracization, derision, or the willful deafness that so often faces the deadly serious critic who cries out to be heard unambiguously.[3] Comedians are committed to irony in its broadest sense, keeping open their escape route through the creation of abiding confidence in the *possibility*, at the very least, that in the end they are saying one thing and meaning another—in a word, that they are *joking*. The successful comedian is necessarily a successful confidence man, and he keeps his inscrutable game going through maintaining a web of ironic tension between falsehood and earnestness, play and criticism, defense and attack, balancing his conflicting and simultaneous urges to be heeded and indulgently dismissed.

My study of American comedy in particular has led me to notice an affliction shared, to varying degrees, by too many comedians to be ignored. Sustaining the comic masquerade apparently does take its toll, and the symptoms can be something more than a mere pain in the neck. If a comedian were to admit in confidence, "Doc, I have this problem . . ." and proceed to outline the symptoms I explore in this book, I would be fairly confident of my diagnosis: "Looks to me like a bad case of irony fatigue." I have coined this phrase—*irony fatigue*—to account for at least one reason why a comedian may lose his willingness or ability to keep up with his necessary confidence game. How pervasive is irony fatigue in American comedy? Pervasive enough to be remarked upon by Kurt Vonnegut, who has observed: "For whatever reason, American humorists or satirists or whatever you wish to call them, those who choose to laugh rather than weep about demoralizing information, become intolerably unfunny pessimists if they live past a certain age."[4]

Now, I would not choose to restrict this condition to American humorists and their work, although my own academic expertise is restricted to this fellowship. I sense that there is more than a touch of irony fatigue affecting the English music hall comedian Archie Rice in John Osborne's *The Entertainer*. King Lear's "poor fool . . . hang'd" might also have succumbed to it—in a recent British production (1995), under Jude Kelly's direction, the fool hangs *himself* just as Cordelia is hanged. Moreover, theoreticians of social play such as Huizinga and Gregory Bateson have ranged far afield in "the real world" to describe the consequences of ultimately dispensing with a requisite mask of play in social settings as diverse as western Europe, Africa, and the Andaman Islands. They don't mention irony fatigue per se, nor do they restrict their attention to professional comedians; but they provide a wealth of instances in which the urge to spoil the sport leads to outraged retribution all over the planet. It is this *urge* that concerns me here, especially among those practitioners whose diversionary—and defining—modus operandi is to make people laugh, whatever their critical intent.

This urge has, explicitly or otherwise, concerned other theorists as well: Max Eastman, who back in the 1930s explored in his *Enjoyment of Laughter* the implicit laws of humor that rely on the shared convention that all is in fun—even if the comedian might wish to suggest the opposite; Umberto Eco, whose analysis of the intermediary comic mask first described by Aristotle focuses on the licensed, *permitted* nature of comic subversion—implying the containment (and thus impotence) of comedy as a force for social change; students of discourse and rhetoric after Kierkegaard, such as Wayne Booth, Linda Hutcheon, Patrick Colfer, Susan Purdie, Benjamin De Mott, D. J. Enright, and C. Jan Swearingen, whose separate treatises on irony as a duplicitous discourse never blot out the image of the critic who might just want to damn the consequences and "say it straight"; political theorists such as Richard Rorty, John Seery, Daniel Conway, and—in all his enigmatic mastery—Thomas Mann, who in their various ways wrestle with the apparent dilemma: irony or political commitment. The problems of irony and frankness, deception and truth, commitment and evasion explored by this disparate group of thinkers—not all of them American—*do* inform the works of the eight American comedians who are the subjects of my study.

An awareness of these problems precedes my choice of the comedians who, to me, seem best to exemplify them. There is no other reason why this book should be devoted particularly to the study of Sinclair Lewis, Garrison Keillor, Ben Franklin, Herman Melville, Lenny Bruce, Bill Hicks, Kurt Vonnegut, and Mark Twain. There is, of course, no compunction upon me to rely on an all-male stable; but I have deliberately not set about a project of either establishing or reconstructing a comedic canon. Rather, my choice of examples has been based on the immediacy with which these particular tricksters struck me as relevant (and revelatory) to the problems of irony fatigue. Perhaps, going the *Iron John* route, I could suggest that some unconscious form of male bonding has been in operation during the writing of this book. If so, I may as well admit it; but I would prefer to think that my choice of comedians is based on their exemplifying capacities as well as my own confidence in writing about them. I have chosen eight American comedians who have spoken most directly to me of the irony fatigue that apparently threatens the longevity of many a comic masquerade.

My designation of the comedian as confidence man comes not from the literary or historical type explored in the unapproachable studies by Gary Lindberg, Warwick Wadlington, Richard Hauck, and Susan Kuhlman—but rather from the problems of deception and frankness fitfully explored by Melville in his last novel, *The Confidence-Man*. While to some degree this designation *might* commit me to an all-male group, my first fictional example is, after all my self-justification, a woman. Carol Kennicott, the sacrificial lamb of Sinclair Lewis's *Main Street*, deliberately avoids any association either with comedians or confidence men: she represents to me the critic who is not prepared to lie with a smile, and who, as a result, faces—like one of Huizinga's "spoil-sports"—the wrath of a community that will not tolerate frankness. I open my discussion with *Main Street*, for—as Max Eastman implied—there is a lesson for any critic who defiantly ignores the injunction of Gary Cooper in *The Virginian*: "Smile when you say that." Carol Kennicott learns this lesson following her exile from Gopher Prairie, Minnesota, whence she returns only after having learned to put her faith in laughter as a critical shield, at whatever the cost to truth. In contrast to Carol Kennicott I offer the fictive personae of Lewis's fellow Minnesotan and self-avowed disciple, Garrison Keillor, who from the outset devotes his full attention to the creation of a duplicitous smoke screen in the stories and broadcasts from Lake Wobegon. These two contrasting figures open my exploration of the comedian's necessarily ironic identity and the price it exacts from that part of the comedian that wants to tell the truth—the straight-shooting critic—even as he is obliged to promise, "Only kidding, folks." It is not, apparently, an easy promise for a social critic to make, let alone to keep. But in Carol's fictional resistance to it, as in Keillor's factual irritation with it, one can detect the earliest signs of irony fatigue.

Assuming that all rules need an exception to prove them, I then look to Benjamin Franklin, a smiling hoaxer well into his eighth decade, who with equanimity could manipulate an ironic legacy from beyond the grave just as he could manipulate the impressions of his contemporaries with a clear and gleeful conscience. His *Autobiography* remained to vex a host of critics maddened either by the thought that it should dare to be taken seriously (such as Mark Twain, D. H. Lawrence, and some of my old American Lit. professors) or by the possibility that it was never so intended (such as Herman Melville and the scholars of the confidence man mentioned above). Franklin is the comedian as confidence man par excellence, the epitome of the "false player"—or so Melville depicts him in *Israel Potter*. But behind Melville's rendition of Franklin as a philanthropic master of deception is the unassailable fact that the same duplicitous mastery is also the weapon of Satan. It is a small step from the comic philanthropy of *Israel Potter* to the comic misanthropy of *The Confidence-Man*, wherein all of Franklin's comedic potential is as likely to be put to the service of an inscrutable evil as an inscrutable good. *The Confidence-Man* is Melville's ultimate disquisition into comedic mendacity, exploring the moral price of laughter and diversion as much as the practical futility of frankness. Franklin may have had the exceptional ability to keep his confidence game going with an undivided conscience until the end of a long life; but in *The Confidence-Man* Melville offers some speculation as to why other comedians may not be so fortunate, nor so undivided, in their subscription to the shiftiness of irony and the dubious promise of play.

With the terms of the discussion established in the first two chapters, I turn to one of the most notable of American comedy's divided unfortunates, Lenny Bruce, whose resistance to the requirements of play to which Franklin had so slyly adapted himself led directly to the fate of the unguarded iconoclast. And if, in *Main Street*, Carol Kennicott effectively declared, "I'm not a comedian," Lenny Bruce actually declared it *on* Main Street, to his great cost. With all his defiant instincts—his devotion to the frank spontaneity of the jazz and drug subcultures, his linguistic improvisations, his intention to lay bare the sexual and moral hypocrisies of the American middle class, his contempt for the totalizing consciousness of the Cold Warrior—it is perhaps not surprising that the requirements of professional comedic convention as handed down to him should have proved such a trial, with all their bases in the implied, the not-said, the naughty-but-nice. When Bruce turned his back on the indirections of comedy—indirections he had also inherited from the evasive traditions of eastern European Jewish humor —he stepped out from behind his comic mask, dropping the guise of the "false player" for the nakedness of the "spoil-sport." Such a move led directly from the comic stage into the American courtroom, where the saving duplicity of irony had to give way to the stark literalness of the law.

Lenny Bruce was overwhelmed by irony fatigue, in contrast to Benjamin Franklin, who was hardly, if ever, touched by it. Irony fatigue infected Melville enough for him to worry about its unchecked germ—irony itself—while Sinclair Lewis portrayed in *Main Street* a character who is ostracized through her determination never to catch it in the first place (no ironic identity: no irony fatigue). Even Keillor's mildest wish that he could sometimes exchange the writing of guarded humor for the pleasures of writing unguarded irritation is an indication that he is aware of his need to resist any further encroachment of irony fatigue, for the sake of his comic voice. Were he to lose that duplicitous voice—even in the 1990s—he could conceivably be silenced as Lenny Bruce was silenced in the 1960s. This is in fact what happened to the late Bill Hicks, a rising American comic star who in 1993 proved that censorship was still alive and kicking in the United States—nearly thirty years after the death of Lenny Bruce—in the guise of "reasonable" editorial procedure. I include Hicks in this study not only because I believe he was an American comic treasure worthy of far greater exposure than he has so far received but also because his case demonstrates the sad fate of American satire at the hands of contemporary network television. Bill Hicks had his share of irony fatigue, to be sure; but he was able to resist it enough to conform to the censorial demands of CBS, from whose David Letterman show he was nonetheless banned upon his twelfth appearance. On the one hand, Hicks was a true heir of Jonathan Swift, a savage idol-toppler with contempt for all mildly ironic diversions offered up by American television—in his words, "Lucifer's Dream Box." But on the other hand, his grudging willingness to submit to the censorial grooming of the Letterman producers is just one indication of the conflict he faced in matching his urge toward unfettered critical speech with his urge to be heard at all—or, at least, to be heard where it mattered the most: not on the free, though marginalized, cable channels, but in front of the largest, most consolidated audience possible. Contributing to Hicks's irony fatigue was the gall of having once more to edit that line, to modify that word, to disguise that reference in the interest of corporate sponsorship. The fact that he was censored *anyway*, after having conformed precisely to the demands of the Letterman producers and their corporate masters, suggests that there was more at stake, in his case, than the mere question of comedic longevity.

But that is, after all, the focus of this book: how long can a comedian keep up with the demands of ironic play in the face of an urge toward unambiguous criticism? All the examples mentioned so far—barring Franklin—demonstrate some degree of difficulty. If this suggests a wider trend, it is that noticed by Kurt Vonnegut, whose crucial observations about the fragility of the comic mask are among the most valuable ever uttered by an American practitioner. In one sense, he has devoted his entire writing career to the exploration of what it means to be a comedian in a world where frankness—however unbearable—is the only agent of awakening. "Jokesters," he says, "are all through when they find themselves talking about challenges so real and immediate and appalling to their listeners that no amount of laughter can make the listeners feel safe and perfectly well again."[5] Yet the highlighting of such challenges is precisely the object of social criticism; and as Vonnegut demonstrates in virtually all his novels, the momentarily saving grace of laughter—and the play that gives rise to it—may well lead directly to the "real," the "immediate," and the "appalling" verities that the comedian is obliged to ameliorate or conceal. Vonnegut has given the world a series of novels in which comedians and would-be comedians are doomed to confront the consequences of their play, and in doing so has illuminated the problems of irony fatigue more prolifically than any other American writer. For this reason he is central to this study, and as indispensable as Melville; for if *The Confidence-Man* asked in the nineteenth century whether a comedian, though "essentially a fool," might be "effectively a knave," such novels as *Mother Night*, *Cat's Cradle*, and *Breakfast of Champions* (among Vonnegut's other works) ask the same in the twentieth.[6]

But Vonnegut has his mentor, as the world knows. He meditates, he says, "with Mark Twain's mind."[7] He named his first son after the depressed Victorian-American iconoclast "who became a world citizen while necessarily disguised as Mark Twain"— the antipatriotic, God-hating misanthrope who cast himself as "an utterly winsome sort of teddy bear, in need of all the love he could get."[8] Clemens called Mark Twain "my hated nom de plume"; and he demonstrated this hatred, not only in his letters and private utterances but in a variety of his published writings. His damnation of a Connecticut Yankee's trickery, whether Hank Morgan's or that of a southern comedian transplanted to Hartford; the inconsistencies of Huck Finn's voice; the defeat of comedy at the hands of the law in *Pudd'nhead Wilson*—all reflect upon what I call the wrestling match between Samuel Clemens and his fictional alter ego, Mark Twain, from under whose necessary comedic shadow Clemens so often, and so desperately, wanted to escape. The examination of this battle draws to a close my exploration of irony fatigue in American comedy, but not before I am led to explore the condition in a more theoretical, less descriptive sense.

Thus, my conclusion relates the symptoms exhibited by my chosen American comedians to the problems of irony and commitment explicitly explored by John Seery, Daniel Conway, Richard Rorty, and Linda Hutcheon—all on the heels of Thomas Mann, whose autobiographical *Reflections of a Nonpolitical Man* and fictional *Confessions of Felix Krull, Confidence Man* respectively pit the crafty ironist against the direct political activist, and the guilty (though guilt-free) comedian against his charmed, benighted dupes. In considering the observations of these theorists, I hope to have illuminated one possible reason for the affliction first named in this conclusion, demonstrated by the eight comedians under discussion, and—perhaps—familiar to any serious critic who is under the abiding injunction, "Smile when you say that."

Sinclair Lewis, Garrison Keillor, and the Dangers of Grumbling through Minnesota

The words could have come from a Jacobean soliloquy lamenting the prevalence of deceit in social relations: "Disguises and lies, surprises and poisons, subversion—a looking-glass universe where nothing is ever as it seems." They could have come from the pages of a behavioral study—say, Eric Berne's *Games People Play*, or Erving Goffman's *The Presentation of the Self in Everyday Life*: "Deceivers have a way of coming between the evidence and the senses." They could have been written by a bitter aphorist condemning the inherent mendacity of the lowest of species, man: "In a world where deceit can be as successful as strength or speed, some animals make a living as impostors." They come in fact from a BBC nature program about the deceptions of the animal kingdom —such as those perpetrated by the pug-mouth caterpillar, masquerading as a twig; the leafy sea-dragon of the Sargasso Sea, donning a seaweed disguise for camouflage in order to eat "the fish that came to eat *it*"; or "the diva of the death act," the hog-nosed snake, with its "lolling tongue," "Shakespearean throes," and a mouth frightening away predators with "the smell of decay." Such trickery, of course, is no joke: "Animals whose disguises don't work, don't live to leave another generation."[1] With animals this is literally the case; with *most* humans, it would be an exaggeration.

But if the metaphor were extended almost intolerably, the case might be made for those humans for whom trickery is *precisely* a joke: comedians whose disguises don't work, don't live to leave another generation. As in many other contexts, Americans may look to the home truths of their popular culture for confirmation: go to Owen Wister's *The Virginian*. Hear the hero called a "son-of-a-bitch" over a poker game, and note his response as he draws his pistol: "'When you call me that, *smile!*'" The Virginian may not *deliberately* be paraphrasing Aristotle's dictum that the comic mask—however distorted and ugly—must not cause pain; but he knows that he has offered the critic "'the choice to back down or draw his steel.'"[2] The grinning "intermediary mask" of comic license, in Umberto Eco's words, is all that allows the violation of rules, conventions, and sensibilities; it is the guarantee that such violation is in jest.[3] Without this promise of play, and its acceptance as such, the comedian is guilty of mere outrage and assault. Hence Mark Twain's ancestor, in his burlesque autobiography: "He was as full of fun as he could be, and used to take his old sabre and sharpen it up, and get in a convenient place on a dark night, and stick it through people as they went by, to see them jump. He was a born humorist."[4] Without the "fun" he would be a rank assassin. With it, he is at worst a trickster, a loveable rogue, a confidence man. He may be playing a game—"only kidding, folks"—but his greatest comedic difficulty lies in *convincing* an audience that he is operating within the bounds of comic license, and that whatever the unspoken rules in a given situation, he is playing by them.

As Johan Huizinga noted in *Homo Ludens*, his study of play in human societies, the rules of play are transgressed at one's peril. The "spoil-sport" who refuses to play by the rules destroys the game and is vilified: "By withdrawing from the game he reveals the relativity and fragility of the play-world in which he had temporarily shut himself with others. He robs play of its *illusion*." It is less hazardous to be "the false player, the cheat" who makes believe—literally *creates the belief*—that he is playing by the rules. A given society, Huizinga says, is much more likely to forgive the successful cheat than the spoil-sport.[5] When this play world is the arena—literary, recorded, or live—in which the comedian challenges the sanctified hypocrisies and conventions of the very society in which he is forced to operate, whatever else he violates he must never trespass against what Max Eastman called "the first law of humor": this is the convention that "things can be funny only when we're in fun. There may be a serious thought or motive lurking underneath our humor. We may be only 'half in fun' and still funny. But when we are not in fun at all, when we are 'in dead earnest,' humor is the thing that is dead."[6] And if the humor is dead, where does that leave the humorist? In his place stands any one of those figures against whom any number of societies, according to Huizinga, are the most vindictive: "the spoil-sports, here called apostates, heretics, innovators, prophets, conscientious objectors, etc."[7] One might also add to the list those social critics whose bitterness or impatience with the status quo is matched by their refusal or inability to maintain an effective masquerade, whether of comedy or general deference. The load-bearing word here is *effective*, for some masquerades don't work. The fact of his having written a novel, and a comic one at that, was not enough to protect Salman Rushdie from the wrath of a particular outraged public. Even within an admittedly deceptive or fictive framework, there is ample room for the mask to slip. It is sometimes not enough to proclaim that you are only at play when you have too successfully convinced people otherwise.

Main Street: The Critic as Spoil-sport

Huizinga's *Homo Ludens* demonstrates in many ways how serious the assurance of play is taken among its practitioners and its objects, as well as the consequences of not taking that assurance seriously. At least one significant American novel also makes this its explicit subject. Sinclair Lewis may well have only *implied* that he was kidding when he published *Main Street* as a novel rather than as a polemical essay, changed the name of Sauk Center, Minnesota, to Gopher Prairie, and put his earnest critical words into the mouth of a fictional iconoclast named Carol Kennicott. This did not protect him from immediate public outrage upon the book's appearance—not that he really cared, since he had never explicitly projected himself as a comedian, satirist though he was. However, he was aware of the hazards of too much critical honesty and too little apparent play, demonstrating it in the fate of his sincere rebel against the complacency of small-town America. Carol Kennicott is one of Huizinga's spoil-sports, guilty of all the crimes he enumerates above; and Lewis knew this as he pitted her against the "comfortable tradition and sure faith" of Main Street. He suggested as much in the rhetorical question of the preface, which sarcastically refers to small-town America as "the climax of civilization": "Would he not betray himself an alien cynic who should otherwise portray Main Street, or distress the citizens by speculating whether there may not be other faiths?"[8] Better Carol than he; and so he condemns her to the defeat of the spoil-sport at the hands of an audience that will accept criticism as play—that is, as an apparent lie—or not at all. As Carol finds in the course of the novel, the rebellion she hopes to incite is actually against *her*, a "credulous, plastic, young" woman with a mission (7): "I'll get my hands on one of these prairie towns and make it beautiful" (11). When she heads toward Gopher Prairie on the old No. 7 way train, "grumbling through Minnesota," one of the most hateful words on her lips is "insincere" (24). By the end of the novel, however, she finds herself driven precisely to insincerity—to the dishonest impression of acceptance, signified by laughter, in a great betrayal of her critical spirit. She is a most unwilling false player, demonstrating the pitfalls of the critic who cannot lie. For this reason, she deserves some attention, as her story bears directly upon the relationship between social criticism and comedy, with its implicit mask of play.

The mediocrity and smugness of the American small-town ethos that Carol Kennicott attacks are, by her own admission, not amusing. "It is an unimaginatively standardized background . . . a rigid ruling of the spirit by the desire to appear respectable. It is contentment . . . the contentment of the quiet dead, who are scornful of the living for their restless walking. . . . It is dullness made God" (257). Such an ethos has been the target of American comedians from Mark Twain in Hadleyburg to Garrison Keillor in Lake Wobegon, but Carol finds that unlike such tricksters she is without strategy in her confrontation. She herself is an outsider, making a bull run at a "savorless people, gulping tasteless food, and sitting afterward, coatless and thoughtless, in rocking-chairs prickly with inane decorations, listening to mechanical music, saying mechanical things about the excellence of Ford automobiles, and viewing themselves as the greatest race in the world" (258). As she admits, she hasn't much of a sense of humor, which is most ironic, since the earliest of her many planned "reforms" is to infuse Gopher Prairie with "the power of play as well as the power of impersonal thought" (77).

What Carol eventually finds, however, is that the townspeople *do* know how to play—even if it isn't her kind of play—and that they do so at her expense. She *works* at making them play, badgering them into bobsled parties or snowball fights, nagging them into skiing or party games with an earnest, evangelical fervor in "an attack on Gopher Prairie's timidity in pleasure" (75). She attaches so much obvious significance to her mission that she alternately sees herself as "a great reformer" if she succeeds and a bitter failure if she doesn't (80). But Carol does not have the makings of a comedian or a prankster, exhausting herself in the effort of "creating hysterical parties" (81). She despises the comic sense of Gopher Prairie, "'the back-slapping jocosity that passes for humor here'" (327), aloof from the comic repartee across the store counters: "Carol had never been able to play the game of friendly rudeness; and now she was certain that she never would learn it" (102). She admits to herself that she is a bad actress, not only in the acknowl-edged play world of amateur dramatics but on the social stage as well, in the eyes of the townspeople: "They were a blurry theater-audience before which she self-consciously enacted the comedy of being the Clever Little Bride of Doc Kennicott" (48). Two of her three closest soul mates are the town's most earnest incomers, Guy Pollock, the lawyer who—to Carol's gratification—offers "no hu-morous remarks" (69), and Erik Valborg, the tortured aesthete who, Carol notes, "'has absolutely no sense of humor'" (327). And, it is with the greatest reluctance that Carol finds herself laughing at the mirage of a movie comedy, guilty at being diverted from her mis-sion of bringing the poetic sense to the "peasants" she had come "to bathe and encourage and adorn" (26): "For a second she loathed her laughter; mourned for the day when on her hill by the Mississippi she had walked the battlements with queens" (121).

Carol's greatest problem is in her own inability to lie, and in her failure to appreciate other people's lies, even if well meant. When her play fails and the local newspaper reports it as a glowing success, she muses ruefully, "'So kindly . . . so well meant, so neighborly—and so confoundedly untrue'" (223). In hiding her brief infatuation for Valborg, she condemns herself: "'I have be-come a liar. I'm snarled with lies and foggy analyses and desires—I who was clear and sure" (353). What Carol cannot accept is the pos-sibility that there are circuitous and deceptive means of implying the truth, and that her safety relies on her resorting to them. This is most apparent in her debates with Vida Sherwin and Sam Clark, re-spectively the local English teacher and hardware merchant, who, as it turns out, are Gopher Prairie's best false players, with much to teach Carol.

Sam has a valuable warning for Carol upon her arrival, which she is for the most part either unable or unwilling to heed. When Carol tells him, "'I want to see people as they are,'" Sam re-plies, "'Well, don't forget to see people as other folks see them as they are!'" (46). This expresses, among other things, a calculated

willingness to set aside what one might *know* for what one is willing to *imagine*—in critical terms, a hypocritical act that disgusts Carol, as she implies in another instance to Vida. Whether about art or
social criticism, Carol and Vida remain diametrically opposed:
"Carol tried to be eloquent regarding honesty of observation. Miss
Sherwin stood out for sweetness and a cautious use of the uncomfortable properties of light" (68). Vida's caution is Carol's anath-
ema. "'Think how much better you can criticize conventional
customs,'" Vida tells her, "'if you yourself live up to them, scrupu-
lously.'" Carol replies in contempt: "'Yes. I've heard that plea. It's a
good one. It sets revolts aside to cool. It keeps strays in the flock. To
word it differently: "You must live up to the popular code if you
believe in it; but if you don't believe in it, then you *must* live up to
it!"'" (359–60). And Carol damns Vida as a liar.

　　　Yet Carol is forced to respect this "liar" when she learns
the truth of Vida's cunning from Miles Bjornstam, the third of her
fellow iconoclasts: "'From all I can hear she's in everything and
behind everything that looks like a reform—lot more than most
folks realize. . . . Miss Sherwin is the secret boss, and nags all the
easy-going dames into doing something.'" Nevertheless, as a
"destroyer," Carol is not content with chipping away from the inside, as Vida is; she has more sympathy with Bjornstam's observation: "'Miss Sherwin's trying to repair the holes in this barnacle-
covered ship of a town by keeping busy bailing out the water. . . .
Me, I want to yank it up on the ways, and fire the poor bum of a
shoemaker that built it so it sails crooked, and have it rebuilt right,
from the keel up'" (116). Yet both Bjornstam and Carol suffer for
their openness, earning the opprobrium that forces them separately
into exile.

　　　Carol's unwillingness to play a role brings her smartly to
the consequences of her refusal. Initially she declares, "Fight or be
eaten. It [is] easier to change the town completely than to conciliate
it!" (111). But conciliation is precisely what she is driven to, amidst
the bizarre circumstances of being cast against her will in the role
she most abhors: the ineffectual comedian at the mercy of a com-
manding audience. She is in fact the *last* to know of Gopher Prairie's capacity to transform her into a performing comedian on its
own terms. "'You're the pluckiest little idiot in the world,'" Vida
tells her. "'I wonder if you understand that in a secluded community like this every newcomer is on test? People cordial to her but
watching her all the time'" (95). Likewise, her husband tells her
that she will *always* have an audience to perform for: "'There's

nothing in this town that you don't do in company with a whole lot of uninvited but awful interested guests'" (380). Initially, this is news to Carol: "In supposing that only she was observant Carol was ignorant, misled by the indifference of cities. She fancied that she was slipping through the streets invisible" (36). But even when she learns otherwise, she is defiant: "'It's infuriating to have to pay attention to what people think. In St. Paul I didn't care. But here I'm spied on. They're watching me. I mustn't let it make me self-conscious'"—which, of course, it does, putting her "offensively on the defensive" (87). Guy Pollock might give her a backhanded compliment about her naive openness—"'I insist that there's only one professional-man's wife in this town who doesn't plot, and that is you, you blessed, credulous outsider!'" (156)—but there is no compliment from the general townspeople who send Carol into a spiral of paranoia. "She had tripped into the meadow to teach the lambs a pretty educational dance and found that the lambs were wolves. There was no way out between their pressing gray shoulders. She was surrounded by fangs and sneering eyes" (100). Carol knows what she has to do; even attempts it in spite of herself as she walks the street with downcast eyes, forced into a hateful theatrical deception: "Always she was acting, for the benefit of every one she saw—and for the benefit of the ambushed leering eyes which she did not see" (100). But she is an incompetent, unwilling comic actress struck with stage fright in the public glare of Main Street's bay windows, fleeing from "a thousand enemies armed with ridicule. She told herself that her sensitiveness was preposterous, but daily she was thrown into a panic. She saw curtains slide back into innocent smoothness" (101). And her imagery impresses upon her the truths of the animal kingdom (to repeat: "Animals whose disguises don't work, don't live to leave another generation"). Carol sees herself as "'a hawk; a tiny leashed hawk, pecked to death by these large, white, flabby, wormy hens'"—both her audience and the objects of her criticism (157).

Criticism, she says, is the "remedy"; but Carol finds that if she won't cast it willingly in the form of comedy, then Gopher Prairie will do it for her. Never mind that Carol's ideas are enlightened and humane; before the denizens of Main Street, *she* is the freak, and *they* do the laughing, however vile their bigotry: "In the manner of one who has just beheld a two-headed calf they repeated that they had 'never *heard* such funny ideas!'" In Carol, they scent "the heretic" and do to her what she refuses to do herself—they take it as a joke: "And with forward-stooping delight they sat and tried to drag out her ludicrous concepts for their amusement. They were like the Sunday-afternoon mob starting at monkeys in the Zoo, poking fingers and making faces and giggling at the resentment of the more dignified race" (238). Vida tells Carol, "'Well, my dear, if I *did* take all your notions seriously, it would be pretty discouraging'" (262). Carol herself laments, "'And Main Street laughs till it aches, giggles till the spirit doubts his own self and tries to give up the use of wings'" (327). When Carol finally realizes that the joke will be on her whether she wishes it or not, she is desolate: "'Is that the real tragedy, that I never shall know tragedy, never find anything but blustery complications that turn out to be a farce?'" (360).

After her year of exile from Main Street, Carol returns, empty and chastened. Once on the offensive against a host of tyrannical enemies—"Polite Society, the Family, the Church, Sound Business, the Party, the Country, the Superior White Race"—she has been beaten onto the defensive, with "unembittered laughter" more of a shield than a weapon (413). "'I can laugh now and be serene,'" she declares (424), "rather proud of herself for having acquired so much tolerance" (425). But the laughter and tolerance have come only with the adoption of an absurdist philosophy and a retreat from criticism: "She knew, a hundred generations of Carols will aspire and go down in tragedy devoid of palls and solemn chanting, the humdrum inevitable tragedy of struggle against inertia" (431). In her newfound tolerance she is herself at last tolerated by her adversaries, committed to comic deceit, having exchanged "humdrum tragedy" for the "farce" that dulls the pain of criticism. By the end of the novel, she has arrived where most comedians begin.

Lake Wobegon Days and the Lesson of *Main Street*

Carol Kennicott is, by her own admission, defeated by Main Street in her ultimate surrender to laughter, either as a substitute for earnest criticism or as a palliative: "'I may not have fought the good fight, but I have kept the faith'" (432). Her fight, she says, is deferred to the next generation, as she points to her newborn baby: "'Do you see that object on the pillow? Do you know what it is? It's a bomb to blow up smugness. If you Tories were wise, you wouldn't arrest anarchists; you'd arrest all these children while they're asleep in their cribs'" (432). At least one child from Minnesota *did* grow up with the words of Carol Kennicott in his ears, and he paraphrased them for a British radio audience in 1995: "The great sin that was not preached about when I was a child—the great sin is smugness and self-righteousness, and the failure to recognize joy and to respond to it, and the failure to use one's own gifts."[9] This could almost have been Carol speaking, if it were not Garrison Keillor. But while *Main Street* closes on the standpoint of admitted defeat, Keillor starts from it, inasmuch as he declares to the world (for those who need to be told), "My cash crop is humor," and inasmuch as he reinforces his partnership not only with Mark Twain but also with "the gentlemen of the old firm of Benchley, Thurber, Perelman & White."[10] He acknowledges his debt to Sinclair Lewis, which extends back to his days reading *Main Street* and *Babbitt* in high school, where he sat picturing himself "a rebel against the materialism and provincialism of the Midwest as Sinclair Lewis described it, the culture of the Shriners and boosters and plumbers and shopkeepers and dull solid unimaginative people who seemed to dominate the landscape."[11] Keillor established himself as a comedian to critical and popular acclaim precisely by carrying his rebellion—inspired, if he is to be believed, by Lewis—to the broadcasts and pages of his Lake Wobegon stories. Yet if we explore, in John Miller's words, "the distance between Gopher Prairie and Lake Wobegon," we may see how Keillor has so far managed to escape generally the resentment that Lewis both depicted in *Main Street* and, to some extent, incurred himself.[12] Lewis recalled receiving letters "denouncing" him "for having sinned against the Holy Ghost" in his attacks on "one of the most treasured American myths . . . that all American villages were peculiarly noble and happy." *Lake Wobegon Days*, in contrast, has hardly had the "success of scandal" that Lewis relished in *Main Street*.[13] Thus, if anything, in addition to teaching him what to rebel against, Lewis may have taught Keillor *how* to rebel—or, through the example of Carol Kennicott, how not to. Certainly, Lewis deliberately set his heroine up to be knocked down; as he recalled, he had "painstakingly planned" that Carol "should be just bright enough to sniff a little but not bright enough to do anything about it."[14] What Carol fatally lacks is a capacity for artful dissembling, the indispensable hypocrisy of a comedian. The same can't be said for Keillor.

I would like to build, then, upon John Miller's work with particular attention to Keillor's highly crafted comic stances—the suffocated insider with an outsider's vision; the prodigal exile with an insider's tolerance; the antifundamentalist wincing at secular emptiness; the shy, articulate sophisticate directing his criticism inward as well as outward, with a multiple voice that is at once his indispensable shield and his critical weapon. Perhaps Keillor hasn't pleased everybody, as he wryly suggested upon the reception of *Lake Wobegon Days* in Minnesota, where "the local newspaper put me in my place but good. They marked my front yard with orange rinds and nailed a dead cat to the porch."[15] Believe it if you wish; the importance lies in Keillor's recognition that a comedian is obliged to fool most of the people practically all of the time, if he is to survive as a comedian. He also apparently recognizes what Mark Twain explicitly stated (and sometimes ignored): "Humor must not professedly teach and it must not professedly preach, but it must do both if it would live forever."[16] By "forever" Twain meant "thirty years"; and while it is tempting to argue over the appropriateness of such a yardstick (which I find quite arbitrary), in the case of a contemporary comedian like Keillor it is more important to consider the more *immediate* consequences of the faulty comic mask. One measure of the distance between Gopher Prairie and Lake Wobegon lies in Lewis's ostentatious declaration, in his preface, that he was describing "the continuation of Main Streets everywhere" (6). Keillor makes no such claim: think what you will, and as plausible or even likely as it otherwise seems, the object of *his* ironic scrutiny is nothing more than "the tiny town that time forgot, that the decades cannot improve"—the Lake Wobegon of ephemeral Mist County, excluded from all existing maps even in its fictional context, and whose Main Street, like its railroad branch, goes nowhere else.[17] This reluctance of Keillor's to generalize and to preach is only one of his many protective narrative strategies.

As much of the English-speaking world knows by now, the Lake Wobegon stories were initially conceived for live radio broadcasts. Because of this, Keillor told his British audience, his storytelling was required to be "more charming" than it might otherwise have been.[18] The word *charm*—and its magical associations—must carry considerable weight in any discussion about comedy, if we understand it in terms of play. The *illusion* to which Huizinga refers is, as he notes, "a pregnant word which means literally 'in play' (from *inlusio*, *illudere*, or *inludere*)." A spoil-sport who refuses to employ play as a charm "must be cast out, for he threatens the existence of the play-community. . . . The spoil-sport breaks the magic world, therefore he . . . must be ejected. In the world of high seriousness, too, the cheat and the hypocrite have always had an easier time of it than the spoil-sports."[19] Sinclair Lewis demonstrated his awareness of this in his contrasting treatment of Carol Kennicott (spoil-sport) and Vida Sherwin (cheat); Keillor demonstrates the same in his acknowledgment of "charm." Moreover, it is a charm he has carried from the exposed standpoint of the live comedian to the only slightly less vulnerable one of the literary comedian. In either case, he must be prepared to answer for what he says, and how he says it.

A comedian with an ineffectual disguise may speak, broadcast, publish, and be damned. Generally, Keillor has been blessed. For sixteen years he hosted one of the most popular weekly radio programs in American broadcasting history—on *public* stations, decades after the heyday of the radio comedians had ended. When *A Prairie Home Companion* ceased its regular broadcasts in June 1987, it became international news, with even the American government, through the Voice of America, treating its European listeners to long excerpts—as though Keillor were a national representative.[20] Keillor still returns to the broadcast microphone with special offerings of the program, as if America will not let it die. In Britain, through the BBC he and Lake Wobegon are household names. His two collections of Lake Wobegon stories, *Lake Wobegon Days* and *Leaving Home*, were best-sellers even in hardcover when they appeared in 1985 and 1987 respectively; and until his break with the *New Yorker* he was one of that magazine's most popular authors. Never mind what publishers' blurbs and Sunday supplement magazines have gushed about the "loving" gentleness of his celebrated homespun homilies; even seasoned, crusty academics seem to have been taken in: "His stories are parables of patience rewarded, of adversity endured. . . . Keillor considers the hopes and fears, the fantasies and dreams of people to be legitimate. He seldom judges but rather accepts and affirms."[21] Some have noted how *others* have been taken in: "Keillor's creation of a mythical place captivated the imagination of American audiences because it addressed a long-standing cultural need . . . for a sense of community and belonging, for reassurance against social disruption and the threat of loss—the need, in short, for a sense of place."[22] Or: "When he spun his dreams and conducted what he called his seance on *A Prairie Home Companion* each week, even sushi addicts drew comfort from the smell of tuna hot dish, soul food of the fifties, emanating from the Chatterbox Cafe. In Lake Wobegon the elm trees still flourished, impervious to the Dutch elm disease that denuded the rest of the Midwest."[23] Some—notably Minnesotans—have *complained* about how others have been taken in: "[Keillor's

work is] for Americans what *All Creatures Great and Small* has been
for the English: a sweet picture of small-town life, misty around the
edges, that panders to the nostalgic and escapist yearnings of a society alienated from the present and aware that it is on the skids."[24]
And—most important—some have noted how *curious* it is that so
many should have been taken in, given the underlying critical design: "Keillor uses the town, its businesses and citizens, to expose
folly, to undermine pretension, to deflate pride, and to remind us of
our human limitations."[25] A French analysis attempts to set the record straight: "Is the narrator too much of an uncritical praise singer
of small-town culture? Some of his reviewers, repeating that here,
at last, was a *wholesome* humorist, a *family* entertainer, have unduly
encouraged this impression. . . . He neatly tiptoes between . . .
le mythe noire (Emile Zola) and *le mythe rose* (George Sand) of rural
literature."[26]

   Keillor has obviously thrown out a smoke screen, both in
print and over the airwaves, and it is this that allows him to with-
draw and observe the ensuing critical battles from a safe distance.
He says as much himself, in spite of admissions to the contrary. The
epigraph to *Lake Wobegon Days* indeed protests his honesty—"Dogs
don't lie, and why should I?"[27] So does his declaration during a
Prairie Home Companion broadcast from Seattle: "It would be very
easy for me to lie to you up here and to make up things, being so
far from home, so that it would be hard for you to check my veracity. I'm determined not to, but believe me, it's a great temptation
for a person who's benefited as much as I have from fiction."[28] Still,
he dares the world to believe him, both in the fictive context of *Lake
Wobegon Days*—"In school and in church, we were called to high
ideals such as truth and honor by someone perched on truth and
hollering for us to come on up, but the truth was that we always fell
short" (6)—and in personal interviews: "People who make a show
of being open and displaying themselves in entirety, are really fooling themselves—they are simply creating another defense and another screen."[29] Keillor's statements combine in the comedian's
paradox: I demand your trust, and I don't deserve it. Like any comedian, his career depends on his keeping the tension between the
two sides of the equation taut—a wearying task that, as the following chapters show, has apparently taken its toll on a number of
American comedians.

   Keillor's other "defenses and screens" have begun to attract critical scrutiny. People have observed his adoption of a pseudonym (from Gary Edward to Garrison), and his reason: "I think I

was trying to hide behind a name that meant strength and 'don't give me a hard time about this.'"[30] Judith Lee has noted that the "distinction between the public and private Keillors, between performer and author, is as blurred as the distinction between Samuel Clemens and Mark Twain." She describes the "many represented (or implied) voices and a single persona" as a disorientating, diverting comic strategy. The result, she says, is a "cacophony [which] cautions against believing too much in any one voice and urges us to focus instead on the essential fictiveness of the storyteller, who continually reinvents himself while narrating the published stories and in the monologues of *A Prairie Home Companion*."[31]

With particular attention to the radio broadcasts, Lee has identified various other strategies of Keillor's, notably the multiple stances that accompanied the development of various routines over the years: the "mock-commercial rhetoric" of advertisements from imaginary sponsors—Jack's Auto Repair, Bob's Bank, and other concerns "whose boasts of small-town friendliness veiled hints of nosiness and interference," and which emphasized a desire to elevate "the unmarketable into the precious"; the "News from Lake Wobegon," which allowed Keillor, through the mask of objectivity, to transform "the mundane into the ritualistic"; and the letters from Barbara Ann Bunsen, which allowed both an inside and outside perspective while allowing Barbara Ann, rather than the narrator, to take the heat for her less flattering observations.[32] Lee has also identified what she calls the "Prairie Home Postures," a series of comic poses that express Keillor's "*implied* attitude toward a particular subject and audience at a particular time." She names them "the Amateur, the Professional, the Shy Person, the Cracker-Barrel Philosopher/Preacher, the Witness, the Exile"—all of which combine into the overall persona of the Companion of the program's title.[33] This bewildering variety of stances and voices allows Keillor the Companion not only to obfuscate the critical field he surveys, it also prevents him from swinging between the wide extremes of naïveté and cynicism that mark Carol Kennicott's observations. On the page as well as in the broadcasts, the narrator from Lake Wobegon demonstrates the craftiness that Carol Kennicott despised, to her peril. How else, as Hans Schreffler asks, can Keillor command the allegiance of *so many* audiences? It would sicken a critic of Carol's directness to be all things to all people; yet, as Schreffler notes, even in the relatively narrow area of religious criticism, Keillor can appeal to at least four types of reader: "anti-secularists, anti-fundamentalists, the spiritually ambivalent, and grace advocates." In providing each of these audiences "with enough potential evidence of a world view consonant with their own," Keillor presents himself as "a kind of spiritual chameleon."[34] *Lake Wobegon Days* suggests that Keillor is a chameleon in other respects as well.

As Jacques Laroche and Claude Fouillade have noted with reference to *Lake Wobegon Days*, "There is an inevitable whiff of deceit in small-town eulogies. Claiming the superiority of ordinary, uneducated folk, they were written by successful professionals who chose not to stay with them."[35] As if to acknowledge just this possibility, Keillor—for that is the narrator's avowed name —points to "some fifteen hundred subscribers" of the Lake Wobegon *Herald-Star*, "most of whom don't live there anymore (and wouldn't if you paid them) . . . the ones lured away by the pleasures of school and good money, who can afford to be nostalgic" (250). What is the distance between this narrator, the people he describes, and the cosmopolitan who created them all? Certainly a fictive one; yet it is credible (at least, immediately), as is the amateurism with which Keillor offers the book. It is, he says, a failure, a "pale and impoverished" shadow of a lost manuscript that preceded it, that manuscript itself having followed a radio career which—he says—had been kept going "because I had no illusion that I was good at it" (ix). Thus, "the lost cause of live radio" becomes the lost cause of comic literature in the hands of an inept amateur who (never mind his popularity on the pages of the *Atlantic* and the *New Yorker*) had made his name wearing hick suits and mumbling monologues into a microphone, buttressed by such incisive qualifiers as *"kinda, buncha, gotta, ya know."* But, as Judith Lee notes, don't kid yourself: what went for the broadcasts goes for the page. "Glitches in the live performances conveyed his authenticity and veracity; the absence of slick performance values gave the impression that he wasn't performing at all." Keillor himself admitted, "'On a lot of the scripts I wrote, we could have used more mistakes'"—betraying, possibly, his recognition that in the face of a pervasive disgust over the values of professional slickness, "amateurishness signified integrity and sincerity."[36]

It is ironic that *Lake Wobegon Days* has the capacity to be seen as "an affirmation of small-town values," given the calculated *reluctance* that so pervades the narrative. Affirmation seems hardly to come into it—another pose that Keillor, the self-proclaimed champion of the Shy Person, has carried from the radio to the page. In addition to the Amateur, as Lee notes, Keillor's Shy Person offers "a second naïve pose with comic potential. A shy radio announcer is even more of an anomaly than an amateur and has commensurately greater capacity to evoke sympathy and sentiment." The same can be said for a shy literary narrator, not only reticent in his own right but clued in to the defensive strategies of highlighting the shyness of others. The issue is not whether Keillor the man is himself shy—again, as Lee says, "Keillor's wide *reputation* for shyness (deserved or not) proves unequivocally how effectively the humorist exploited the pose. . . . Like the Amateur, the Shy Person succeeds as a comic device because we recognize it as a comic posture, because Keillor connects it to a *feigned* ineptitude."[37] Hence the shyness with which Keillor sets out to describe Lake Wobegon, a target you can't hit because you can't see it: "It would make quite a picture if you had the right lens, which nobody in this town has got" (3). Lake Wobegon's history is a parody of Rolvaag's *Giants in the Earth*, depicting a retreat peopled by befuddled Norwegians (and their reluctant descendants) for whom grandeur is an alien concept. *Sumus Quod Sumus* is the town motto: We Are What We Are. Like the rest of Mist County, Lake Wobegon isn't even on the map, due to a surveying team's error in 1866; but as the state legislators explain: "We doubt that its absence would be much noticed." Over a century later, when the governor dedicates the town's Statue of the Unknown Norwegian and salutes Lake Wobegon's "patience in anonymity," he gets the reply that it has been "no sacrifice, really, but a true pleasure" (90–92). Even the statue itself is a monument to shyness and reluctance, cast as it is in an attitude that says, "Wait here. I think I forgot something" (93). As Bruce Michelson notes, "The whole book seems reluctant to say anything for sure about inherited mythologies and their shifting relationship to the present."[38] Lake Wobegon is where people "go straight for the small potatoes," where "majestic doesn't appeal to us" (7), and "where smart doesn't count for so much" (97). In Lake Wobegon it is best *not to be noticed*.

Deliberate self-effacement is, perhaps, Keillor's greatest strategy in *Lake Wobegon Days*, nowhere more evident than in the damning swath of criticism that counters and ironically underpins the entire eulogy: the "95 Theses," which run for twenty-four pages of small print in footnote form. Surely the most sustained indictment of Lake Wobegon's suffocating ethos and hypocrisy, the 95 Theses are not only a parody of Martin Luther's protests nailed openly to the church door at Wittenberg; they are yet another indication of the narrator's reluctance to make the sort of open protests that put Carol Kennicott at the mercy of the vengeful spirits of

Gopher Prairie. Keillor himself recently backed away from the question put to him as to whether he had depicted himself as this timid protestant: "It wasn't me. It was somebody who I understood and could sympathize with, and whom I gave voice to; but those were not *exactly* my complaints"—and one can imagine the smooth chuckle that easily could have followed from a less able trickster.[39] Hans Schreffler has noted the "thin three-piece veil" that characterizes and purports to diminish the impact of the 95 Theses: the supposed anonymity of the protestant; his Lutheranism (Keillor himself is not a Lutheran); and "the traditionally secondary status of the footnote."[40] In addition, one can note the casual way Keillor introduces the Theses, in an apparent afterthought during a discussion of the town's newspaper. This great piece of criticism remains the private, unpublished protest of a timid former resident—so timid that, though he had intended "to nail the 95 to the door, a dramatic complaint against his upbringing . . . something in his upbringing made him afraid to pound holes in a good piece of wood." The Theses lie forgotten, buried on the newspaper editor's desk "in a lower stratum of stuff under council minutes and soil conservation reports," the author himself reduced to a buffoon who whines and pleads for their return: "'I simply can't understand despite repeated requests. . . . This is very important to me. . . . The ms. is *mine* and I need it *now* for a longer work I'm writing" (251–52). As Laroche and Fouillade suggest, the presentation of the 95 Theses not only demonstrates Keillor's awareness "of the serious risk presented by the *petit-bourgeois* paradise in the mental development of its children," but also of his need "to keep the peace between his early condition and adult sensitiveness, and avoid the 'angry young man' pose of the rebel."[41] Thus, above the footnote line Keillor can milk the nostalgia of a small-town boy playing with his animal friends in the fullness of his imagination ("Children wished for things and animals brought them. It was better than Christmas, you got what you wanted, and nobody argued since there was plenty for everyone") but below the line simmer the 95 Theses, testifying to the legacy of an emotionally and psychically wrecked childhood (262). Above the line, Keillor can note the peaceful humdrum of a blessed town with no bad news to read about: "A sale at Skoglund's, Ralph's new meat counter—those deserve a photo and also a hundred words or so. A girl who makes the Dean's List at college, a boy who finishes basic training—people like to have a nice little article they can send to relatives." But below the line, he reveals what the paper doesn't print: the presence in Lake Wobegon of a bigoted god whose Sabbath "is cloudy and deathly still and filled with silent accusing whispers"; a repression that imposes "shame and disgust" upon the human body; a "fear of becoming lost, which has killed the pleasure of curiosity and discovery"; and the fear of "strangers and their illicit designs" (254). This, too, is the News from Lake Wobegon—even if the Voice of America missed it.

"Only kidding, folks": The Ironic Identity

It is impossible to say precisely where Garrison Keillor will end up in terms of his ability to maintain the comic masquerade required of him if he wishes to continue satirizing the bigotry and strangulation of small-town America with the relative impunity he has enjoyed until now. Keillor himself—in his introduction to *We Are Still Married*—says that he is beginning to grow tired of the demands of this confidence game: "Sometimes I wish I could quit writing humor and just write irritation for a while. I grow old and irritable."[42] But as a comedian, Keillor has no such option; for he is committed to a particular identity; and if he wishes to remain part of that old firm of Benchley, Thurber, et al, he is obliged to keep it going. This identity is ironic in a sense that I hope to make clear.

I am not referring to irony merely as a rhetorical strategy, a voice, or a stance, for these suggest something that can be momentarily assumed or dropped at will. An identity is harder to dispense with—it sticks to one, defines one. To be sure, not all comic or humorous artists share the same kind of ironic identity: but self-avowed comedians like Keillor and most of the others in this study are in various ways constrained by their identities *as* comedians. (Franklin, as we shall discuss, was not; he assumed a stance rather than forged an identity as a comedian. Melville, too, was another story altogether.) However much they might periodically wish it, self-avowed comedians cannot shuck off their ironic identities as they can adopt or drop a rhetorical strategy, a voice, or a stance—all of which they in fact do at times in their work. There is more latitude for artists who are not self-acknowledged comedians, even though their work may at times be as comic as otherwise. Such artists, like Melville and Sinclair Lewis, have still forged for themselves an ironic identity inasmuch as they must propose that their life's fragile work—the fictions of art—actually matter in the face of death. But this is an irony they share with all artists (and perhaps all people). For certain comedians, however, the defining qualities are much more restrictive.

While I would never suggest that irony is the total defi-nition of comedy, or that a comedian's every utterance is necessar-ily ironic *in itself*, I start from the standpoint that the paradoxical makeup of the comedian as social critic is unavoidably an ironic one, and as such, subjects him to all the hazards and pitfalls of ironic interpretation and misinterpretation. The ironic identity en-velops all his utterances, compromising the literal—and thus, the immediately believable—in everything he says. As Wayne Booth notes, an ironic voice will infect *all* its utterances with the germ of irony: "As soon as an ironic voice has been used to any extent in any work of any kind, readers inevitably begin to take interest and pleasure in that voice—in the tasks it assigns and the qualities it provides; *it thus becomes a part of whatever is seen as the controlling context*" (my emphasis).[43] As I shall argue with reference to particu-lar comedians, the apprehension of irony is not always a grounds for pleasure, and the misapprehension of it may be even worse, for both comedian and audience. But the point I wish to make is that the identity of a comedian who wishes to utter serious truths by way of comedy must necessarily be ironic, and it threatens—as *the* "controlling context"—to affect all utterances with both the plea-sures and pitfalls of irony. Careful readers will note that Booth only refers to ironic *voice*: in talking about *identity*, I am taking it a step further, restricting the element of choice or waywardness that ac-companies the adoption of a voice (which, after all, modulates fre-quently in any given work). However strong the temptation toward truthfulness, a comedian cannot drop his identity as a trickster without the gravest of repercussions. However much he might wish to escape from the "controlling context" of irony, the choice may not be his as long as he remains a comedian.

What are the pleasures and pitfalls of the comedian's ironic identity? They are those that accompany the obligations of "saying one thing and meaning another." This is the stock defini-tion of irony that has come down from Cicero (*"aliud dicere ac sentias"*), barely changed by Samuel Johnson ("A mode of speech where the meaning is contrary to the words"), and broadened out over the centuries from mere utterance or "discursive strategy," in Linda Hutcheon's words, to something more encompassing, whether it be "dramatic irony, cosmic irony, irony of fate, irony of character."[44] Like comedy itself, which after centuries of tortured at-tempts at definition always threatens to return to the tautology,

"It's comedy because it makes us laugh," irony has been beset with the problem of definition.[45] The sheer multiplicity of definitions has forced even the bravest into retreat, as Erich Heller wrote back in 1958: "Every attempt to define irony unambiguously is in itself ironical. It is wiser to speak about it ironically."[46] Judging from the gleeful irony of most postmodernist definitions, which in their fashion celebrate the unlimited deferral of meaning, the situation hasn't changed much; but all definitions—even postmodernist ones—seem somehow to revolve around the concept of "the clash between appearance and reality in events or language," even if reality itself is deemed inaccessible.[47] Lately, the urge to define irony has returned to the easier task of describing the ironic process, such as in its "avoidance of head-on assertion" in hopes of "discomposing, if not winning over, the person addressed."[48] But the element of *shiftiness* in irony has remained in place for centuries. Wayne Booth's emphasis on its "covert" quality—its intention "to be reconstructed with meanings different from those on the surface"—corresponds with its earliest association, that of the ancient Greeks, whose *eironeia* referred to the sly self-deprecation of Socrates.[49]

Irony's shiftiness is in a real sense a satirist's refuge. Rhetoricians have long focused on its transformative nature, that is, its part in tempering *anger*—the motivating force of satire—into comedy. Anger, as Patrick Colfer notes, stems from a desire to make an affirmation against a perceived injustice—an injustice against either oneself or another—and is generally the primary urge that opens up a host of possibilities for social change. But it may also be the critic's worst enemy: "We know how, when anger swells up in us, we find it difficult to speak justly, to provide grounds for our affirmations, or to care about inviting anything other than anger in return. Anger involves the seemingly irresistible urge to appeal to self-evidence, and to become a mere polemicist."[50] This, of course, a comedian cannot do *as* a comedian—and this goes even for Benjamin Franklin, who, alone among the subjects of this study, could drop comedy (and thus irony) altogether and step into the heart of political activity and nation-making, whereby he could appeal in all seriousness both to polemics and self-evidence (as he did in contributing the latter concept to the Declaration of Independence). Other satirical comedians, however, are obliged to appeal to what Schlegel called the "transcendental buffoonery" of irony to temper their anger and disguise their intent.[51] In doing so, they open themselves up to a variety of practical and ethical problems.

A comedian whose urge is social criticism through satire (as opposed to the politically uncommitted clowning that relies on incongruity or other comic situational aspects) must perform a wearying tightrope act. As Susan Purdie notes, his satire must "steer its audience in and out of serious implication; control the degree and balance of optimistic and pessimistic judgments it offers about the actual world beyond the performance; and manipulate the connections audiences experience between its implicating and joking elements."[52] The satirist must instigate and negotiate two conflicting states of mind in his audience: the belief that he is offering more than mere comedy, that is, that "there is more here than meets the eye," and, in the interests of self-defense, "the suspicion that there is less."[53] He operates in a minefield because so much of his communication is based upon the hopeful assumption that there are "unspoken understandings" between his audience and himself, that there is a strong degree of silent "ideological complicity—an agreement based on shared understandings of 'how the world is.'"[54] Of course, this is a dangerous assumption to make, given the multiplicity of "understandings" residing in any one audience a satirist may reach. Moreover, he is actually obliged to hope that his intended targets have *missed* his ironies—at least for long enough to give him the chance of being heard again (and this applies to Swift and Defoe as much as to Bill Hicks and Lenny Bruce, all of whom faced the threatened or actual gag of the censor). This must be a galling realization for the social critic who is out to be *heeded* by those that matter, and who hopes to effect a commitment to change from the objects of his satire. Moreover, none of these particulars exempt the satirist from the other intricacies of the delivery and apprehension of meaning that are faced by all communicators: for the utterer, the ability to gauge the ingenuity or competence of the audience members in making sense of his strategic effects, *let alone* determining their sense of humor; for the audience, the ability to perceive the intentions of the speaker or writer behind the effects, with all their vagaries of tone, vocabulary, implication, explication, and inscrutability. What sets the ironist apart from all other communicators, however, is his intention to confound the literal-minded, to affirm positively in words while negating somehow his very affirmations. As Benjamin DeMott notes, the ironist "means only part of what he says, and says a good deal that he does not fully mean."[55]

Given that irony constitutes, in Peter Conrad's words, a "double-plot"—a vacillation between "prophetic self-assertion and emphatic self-effacement"—it is not surprising that through all the centuries-long struggle to define the ironic, the ethical dimension has never been absent.[56] This is perhaps the most important problem for the comedian as social critic. As Linda Hutcheon observes, "irony might well mean never having to say you really mean it," turning the "healthy suspension of certainty" into an outright, "morally suspect evasion."[57] In no other area have rhetorical, ethical, and political theories been brought so close together as in the examination of irony. C. Jan Swearingen notes that "the Western aesthetic and ethical scrutiny of irony, and of related notions of linguistic deceit and lying, is as old as rhetoric and literacy," yoked in its early Greek infancy to questions about the corruption of the individual and the state.[58] Daniel Conway and John Seery have pointed out that while irony may provide "a much-needed critical perspective and even underwrite a minimal political agenda, it is generally regarded as irredeemably parasitic and antisocial" among the theorists who have explored it. "The individual's ironic triumph is often achieved at the expense of others and is liable to vitiate the public ideals of the society as a whole. Echoing the judgment of Socrates' accusers, political theorists often warn that an unchecked irony can poison and potentially topple the body politic."[59] In reviewing the line of critical inquiry from the Preplatonics, through Plato, Aristotle, and Cicero to St. Augustine's "critique of mendacity," Swearingen has shown that the associations between irony and moral culpability have rarely wavered—associations that still linger today, in spite of the recent attempts of political theorists and philosophers, most notably John Seery, to rescue irony from the camp of political evasion and place it in the service of political commitment. They have an uphill battle, for as Swearingen shows, contemporary scholarship—postmodernism notwithstanding—has failed to dislodge the associations between irony and the highly suspect "deception, double meaning, and strategic understatement" explored most fully by Aristotle. "The double bind; the confidence game; the ironic narrator; the schizophrenic personality . . . each of these modern *koinoi topoi* borders directly on issues and phenomena that were examined in classical treatments of both *ethos* and irony."[60]

It is small wonder, then, that the shiftiness of irony as the satirist's refuge may also be the satirist's nemesis. Small wonder that he may have the urge to stop smiling. For he may once have been confident, as Malcolm Bradbury apparently is, that comic forms—and satire in particular—are "among the greatest forms of human intellectual energy." He may once have agreed that the indirections of irony have the power to "displace, distort, subvert and dispel the familiar structures of reality, truth and history, replacing these rule-making systems with the rule-breaking laws of humor, at once the most humane and subversive of our impulses." He may have felt that his ironic criticisms could actually "intervene in reality and history."[61] Such things have been argued; but why, then, would Graham Greene have the sinister Concasseur say in his novel, *The Comedians*, "I am in favor of jokes. They have political value. Jokes are a release for the cowardly and impotent"? Why would the newspaper cartoonist Herblock feel so utterly dismayed upon being asked by Richard Nixon's hatchetmen, Haldeman and Erlichman, for the originals of his grotesque caricatures of them—not to destroy these caricatures but to gleefully display them in their offices? And why, after expending so much of his satiric energy against Nixon, would Kurt Vonnegut conclude after his renomination, "Clowning doesn't throw off the timing or slow down cruel social machinery. In fact, it usually serves as a lubricant"?[62]

　　Such questions are indicative of the internal conflict that stems from the ironic identity of the comedian as social critic. Even without access to a given comedian's individual circumstances, one can speculate generally upon a number of possibilities that would contribute to the conflict: the grimness or seriousness of the issue at hand in the face of the continued demand to *smile, smile, smile* (either literally or by comic implication); the moral and critical premium placed upon truth over falsehood; the strain of keeping up appearances; the liberality or conservatism of the cultural milieu in which the comedian operates; the stigma of the buffoon against the respect of the serious observer; and the desire to effect a change rather than to get a laugh. These and other considerations find their way into the following discussion, to reflect upon questions of comedic longevity that have yet to be introduced. What follows is an examination of six more comedians whose conflicts, both internal and external, have struck me as immediately relevant to the main subject of this study: the war of attrition between the social critic who demands to be taken seriously and the comedian who cannot be.

CHAPTER 2

Ben Franklin and Herman Melville: The Comedian as Confidence Man

It is April 2, 1722, in Cambridge, Massachusetts. You have set aside the lecture you are writing for your Harvard students and have picked up a copy of *The New-England Courant* to learn that a new contributor has added her pseudonym to the paper's writing stable, joining the likes of Ichabod Henroost, Timothy Turnstone, Homespun Jack, and Betty Frugal. You know her name is not *really* Silence Dogood, but you don't know who she is, other than that she is supposedly a country widow with a smattering of self-taught education, horse sense, and an inclination to speak her mind. The following week, you chuckle along with her recollections of her early days as a single woman courted by an awkward bachelor, whom she used to deflate with "an unmannerly Laughter." Because she is such a jumped-up, rustic clown, you do not take too seriously her declarations of being "an Enemy to Vice, and a Friend to Virtue," or "a mortal Enemy to arbitrary Government and unlimited Power." You do not tremble much at her warning: "I have likewise a natural Inclination to observe and reprove the Faults of others, at which I have an excellent Faculty. I speak this by Way of Warning to all such whose Offences shall come under my Cognizance, for I never intend to wrap my Talent in a Napkin." Upon your third encounter with her, you learn that she is aware—if only in the basest degree—of the various rhetorical strategies a disputatious writer will employ to win over an audience: "He must one while be merry and diverting, then more solid and serious; one while sharp and satyrical, then (to mollify that) be sober and religious." She has so convinced you of her barnyard harmlessness that you are utterly blindsided in the fourth week, when she savages your beloved Harvard as a place where "every Beetle-Scull [seems] well satisfy'd with his own Portion of Learning," where "they learn little more than how to carry themselves handsomely, and enter a room genteely, (which might as well be acquir'd at a Dancing-School)," and from where they will depart, "after Abundance of Trouble and Charge, as great Blockheads as ever, only more proud and self-conceited." You are so stung that you scribble off an angry protest to a rival newspaper over the signature "John Harvard," unaware that in all your pompousness you have been duped by a sixteen-year-old boy who is right now probably whistling as he cleans the ink off his older brother's printing press.[1]

Eight years later, somewhere in Pennsylvania, a newspaper reports *as news* the proceedings of a witch trial at Mount Holly, New Jersey, and invites you to believe the slapstick of the accused being weighed in balancing scales against the books of the Bible, whereupon "to the great Surprize of the Spectators, Flesh and Bones came down plump . . . and their Lumps of Mortality severally were too heavy for Moses and all the Prophets and Apostles."[2] You may sense that a blow against religious fundamentalism has been struck, but you don't know by whom, nor will anyone in your lifetime ever know. You will never be certain whether the report is true. It is possible that it implies an appeal to *reason*, but you are not absolutely sure because the report refuses to say. In another three years, you may experience a sense of déjà vu: in the first edition of an almanac put together by a man writing as "Poor Richard" Saunders, you read the sober prediction that a rival almanac-maker and astrologist, one Titan Leeds, will die at 3:29 P.M. on October 17, 1733—based upon a calculation *reluctantly* made by Saunders at said Leeds's *own request*. Not only will you be unable to resist checking the obituary notices for a while after that date, but you will also be expected to believe that the maxims of "Poor Richard" reflect the native wisdom of an unlettered, cracker-barrel Yankee rather than the manipulations of, say, a sophisticated journalist who has lifted and reworked the literary aphorisms of Virgil, Montaigne, Bacon, Herbert, and others.

On April 15, 1747, readers of the London *General Advertiser* will encounter a speech by an unmarried woman named Polly Baker, delivered by her "before a Court of Judicature, at Connecticut . . . where she was prosecuted the Fifth Time, for having a Bastard Child." They will read her reasonable and eloquent argument against the hypocrisy of the charges made against her by a body of men, one of whom—now a magistrate—is too cowardly to own up to his paternity. They will read her appeal against the excesses— even the sadism—of the law ("You believe I have offended Heaven, and must suffer eternal Fire: Will not that be sufficient? What Need is there, then, of your additional Fines and Whipping?"). They will see her turn the tables on her male accusers, who have perversely turned her "natural and useful Actions into Crimes" by their prohibitions: "But take into your wise Consideration, the great and growing Number of Batchelors in the Country . . . [who] leave unproduced (which is little better than Murder) Hundreds of their Posterity to the Thousandth Generation. Is not this a greater Offence against the Publick Good, than mine? Compel them, then, by Law, either to Marriage, or to pay double the Fine of Fornication every Year." The *General Advertiser*'s readers will note her defiant closing statement ("[I] ought, in my humble Opinion, instead of a Whipping, to have a Statue erected to my Memory") and learn that her speech had "influenced the Court to dispense with her Punishment, and induced one of her Judges to marry her the next day."[3] The speech will produce "an explosive chain reaction in the British periodical press" and will be reprinted immediately in five other London papers as well as in Edinburgh, Dublin, Boston, New York, and Annapolis.[4] Twenty years later, papers from Philadelphia to Sweden will still be printing Polly Baker's speech as fact. The French historians Denis Diderot and the abbé Reynal will cite it in all seriousness in their revolutionary writings. Reynal, for one, will walk away from a meeting with the true author of the speech with egg on his face, having admitted, "Oh, very well, Doctor, I had rather relate your stories than other men's truths."[5]

But with the speech of Polly Baker, Benjamin Franklin is still just warming up. He has decades of literary deception before him. Balzac will call him the father of three things: the lightning rod, the republic, and the hoax. In his fifties, Franklin will present to the world "A Parable Against Persecution," convincing many dupes, time and again, that it comes straight from the fifty-first chapter of Genesis—until they realize that there *is* no fifty-first chapter of Genesis. In 1761, afraid that England will sign a peace treaty with France before the French have been rendered powerless to block American colonial expansion, he will print in the *London Chronicle*—over the signature, "A Briton"—a bogus discourse purportedly from an old Spanish treatise, entitled "Of the Means of disposing the Enemie to Peace." (Its object will be to demonstrate the craftiness with which the Spanish hope to foster a peace movement in England, in order to soften *them* up for conquest.) In 1765, as "A Traveller," Franklin will report in the London *Public Advertiser* about the American sheep whose tails "are so laden with Wooll, that each has a little Car or Waggon on four little wheels, to support & keep it from trailing on the Ground"; as well as describing the cod and whale fisheries that flourish even in the Great Lakes, with "the grand Leap of the Whale" up Niagara Falls being "one of the finest Spectacles in Nature."[6] A self-styled "modern simpleton" named "Q.E.D." will offer the *Gentleman's Magazine* in September 1773 twenty "Rules By Which a Great Empire May Be Reduced to a Small One"—a warning to the British establishment that the troubles brewing in the American colonies are of their own making. The following month, as American resentment intensifies, the same magazine will print a leaked "Edict by the King of Prussia," apparently issued at Danzig, which argues that Prussia, as the "mother-country" of German George's Britain, has the right to tax and command *her* colonies just as Britain does with America. An English gentleman will rush into Lord le Despencer's parlor, waving the magazine and spluttering, " *'Here's the king of Prussia, claiming a right to this kingdom! . . . Damn his impudence, I dare say, we shall hear by next post that he is upon his march with one hundred thousand men to back this.'* " He will then notice Ben Franklin standing by, rocking on his heels—and reddening, will say, " *'I'll be hanged if this is not some of your American jokes upon us.'* "[7] In 1774, Franklin will satirize anti-American extremists by pseudononymously calling in the London papers for the castration of all American males in order to solve the problem of the rebellion ("*'In the course of fifty years it is probable we shall not have one rebellious subject in North America.'*")[8] He will wait another eight years—by which time he will be seventy-six —before printing a fake supplement to the *Boston Independent Chronicle*, accurate to the last detail in its appearance, quality of paper, printing, and the placing of advertisements, to be distributed in England as hostile propaganda. In addition to its other convincing documents, such as fabricated despatches from colonial officers and a forged protest from John Paul Jones to the British Ambassador in Canada, the "supplement" will include a detailed inventory of an intercepted shipment of 1,062 colonial scalps taken by Indians in the paid service of the British. By now the American Ambassador to France, Franklin will write to Charles Dumas, in all shiftiness, "Enclosed I send you a few copies of a paper that places in a striking Light the English barbarities in America. . . . The FORM may perhaps not be genuine, but the *substance* is truth. . . . Make any use of them you may think proper to shame your Anglomanes, but do not let it be known through what hands they come."[9] In 1782, officials of the Royal Academy of Brussels will receive an apparently serious proposal to "discover some Drug wholesome & not disagreeable, to be mix'd with our common Food, or Sauces, that shall render the Natural Discharges, of Wind from our Bodies, not only inoffensive, but agreable as Perfumes." (This momentous discovery would make those of all preceding science and philosophy "scarcely worth a FART-HING.")[10] Three weeks before Franklin's death at eighty-four, readers of the Philadelphia *Federal Gazette* will encounter an essay by "Historicus," in which is reprinted a one-hundred-year-old speech by a member of the Divan of Algiers arguing for the enslavement of European Christians in exactly the same terms as the arguments made by southern congressmen for the perpetuation of African slavery. The essay will send readers to the bookstores and libraries to find the ancient text from which the speech is taken, just as the "Parable Against Persecution" will have sent them looking for the fifty-first chapter of Genesis. And in between all these later efforts, Franklin will find time to devote his attention to his most sustained hoax, begun when he was fifty-five and continued for three decades: his *Autobiography*.

In total, the writing career of Benjamin Franklin demonstrates earlier than any other in America the potentially sinister side —as well as the philanthropic side—to the dilemma in which comedians are placed by virtue of their ironic identities. Going back to the masquerades of the animal kingdom: prey and predators *both* adopt disguises, not only to protect themselves from each other but also to exchange places with each other; one animal's prey is another's predator. "The trick is in confidence and credulity" and the manipulation of both.[11] The comedian who, as a social critic, wants to be taken seriously must frequently adopt the same sort of hypocrisies, employ the same kinds of fictions, that he condemns through his comedy—and is thereby open to the charge of doing so. Moreover, scoundrels and saints can both be comedians; the nature of the masquerade can eventually make it impossible to determine with surety who is who.

This potential impasse is the basis of what I believe is one of American comedy's most important examples of comedic action and critical reaction, grounded as it is among the implications of masterful comedic deception in a world that professes to place its highest premium on the truth: I refer to the ironic capacity of Benjamin Franklin, and the reaction to it by Herman Melville. Historians of American comedy such as Constance Rourke, Blair and Hill, Warwick Wadlington, Richard Hauck, and Gary Lindberg (among others) have convinced more people than myself that the first national comic figure of any stature was Franklin, the prototypical example of Yankee thrift and hard work, reaping the rewards of prosperity and renown, and advertising the process most famously in his revered *Autobiography*. But this book, presenting a model lesson in the building of a new society and a new American identity, is also the first major text to call attention to the contrivance of the very identity it asserts, and as such merits attention at the beginning of a discussion about American comedians and the lies they are obliged to tell. Through the power of implication in Franklin's frequently comic, deadpan voice, the austere countenance itself is proudly held up as a mask, and the industrious persona as much a sleight of hand as an example of perseverance. However tall he may stand historically in terms of the Puritan work ethic and self-reliance, he is also extremely deft in the adoption of a multitude of roles and the comic mythologizing of himself—and this is where Melville's damning reaction becomes important. As the numerous hoaxes outlined above demonstrate, in the comic persona of Ben Franklin (as distinct from the truly unknowable historical personage) one can identify an American confidence man in full glory, not only as one who inspires confidence but, more to the point, one who comedically manipulates it. The source of Franklin's comic success, however, is the source of Melville's worry: the more deft and artful Franklin's deceptions, the more disturbingly Melville waxes over the implications of—well, the *mastery* of it. As I hope to show, Melville's speculations over all that Franklin represents in terms of comic deception does not end with his rendering of the sly fox in *Israel Potter*, but gains its fullest expression in his next and final novel, *The Confidence-Man*. Moreover, they continue to reverberate into the present century, raising troubling questions for those later American comedians—living and dead—who were and are unable to accomplish what Franklin did: namely, survive into old age with their faith in their jokery undiminished, their comic voices and ironic identities intact.

Kurt Vonnegut recently surmised, "If Lloyd's of London offered policies promising to compensate comical writers for loss of sense of humor, its actuaries could count on such a loss occurring, on average, at age sixty-three for men, and for women at twenty-

nine, say."[12] Like Twain's thirty-year yardstick regarding the im-
mortality of humor, Vonnegut's average might not withstand too
much scrutiny. But if he is right, Franklin is surely one American
"comical writer" who would have confounded the actuaries. It is
doubtful that many other Americans besides Franklin have been
able to *begin* a major comic opus at the age of fifty-five and continue
working on it for another thirty years, stopping not because of any
crisis of confidence but rather because of ill health. When Franklin
set his pen aside for good, he was "tormented with the stone,"
wasted in body from the opium that, he said, had left him "'but a
Skeleton covered with a Skin.'"[13] His self-assurance, geniality, and
wit, however, remained. Adams and Jefferson marveled at—and
were considerably vexed by—the sustained constitution of his mischief and playfulness. No other American career has demonstrated
such a capacity; and in historical terms, no other revealed so early
the extent to which the promise of play is at once a comedian's licensed weapon and his greatest shield. In the aggregate, the voices
that condemned Franklin belonged to a few—Melville, Hawthorne,
Mark Twain, D. H. Lawrence, Max Weber, William Carlos Williams
—and their objections were based not on any apparent failure of his
humor to mask the outrageousness of his observations, but if anything, the opposite. The mask was *too* effective: as Kenneth Silverman suggests, these critics were most disturbed by "the absence of
a sense of the harshness and the inexplicability of life"—as though
no man who had lived so long could have the right to such playful
optimism.[14] If there was any skepticism, cynicism, or iconoclasm on
the part of Benjamin Franklin, his most earnest critics missed it. If
there was any gambit on Franklin's part—the eye-twinkling challenge to take him at his word—they missed it. One important exception was Mark Twain; the *most* important was Melville.

     After all, it is one thing for Franklin to have proven that
lightning is electricity, to have devised musical instruments and
stoves, to have plotted the Gulf Stream and invented bifocals, to
have established his country's first public library or fire department
or philosophical society, and to have been one of the leading revolutionary statesmen of his era. As Gary Lindberg notes, it is another
thing to write it all down and offer it to the world with the suggestion that, really, it was nothing. Lindberg calls Franklin's *Autobiography* "one of the major how-to-do-it-manuals in American history,"
artfully constructing a national role model made up of more or less
equal parts of the self-made man, the promoter, the jack-of-all-
trades, the gadgeteer, and the shrewd Yankee peddler.[15] But it is

also a milestone in one other sense: as Warwick Wadlington notes, with its deadpan narrative voice masking the sheer audacity of its claims, the *Autobiography* is the earliest major American comic work to set up an icon of success that simply cannot be believed, and to subvert it by calling attention to the *fact* of its incredibility. The scholars mentioned above have argued so persuasively that the comedian and the confidence man meet in the model self of the *Autobiography* that it would be pointless to repeat their arguments to any great extent. What most interests me is the reaction of Franklin's critics, especially Melville; for unlike, say, Lawrence, who apparently failed to notice or appreciate Franklin's irony and self-mockery as comic devices; or Twain, who was too ready to dismiss them, Melville knew full well that Franklin was a subtle comedian, was impressed by the ease with which he would set out to deceive, and was disturbed by the implications of his success.

A few examples from the *Autobiography* are needed to lay the groundwork for such criticisms, given that they were based almost exclusively on this one influential text (and I risk discussing it in the knowledge that others have done it in much greater depth). While it certainly emphasizes the necessity of doing the job right—whether printing, bookkeeping, conversing, lighting the streets, or forming a government—the *Autobiography* both implies and proclaims outright that the manipulation of the *impression* matters at least as much as the reality. Franklin happily admits that his early reputation for industry and frugality was in no small way owing to his detailed plan "to avoid all *Appearances* of the Contrary." He would, for instance, time his hours in the print shop to be seen working when everyone else was going home; and, as he confided, "to show that I was not above my Business, I sometimes brought home the Paper I purchas'd at the Stores, thro' the Streets on a Wheelbarrow. Thus being esteem'd an industrious thriving young Man. . . ."[16] He savors his success in creating this estimation with more relish than he betrays for his accomplishments as a printer, lingering over the impression of an observer: "the Industry of that Franklin, says he, is superior to any thing I ever saw of the kind: I see him still at work when I go home from Club; and he is at Work again before his Neighbors are out of bed" (67).

The *Autobiography* is elsewhere replete with Franklin's admissions of play acting, and these admissions *must* act as part of an implicit dare for the reader either to believe or condemn him. For example, having learned to "work" the opposition and deflect criticism with his crafty "Socratic Method" in debate, Franklin reveals his deliberate imitations of Jesus and Socrates, and how he had "put on the humble Inquirer & Doubter" (18). If he can't rouse *Lawrence's* amusement, he at least betrays his own over the facility with which, as a young man, he one day "conceive'd the bold and arduous Project of arriving at moral Perfection" (90). It was easy once you knew how: thirteen step-by-step instructions to attain the proper mixture of Temperance, Order, Frugality, Sincerity ("Use no *hurtful* Deceit" [my italics]), Chastity, and Humility (92); and if Franklin couldn't in the end quite succeed "in acquiring the *Reality*" of this last virtue, he "had a good deal with regard to the *Appearance* of it" (102). Lindberg and others describe these sorts of Franklin's machinations in much greater detail; but with such implicit and explicit emphasis placed by Franklin himself on adaptability, manipulations of appearance, and the importance of play, the *Autobiography* offers enough clues as to the peril of taking it at face value —that is, as the earnest self-congratulation of a smug, abstemious literalist rather than the playful execution of an unbelievable ironic masquerade.

As a result of falling into the trap of taking Franklin at his word, D. H. Lawrence allowed him, famously, to get under his skin, pouring his irritation into a savage, angry essay in *Studies in Classic American Literature*. Its short exclamations betray his contempt for Franklin's ease in mechanical self-creation, and his apparent refusal to see that the "soul is a dark forest" and that the "known self will never be more than a little clearing in the forest." Lawrence's disgust with Franklin's apparent nonchalance with the world leads him to declare: "I, at least, know why I can't stand Benjamin. He tries to take away my wholeness and my dark forest, my freedom."[17] Most strikingly, Lawrence—in his foolhardiness— avows that he will no longer be duped: "Oh Benjamin! Oh Binjum! You do NOT suck me in any longer."[18] But ironically enough, Lawrence is all the *more* sucked in for earnestly taking Franklin at his word rather than for allowing himself to be the butt of a practical joke—especially as he was able to identify Franklin's masterful capacity to juggle "policy" and "honesty." If the apoplectic spluttering in *Studies in Classic American Literature* doesn't indicate how wholly Lawrence *was* taken in, a lesser known, more reasonably argued essay in *The Symbolic Meaning* does so. Here, in taking Franklin at face value, Lawrence surmises that the only "voluptuous pleasure" Franklin ever enjoyed lay "in subduing and reducing all his feelings and emotions and desires to the material benefit of mankind" (which is odd, since Lawrence was well aware of Franklin's legendary use of "venery" for other than "health or offspring"). He saw Franklin as "purely self-congratulatory" in his recounting "in detail how he worked out the process of reducing himself to a deliberate entity." And he concluded that this "deliberate entity, this self-determined man, is the very Son of Man, man made by the power of the human will, a virtuous Frankenstein monster."[19]

Yet Franklin's self-congratulation is not pure, and neither is the "deliberate entity" so monolithic. Kenneth Silverman points to the readiness of Franklin to describe his "Errata," or "missteps." More importantly, he notes the distinctions between the many "Franklins" negotiated within the *Autobiography*—not with reference to the "easy variety of pursuits" which so mystified Melville, but rather to the book's "earnest young protagonist," its "avuncular narrator," the historical Franklin who created both, and the legendary reputation that had already preceded the writing (and which would surely pervade the consciousness of reader, writer, narrator, and narratees—Franklin's "Dear Son" and "the Public" of the present and future).[20] Perhaps Lawrence was not prepared to view the *Autobiography* in the light of such theoretically informed distinctions; perhaps, as Hauck suggested, he merely lacked a sense of humor, refusing, like Huizinga's spoil-sport, to play along with Franklin. It is likely, however, that what most angered Lawrence was Franklin's capacity to represent the confident, rational, and, as Lawrence would have it, *arrogant* assumptions of the Enlightenment which he (Lawrence) so despised for its supposed lack of mystery. It was Franklin to whom he sarcastically referred in declaring, "The idea of the perfectibility of man, which was such an inspiration in Europe, to Rousseau and Godwin and Shelley, all those idealists of the eighteenth and early nineteenth century, was actually fulfilled in America before the ideal was promulgated in Europe."[21] On the page, at least, yes; it is well within Franklin's power to represent this idea. But the deadpan irony in his voice, as well as the repeated emphasis he places on "imitation" and the avowed ineptitude of his own humility, undercuts any such grand assumption of perfectibility. With only the capacity to half-appreciate Franklin's humor, Lawrence could only half-acknowledge the way it worked: "Franklin had his humour, but it was always of the 'don't-put-all-your-eggs-in-one-basket' sort. It always derided the spontaneous, impulsive or extravagant element in man, and showed the triumph of cautious, calculated, virtuous behaviour."[22] It is true that the *Autobiography* not only demonstrates the triumph of calculation but in fact relies on it; but to deny extravagance on the part of one of the most extravagantly (and, as such, unbelievably) rendered icons of industry and success is to lose sight of Franklin's comic challenge—the same challenge he offered in all his hoaxes. It is the failure truly to *appreciate* Franklin as a comedian or a confidence man.

Mark Twain, on the other hand, could at least *identify* Franklin's comic challenge, if not appreciate it. He thought the *Autobiography* "pernicious," but he obviously recognized Franklin's capacity for outlandish exaggeration. He implied as much in his treatment of Franklin's famous boast of having arrived in Philadelphia "with nothing in the world but two shillings in his pocket and four rolls of bread under his arm. But really, when you come to examine it critically, it was nothing. Anybody could have done it."[23] It is less certain, however, how many other American comedians could have remained so consistently playful, and so confident in their powers to deceive, until well into their seventh decade. Mark Twain, for one, could not, and—perhaps—was prompted by a touch of professional jealousy.

But, more likely, Twain was saying something else entirely: trickery was trickery, humorous or not; deceit still deceit, hurtful or not; and the confidence man could either be a revered Founding Father or a second-rate Yankee peddler. Certainly the first half of the nineteenth century saw just such a debate unfold, as the confidence man established himself as a national type, not only in comedy, but in life. While from the Revolution to the Civil War the illusions of comedy might make the confidence man the most popular imaginative figure—whether Brother Jonathan or Sam Slick, the Yankee peddlers, or the backwoods rogue, Simon Suggs (his motto: "It Is Good to Be Shifty in a New Country"), or Jim Crow, the implausibly genial "darky" minstrel—the realities hidden behind these characterizations inspired a wealth of comment. However much vicarious pleasure might be had through the sly bargainings and audacious deals of Brother Jonathan and Sam Slick, there were still real peddlers traversing the land, swindling farmers and widows, turning fraud into a commercial skill. There was still the terror and mutilation of the frontier towns and river skiffs, however gleefully transformed into the rough-and-tumble brawls and braggadocio of the western tall tales; and however genial and long-suffering was the banjo-strumming clown with the burned cork all over his face and the starred-and-striped outfit, there was still an entire race of human beings in chains beneath the

American flag, still the Prossers, Veseys, and Nat Turners to remind the nation of the human realities and potentials behind the grinning mask.

But with a grin, of course, one could get away with almost anything. So wrote Poe in 1845, when a confidence man was still a "diddler." The grin would not be enough on its own, to be sure. The successful diddle, or swindle, would require "minuteness," or unambitious, "small scale" operations (otherwise the diddler is inflated into a "financier"), "self-interest," "perseverance," "audacity," "nonchalance," and "originality." It requires "impertinence," for a diddle is by definition an outrage: the diddler "sneers in your face. He treads on your corns. He eats your dinner, he drinks your wine, he borrows your money, he pulls your nose, he kicks your poodle, and he kisses your wife." But all of these qualities are no diddle without one other essential ingredient: "Your *true* diddler winds up all with a grin."[24] As if to bear out Poe's theories, only four years later there appeared in the news the case of one William Thompson, whose place in American history and lore clearly indicates the covert appreciation much of the populace held for the diddler as described by Poe. Thompson had been arrested in New York, having been for the previous two months stopping strangers on the streets, engaging them in genial conversation, and asking them to demonstrate their brotherly and sisterly confidence by leaving their valuables with him for one night. The *New York Herald* publicized the case and the name Thompson earned for his enterprises. He was dubbed "The Confidence-Man." The coinage took hold so quickly, and assumed such broad implications, that only a week after his arrest a *Herald* editorial referred to the stock market as "The Confidence-Man on a Large Scale." One month later, in the *Literary World*, Evert Duyckinck eulogized the act of faith that had enabled Thompson to operate: " 'It is not the worst thing that can be said of a country that it gives birth to a confidence man. . . . It is a good thing, and speaks well for human nature, that . . . *men can be swindled.'* "[25] Other famous American confidence men were soon diddling their way with greater and greater magnitude across the ante- and post-bellum scene, to the delight and awe of the public: P. T. Barnum, who, as a national jokester could admit with impunity that every minute a sucker was born; Jay Gould, Cornelius Vanderbilt, and the other robber barons gamesomely and energetically outmaneuvering each other for control of the national wealth, the railroads, and the future of the working class, turning each newspaper headline into another unbelievable tall tale, leaving Sam Slick, Brother Jonathan, and Franklin himself far behind with the magnitude and crassness of their manipulations. Duyckinck had said the act of faith was "a good thing." Under the circumstances, his friend Melville was not so sure.

Diddling in Good Faith

One of the great ironies surrounding Herman Melville's legendary suspicion of the act of faith—the willingness to risk being diddled—is that he was a novelist and, until his comic voice was silenced by bitterness and old age, a comedian. He repeatedly tormented himself with the agonizing problem of trying both to please people and be frank with them. This use of the term "agonizing" is not an exaggeration, if Melville is to be taken at his word: "What a madness and anguish it is that an author can never—under no conceivable circumstances—be at all frank with his readers."[26] His preoccupation with truth, appearance, confidence, and the manipulation of all in games both divine and demonic runs through his work, from his first to his last novel, spilling over into his essays, letters, and reviews. Telling the truth, he maintained, was the great Art; yet "even Shakespeare was not a frank man to the uttermost. And indeed, who in this intolerant Universe is or can be?"[27] Whoever would, would be doomed to critical failure. Even if failure was, to Melville, "the true test of greatness"—as he wrote in "Hawthorne and His Mosses"—he would *prefer* not to fail.[28] For one thing, dollars damned him. For another, he felt that failure was suicide for an author; one might be left like his character, Bartleby the scrivener, whose uncompromising frankness and obstinacy made him, in his own obscure way, both great and dead. So, if one were to court critical success (and Melville surely tried) one must either dispense altogether with truth, or like Shakespeare and Hawthorne, be content to reveal it only in "cunning glimpses"—sneakily, "covertly, and by snatches."[29]

To say that Melville was himself cunning is certainly not to say that he suffered from the "philosophical levity of tranquillity" of which he accuses Franklin in *Israel Potter*, however much he attempted to equal it. He knew that a comedian, with all his cunning, employs such levity like a tool. As a comedian—*and* as a self-confessed confidence man—Melville was able to appreciate Franklin's cunning, and in fact knew only too well what it could accomplish. Consider his own earliest attempts: he had presented his first two novels, *Omoo* and *Typee*, as truthful travel narratives. A skeptical public disbelieved him. With his third book, *Mardi*, he resorted to the time-honored comedic deception: he would admit the joke. However galling it may have been for one whose highest artistic ambition was to tell the truth, he admitted in the preface to *Mardi* that he was now offering a Polynesian *romance*, "to see whether the fiction might not, possibly, be received for a verity: in some degree the reverse of my previous experience."[30]

In *Mardi*, Melville asks outright, "'If all things are deceptive, what is truth?'" The conclusion is never reached; the interrogator is told, noncommittally, "'That question is more final than any answer.'"[31] The poker-faced tranquillity of such a reply might just cover the "madness and anguish" of a divided consciousness, that of the comedian at play and the truth teller in earnest. Yet Melville himself felt, at any rate, that his creative responses to whatever bleak discoveries he encountered depended on at least the *attempt* to imitate the spirit of play, or, as Ishmael calls it in *Moby-Dick*, "godly gamesomeness." Ishmael declares his intention to consider the universe "a vast practical joke," and to see himself as the butt of it. A "free and easy sort of genial, desperado philosophy" is what on the face of it allows him the adaptability that Ahab fatally lacks.[32] Of course, one might see that a certain "madness and anguish" lie *behind* Ishmael's play, for he is sensitive and sympathetic enough to reflect credibly the bitterness of Ahab, as though he remembers such feelings in himself. The importance is that he *employs* levity, creates the *impression* of it; and it is possibly even this that allows him alone to survive and tell the tale.

The fabrication, Ishmael, was apparently more successful in maintaining this impression than his creator was. The duality of Ishmael's narrative voice—its capacity to contain both the "godly" play and the wicked, hellish winds that Melville said blew through the book's riggings—itself became a preoccupation of Melville's before he gave up writing fiction altogether. He had confessed to Hawthorne after finishing *Moby-Dick*, "What I feel most moved to write, that is banned—it will not pay. Yet, altogether, write the *other* way I cannot."[33] Through the ambiguities of *Pierre* and the deadly masquerade of "Benito Cereno," among other fictions, he continued to voice his preoccupation with the manipulation of impressions; with "Bartleby" he implied his recognition of the futility of frankness. By the time he came to his final novel, *The Confidence-Man*, he would devote his full attention to the mechanics, rewards, and consequences of lying, and their relation to comic practice. This, more than anything, justifies the centrality of *The Confidence-Man* in this discussion; for in this book the comedic convention itself is put under explicit scrutiny. Melville seems to ask: If one is only playing, then even within the charmed circle of an acknowledged game, how much can be attempted? If we accept that much good can be executed under the guise of play, or of irony, then what mischief, or even evil, can also be released—and what are the consequences for both comedian and audience? Without knowing it, Lawrence implied the same questions—and the same concern with their paradoxes—in his assessment of Franklin: "So far as affairs went, he was admirable. As far as life goes, he is monstrous."[34] But Lawrence had no ludic fellowship with Franklin; Melville, on the other hand, very likely had his fellow trickster in mind when he began *The Confidence-Man*. He did not attempt to render the trickery of his Great Comedian in the last novel until he had both doffed his hat and sounded the alarm over Franklin's success in the previous one.

"Every time he comes in here, he robs me"

It has been almost commonplace for critics to dive into one passage of *Israel Potter* and to conclude from it that Melville held Franklin in contempt. "Having carefully weighed the world," they repeat, "Franklin could act any part in it." In citing Melville's catalog of Franklin's "easy variety of pursuits" ("Printer, postmaster, almanac maker, essayist, chemist . . . statesman, humorist, philosopher, parlor-man . . . maxim-monger, herb-doctor, wit"), and finishing the discussion with his summation ("Franklin was everything but a poet") it is possible to conclude, as Kenneth Silverman does, that Melville was implying the same thing as Lawrence —that "like America, he [Franklin] lacked a soul."[35] I must confess to having thought this myself; but upon returning to *Israel Potter*, I think differently. While I cannot account precisely for Melville's use of the word *poet*—whether or not he may have been referring to an earnest revelator—I don't believe the lack of a soul was his implication, but rather Franklin's deliberate inscrutability of soul, effected through his multifarious camouflage. Somewhere, the soul is there, all right: "a soul with many qualities," ultimately as inaccessible as the soul of all collective humanity, needing "the contact of just as many different men, or subjects, in order to the exhibition of its totality" (479). It is a soul that, if shown at all, reveals itself only as a strategy, a "defensive bloom" (469). Rather than contempt, I believe that what Melville shows are both his awe and his unease with Franklin's manipulative capabilities. He speculates over a power that, however beneficently assured in the person of his wise Doctor Franklin, is disturbingly less benign in the person of his next and equally masterful practitioner of comic deceit, the Confidence-Man.

That Melville's Franklin is a wizard, there is no doubt, first appearing as he does, "wrapped in a rich dressing-gown . . . curiously embroidered with algebraic figures like a conjuror's robe," his table "round as the zodiac," his cluttered study "necromantic" (468). In Franklin, the admirable though common enough human qualities of "far foresight, pleasant wit, and working wisdom" are combined and magnified to the point of "supernatural lore." In his venerable age he has waxed potent, "keen, spear-pointed, and elastic," at once bearing "the incredible seniority of the antediluvian" and the timelessness of the immortal: "His white hairs and mild brow, spoke of the future as well as the past" (469). In such supernatural and ubiquitous respects, Melville's Franklin foreshadows the Confidence-Man. That he is—fortunately—*philanthropically* two-faced in his command of the arts of manipulation, there is also no doubt. With his ancient inscrutability —his "primeval orientalness," as Melville describes it—and in his mastery in the creation of an impression, Franklin has his parallel in the Jacob of the Old Testament, "interesting not less from the unselfish devotion which we are bound to ascribe to him, than from the deep worldly wisdom and polished Italian tact, gleaming under an air of Arcadian unaffectedness." In Jacob, the calculated politic and the philanthropic are combined: "The diplomatist and the shepherd are blended . . . the apostolic serpent and dove. A tanned Machiavelli in tents." So it is with Franklin. He may write with the "perspicuity" of Hobbes, but such apparent frankness and clarity is a screen for the workings of a consciousness much less transparent, however socially devoted. History, concludes Melville, offers no greater kinship than in the trio of Jacob, Hobbes, and Franklin, possessed as they are of uncanny powers to persuade and manipulate in the interests of what they perceive as the common good. They are "three labyrinth-minded, but plain-spoken Broadbrims, at once politicians and philosophers; keen observers of the main chance; prudent courtiers; practical magians in linsey woolsey" (477).

What both impresses and disturbs Melville, as Plato and St. Augustine before him, is the tyrannical potential of a confidence man to dominate artlessly and to dispense with truth for whatever his noble or ignoble ends. Thus, when Franklin attempts to instruct Israel in the arts of caution—as befitting a budding spy for the American rebels—he also demonstrates his capacity to work his will upon the protagonist. In both the instruction and the demonstration, he reveals Melville's concerns about honesty versus falsehood, frankness versus inscrutability, trust versus suspicion, and the use of jokery as a calculated device—themes to which he returns in greater detail, though with more cynicism, in *The Confidence-Man*. "'All of us, my honest friend,'" Franklin counsels Israel, "'are subject to making mistakes. . . . Now one remedy for mistakes is honesty.'" But it is only *one* remedy in a whole bag of tricks, and one that, Franklin implies, should be used sparingly. He attempts to teach Israel the art of the poker face: "'At the prospect of pleasure, never be elated; but, without depression, respect the omens of ill'" (472–73). He delivers "didactically waggish" lectures, just as the Confidence-Man does, on the paradoxical indispensability of trust and suspicion (479). "'Sad usage has made you sadly suspicious, my honest friend,'" he tells Israel. "'And though want of suspicion more than want of sense, sometimes leads a man into harm: yet too much suspicion is as bad as too little sense'" (471). Yet the demands of suspicion are at least as urgent as those of the trust which they both—like all spies, envoys, and confidence men—seek to elicit: "'I know it, my honest friend; the sweeter, the more dangerous. Arsenic is sweeter than sugar'" (485).

Franklin is the first American diplomat, "first, both in point of time and merit"; and if the truism stands that a diplomat is a good man sent abroad to lie for his country, then he is a proper mentor for an aspiring spy (477). His instructions to Israel about the calculated employment of a joke—to be used only in the effect of policy or gain—go right to the heart of Melville's later, and fuller, speculations about the comedian as confidence man. Although Franklin is always and ultimately at play—toward whatever the ends—it is to him a valuable weapon, not to be trusted in the hands of inept amateurs. "At times he had seriousness—extreme seriousness—for others, but never for himself" (479). *He* is the master comedian; Israel is the novice. After a pathetic attempt of wit at Franklin's expense, Israel is forced to explain, "'Oh, I was only joking, Doctor.'" "'I knew that,'" Franklin replies. "'It's a bad habit, except at the proper time, and with the proper person'" (483). Israel is in no position even to *think* of teaching his grandmother to suck eggs, until he can become, like Franklin, profoundly, "sagely mischievous" (491).

As if in rebuke for Israel's presumptuousness—or as an object lesson—Franklin goes to work on *him*, suavely divesting him of various luxuries and his own self-possession, leaving Israel "to surmise the mild superiority of successful strategy which lurked beneath this highly ingratiating air" (484). It is a strategy of diversion and flattery—again, central to Melville's discussion in *The Confidence-Man*—which leaves Israel at once perplexed and duped, with Franklin's recurrent appellation of "my honest friend" echoing in mockery. "'Every time he comes in here he robs me', soliloquised Israel, dolefully; 'with an air all the time, too, as if he were making me presents.'" Israel can only conclude, poorer, sadder, and wiser, "'Depend upon it, he's sly, sly, sly'" (486). Of this, Franklin himself is well aware, as in one instance in which he works his art of disarming flattery to soothe and divert the highly inflammable John Paul Jones. "'Thank you for your frankness,'" says Jones, unwittingly outmaneuvered; "'frank myself, I love to deal with a frank man. You, Doctor Franklin, are true, and deep; and so you are frank.'" In the confident knowledge of his own abiding mastery in the creation of an impression, Franklin offers in reply only a sedate smile, "a queer incredulity just lurking in the corner of his mouth" (492).

The Comedian as Confidence Man

In conclusion, *Israel Potter* seems to demonstrate that, far from holding Franklin in contempt, Melville sees him as a master comedian. Moreover, he takes repeated pains—as even Lawrence does—to emphasize Franklin's devotion to the improvement of his society. His narrator even confesses to a certain sheepishness, feeling "more as if he were playing with one of the sage's worsted hose, then reverentially handling the honored hat which once oracularly sat upon his brow" (479). And in accepting Franklin's doubleness—his "slyness"—along with the obvious fact of his social conscience, the duped though grateful Israel takes his leave, carrying with him Franklin's ideas for the mechanical improvement of his own farm. This is, perhaps, the most fitting tribute to Franklin, and Melville's means of making amends for having exposed the workings of his confidence game.

But what if it were not a revered sage such as Franklin under scrutiny? Supposing somebody else could acquire his powers of persuasion? If persuasive, genial trickery—sheer performance—could be mastered by Franklin in the interests of creating a new self or a new society, might it not be employed in either direction, toward goodness *or* corruption, in both self and society? This is what Thomas Mann asks in his allegorical tale about the rise of Fascism, "Mario and the Magician"; and it is what Melville asks in *The Confidence-Man*. To be sure, Melville does not explicitly refer to the surreptitious rise of authoritarian tyranny as Mann does; if anything, the world of *The Confidence-Man* is one without authority, practically devoid of violence and savagery. But it is a world in which, "where the wolves are killed off, the foxes increase."[36] It is a world, too, in which the prime manipulator and purveyor of fiction—the arch liar—is an artist, a patron of the arts, and a comedian.

Just as they have offered conclusive analyses of Franklin's masquerades in the *Autobiography*, Gary Lindberg and Warwick Wadlington, among others, have turned their attention to the implications of convincing play in *The Confidence-Man*. Both deal specifically with the historical context of a still-young America—in Lindberg's words, "the daily fictionalizing—the creating and erasing of characters—that makes up the game of identity in a new and protean society." Lindberg in particular also concentrates on the textual implications—on how, "by baring his own literary devices, emphasizing the problems of fiction, [Melville] estranges us from that fiction-making world and allows us to see it and ourselves anew."[37] A substantial body of scholarship has already focused on Melville's allegorical devices: the setting—the riverboat-cum-gambling-den ironically named the *Fidèle*; the generic Confidence-Man himself, shape-shifting through the tale in a series of performing avatars, engendering and exploiting trust, instigating or exorcising distrust with no accompanying assurance of his motives. Again, I would not wish to repeat or compete with earlier arguments: what I would like to do is to narrow the focus, and explore what *The Confidence-Man* says and implies about the mendacity of comic practice in particular. I would like to examine Melville's speculations about the rules, consequences, and the intolerable paradoxes of serious play that seem to have led so many American comedians to give up the game in the end, comedians—like Lenny Bruce, Mark Twain, Vonnegut, even Melville himself—who somehow couldn't keep up the masquerade with the equanimity and poise of the aged Franklin.

In terms of comedy, *The Confidence-Man* might imply more than it states outright, but it is relevant to this discussion because it foregrounds, even if metaphorically, a host of comedic problems: the precarious balancing of earnestness and play, or at least the *impressions* thereof; the double-edged status of the comedian as both philanthropist and misanthrope, critic and buffoon; the potential of laughter as both shield and weapon; the limits of the implied contract or convention between players in a play-world (comedian *and* public); and the consequences of both seeking and ignoring the truth—or at least the serious intentions—behind a comedian's ironic play. In plotting the intercourse between what one character calls this "'flock of fools, under this captain of fools, in this ship of fools,'" Melville suggests the difficulty of knowing where among the players to apply the epithet of "fool" (855). He does this at the very outset, with the introduction of the first three major characters, who by contrast demonstrate not only how a comedian might or might not manipulate an audience toward his own ends but also the consequences of both the successful and the inept masquerade. At first, a deaf and mute "lamb-like figure" appears onboard, making earnest appeals for charity, through biblical injunctions scrawled on a slate with chalk (844). In Melville's comic world, as in any comedian's, charity implies trust, the giving and receiving of which is central to the intercourse between the duped and the trickster. As Max Eastman emphasized, the crucial item held in trust is the assurance of play, explicit or otherwise; for play —on the face of it—implies safety. The deaf-mute's appeals, however, do not appear playful, at least as far as the audience—the other passengers—can tell. His earnest injunctions both wound their consciences and threaten their selfish prosperity. As a result, he is mocked, jostled, and jeered, but not severely molested because he presents the aspect of "some strange kind of simpleton, harmless enough" (842). He operates, however, on the borderline of resentment, and is humorless except to the extent that he patiently allows himself to be mocked, bearing it as a martyr rather than inviting it as a clown. His aspect and his appeals are in their intrusiveness "not wholly unobnoxious" to the passengers, and give him, at best, the protective mantle of a derisory fool; but they earn neither him nor the world any charity. Ironically, Melville posits at the same time another written appeal—to *suspicion* rather than charity—in the form of a posted barber's notice declaring "NO TRUST." Although at least as intrusive as the deaf-mute's appeal, it provokes no resentment on the part of the passengers, nor does it earn the barber the reputation of a "simpleton." Whatever this may signal about the uncharitable nature either of American capitalism or humanity in general, it also signals something else. The barber succeeds because his appeal is not contrary to the expectations—or even the *mores*—of his society; and therefore he need adopt no ruse. The deaf-mute, however, is a failure: because of the apparent earnestness of his disturbing supplication, he is rebuffed. Perhaps this is one reason for the critical disagreement over whether or not he is the first avatar of the Confidence-Man, for he is a singular failure as one.

There is an instructive contrast in the next character, *unquestionably* an avatar of the generic Confidence-Man: "a grotesque negro cripple, in tow-cloth attire and an old coal-sifter of a tambourine in his hand" (849). It is significant that Melville puts the confidence game into operation with this minstrel figure, considering all that he implies about comic deceit for both the comedian and the audience who is duped by him. He too is a supplicant for charity; but he is accepted as an avowedly comic figure from the outset. He performs the darky act, shuffling to and fro, making music, and —as though conscious of Poe's advice—is always grinning. He succeeds where the deaf-mute fails, but at a price: just as his crippled limbs have reduced his physical stature to that of a dog, so does his darky act "put him on a canine footing." In what the narrator calls "a singular temptation at once to *diversion* and charity" (Melville's emphasis), Black Guinea sets out to provide the first and obtain the second—even if it means he will be treated like a performing animal. He scrapes along the deck, stopping to throw his head back and open his mouth "like an elephant for tossed apples at a menagerie"; only what he catches between his teeth are the coins pitched at him by gleeful passengers. As the narrator pointedly observes, "To be the subject of almsgiving is trying, and to feel in duty bound to appear cheerfully grateful under the trial, must be still more so, but whatever his secret emotions, he swallowed them" (850).

Why is the minstrel figure such a potent avatar of the Confidence-Man, and so charged with negative and positive implications for both the trickster and the audience? Why is he such a fitting figure to begin Melville's disquisition on the consequences of the comic masquerade? As Ralph Ellison notes in *Shadow and Act*, in addition to conferring such a demeaning status upon the African character it purports to reflect, the darky act also successfully blinds an appreciative audience to the dangers of participating in, and perpetuating, the act. Ellison writes that the purpose of the act is "to

veil the humanity of the Negroes thus reduced to a sign, and to re-
press the white audience's awareness of its moral identification
with its own acts and with the human ambiguities pushed behind
the mask."[38] The more the audience laughs, the more *diverted* they
are from the moral and social consequences of the racial crimes that
enable the darky act in the first place. Hence the exploration of the
act in Ellison's own *Invisible Man*: "'I want you to overcome 'em
with yeses, undermine 'em with grins, agree 'em to death and destruction, let 'em swoller you till they vomit or bust wide open'";
and hence the historical fact that the most popular American comic
figure in the 1830s was the minstrel "Jim Crow" Rice, who got the
most laughs when the terror from Denmark Vesey's slave revolt
was still fresh.[39] Thus, having already taken the successful darky
act to its ultimate, bloody conclusion in "Benito Cereno," Melville
returns to it in *The Confidence-Man*, if only to imply the double-
edged potential that it demonstrates in the previous tale. It is important for a later avatar of the Confidence-Man—whose
manipulations depend on the credulity that Black Guinea first establishes and exploits—to reinforce the impression of the former
avatar's harmlessness. "He added that negroes were by nature a
singularly cheerful race . . . that even from religion they dismissed
all gloom; in their hilarious rituals they danced, so to speak, and, as
it were, cut pigeon-wings." It is imperative for this all-white audience, if they are to be successfully duped—as they were historically
and as they are in the novel—to believe it impossible "that a negro,
however reduced to his stumps by fortune, could be ever thrown
off the legs of a laughing philosophy" (902).

Going beyond the racial distinctions alone, Melville illustrates here a major conflict—if not *the* major one—faced by all
comedians who are obliged to negotiate the persona of the buffoon,
whose apparent goal is the *diversion* of laughter, and the serious individual who is so reduced to the persona. To the extent that the
deaf-mute cannot maintain a mutually accepted comic aspect, however much he may retain his self-respect, he fails in his appeal to
charity. To the extent that Black Guinea convinces his audience of
his play, he succeeds in his appeal, but at great cost to his stature in
the eyes of his fellows. And in both instances, the audience is morally endangered by their own reactions: by refusing to believe the
deaf-mute's earnest appeals, and by accepting the comic gratification of the darky act, they are in fact the poorer. In these respects,
the epithet of "fool" is applicable to all players.

Black Guinea also exemplifies another hazard faced by the comedian: he must be convincing, not only in his role, but in his assurance that it *is* a role (even if it isn't), that he *knows* it is a role (even if it isn't), and that he knows his audience knows. In this respect, this avatar of the Confidence-Man almost fails, for at least one person not only suspects him but resents his attempt to dupe him. This is the third character mentioned above, a "limping, gimlet-eyed, sour-faced" man, a cynic with a wooden leg (850). He accuses Black Guinea of failing to cover the truth, namely, that not only is he a "'white masquerading as a black'" but that his motives constitute robbery (873). He, too, shows himself as Huizinga's spoil-sport, wrecking the game of the false player as he makes two distinctions. "'Charity is one thing, and truth is another,'" he says, as though the trust begged by the comedian is, on basis, incompatible with the reality behind his masquerade; and "'Looks are one thing, and facts are another'"—again, as though the impression of play or jokery were a moral outrage, masking a grimmer reality that one ignores at one's peril (853). This wooden-legged skeptic represents the most vindictive spirit in the ludic circle, the one who is not taken in or charmed by the promise of play, and who tries to break the spell cast upon all others. Himself the butt of mockery by his fellow passengers who are indeed disarmed by Black Guinea's buffoonery, the spoil-sport vows, "'But trust your painted decoy . . . and I have my revenge'" (855). The sting in the tail is that, in spite of his offensive refusal to play, he is probably right.

Yet not only is the wooden-legged man an unwilling dupe and fool on the *receiving* end of the comic masquerade, he also portrays the *comedian* as spoil-sport, refusing or unable to utilize laughter in an assumed spirit of play. Incensed by the laughter at his own expense, he can neither employ it defensively nor mask it as an offensive device. The most he can deliver is "a sort of laugh more like a groan than a laugh," which is at best "intended for a laugh." His laughter is too obviously used as a weapon of spite, and that of a man "morosely grave as a criminal judge with . . . the memory of certain recent biting rebuffs and mortifications" (871). A later avatar of the Confidence-Man, the man in gray, denounces this failure. Apparently vexed by the wooden-legged man's cynical laughter at Black Guinea's expense—"a long, gasping, rasping sort of taunting cry, intolerable as that of a high-pressure engine jeering off steam"—he condemns precisely that kind of laughter which "'would make truth almost as offensive as falsehood'" (873). The cynic's laughter has failed to sweeten momentarily the offensive-ness of the truth; and ultimately the man in gray is forced to demand the only clarification that could restore the good will the comedian has lost, namely, the explicit promise of play: " 'In short, would you tell me now, whether you were not merely joking in the notion you threw out about the negro? Would you be so kind?' " In denying jokery, and affirming his status as a spoil-sport, the wooden-legged man replies, " 'No, I won't be so kind, I'll be so cruel' " (873).

The assurance that the man in gray demands ("Smile when you say that") is the same demanded of every comedian who would both utilize laughter as a critical weapon and invoke it at his *own* expense rather than resentment or retribution. The man in gray in fact demonstrates this earlier in the novel as he solicits funds for what may (or may not) be a fictitious widows' and orphans' asylum. Adopting a grave, sanctimonious aspect as he makes the rounds, he is at one point rebuffed by another spoil-sport, a "hard-hearted old gentleman" who demands "less hypocrisy" in reply to the avatar's appeal for "more charity" (870). Yet, as both the deaf-mute and Black Guinea demonstrate, a trickster's audience doesn't require less hypocrisy, but *more*—comic rather than grave, convincing rather than inept. Perhaps the efficacy of this lesson is in this avatar's mind when he shortly comes upon the wooden-legged skeptic and demands of him, of all things, the explicit assurance of a joke. Certainly the Confidence-Man is for the most part canny enough to avoid the impression of too much earnestness in public; for him the earnest endeavor is the failed one—unless, of course, one accepts that he *plays* in earnest. This paradox, which maddeningly places the comedian in an interpretative hall of mirrors, captures the narrator's attention at more than one point in the book. Chapter 5 shows us another avatar, the man with the mourning weed, privately reflecting on his recent triumph in obtaining charity with an inflated, "almost painful," though hardly grave tale of woe. The narrator ironically muses over the cool manner in which this avatar subsequently underplays his victory in public, concluding that "to be full of warm, earnest words, and heart-felt protestations, is to create a scene; and well-bred people dislike few things more than that . . . because the world, being earnest itself, likes an earnest scene, and an earnest man, very well, but only in their place—the stage" (865). In other words, for good or ill, in Melville's comic world the impression of being in earnest, if there is one, must be at once convincing and identifiably false—an act, a joke. In this case, the implications are disturbing, for while the Confidence-Man's public success in impersonating earnestness connotes a certain put-on, so may his private sincerity. In the seclusion of his cabin, this avatar throws off his "cold garb of decorum," adopting a "melancholy unreserved," which "still the more attested his earnestness" (866). But with no one besides the reader to appreciate this transformation, it may be a joke for *our* benefit, on the part of an undeniably playful narrator challenging us to believe the Confidence-Man's sorrow over his victims' credulity.

Thus the deaf-mute, the wooden-legged cynic, and all the avatars thus far mentioned demonstrate the importance of the genial fiction, indispensable for the exploiter who would hope to use the assurance of play as a weapon and a defensive mechanism. The underlying, bleak implication is that the philanthropic confidence man is no more a respecter of persons than the misanthropic one: it might be Franklin, it might be Tartuffe. Both are genial. Thus another avatar, the ironically named "John Truman," transfer agent for the Black Rapids Coal Company (with its hellish associations), condemns the "destroyers of confidence, and gloomy philosophers of the stock market," not for their fictions, but for their gloom. "'Why, the most monstrous of all hypocrites are these bears: hypocrites by inversion; hypocrites in the simulation of things dark instead of bright, souls that thrive, less upon depression, than the fiction of depression'" (891). He, of course, would bullishly set out to simulate things bright, toward his own ends and at any investor's peril; but *he* is never the bear. Rather, he rhapsodizes on a world of games "in which every player plays fair, and not a player but shall win" (898). Such a world may be "uninvented," as he is pointedly told; but in emphasizing his willingness to play, even if he lies about his fairness at play, this avatar reveals himself outright as a most dangerous sort of "false player." He is the liar or cheat who may well stand higher in human estimation than the "spoil-sport" who will not play at all, but who is all the more misanthropic even in his "simulation of things bright." He puts the price of one hundred dollars on an old miser's confidence, with the uncertain promise of trebling it in investment; but the sum is paltry in comparison with the victory of crushing suspicion in the most suspicious of characters. When he tells the miser, "'Honesty's best voucher is honesty's face,'" he knows the truth of the miser's reply: "'Can't see yours, though'" (919). Truman, like all the Confidence-Man's avatars, calls attention outright to the *possibility* of his own fictions; yet his assurance of play (explicit or not, honest or not) is the charm that hooks his mark, with the object just as easily being utter divestment rather than investment.

The first half of *The Confidence-Man* suggests that the comedic sting can go both ways. The deaf-mute, Black Guinea, the wooden-legged skeptic, the man in gray, and the man with the mourning weed all reveal the confidence game backfiring either on the instigator—the comedian—or the public he dupes. Another avatar, the herb-doctor, fails at one point to convince a passenger of either his harmless play or the truth that *might* lie behind it (the questionable efficacy of his "Samaritan Pain Dissuader") and as a result is the victim of the book's only act of physical violence. But his ostentatious application of his own medicine to his injury then places his audience in the position of having to reevaluate their own interpretative stances. The passengers debate over whether he is a "fool" or a "knave," or, more critically, "essentially a fool, though effectively a knave" (935). After learning that he has given half his proceeds away, they nearly short-circuit themselves in trying to determine whether he is fool, knave, or genius. Their three-way debate, or "triangular duel," can end only in "a triangular result" (938). In the passengers' failure to conclude definitively where they stand in relation to the comedian's manipulations— whether they themselves are victims or beneficiaries—they are examples of his warnings against searching too deeply for reality behind his play. He boasts earlier of a potion that "'kills pain without killing feeling,'" employing the terms so frequently applied to the sugar-coated pill of comic pleasure (933). He warns that to demand the ingredients of his potion may be "'the mark of a philosopher,'" but carries with it "'the penalty of a fool'"—that searching too closely for the truth behind the joke will cause pain (925).

Increasingly this is Melville's underlying theme, with the comedy growing more dismal as the reader approaches the center of the book—chapter 23—in which the lesser avatars of the Confidence-Man give way to the one whose powers dominate the rest of the novel, demonstrating with all his inscrutability the misanthropic potential that Franklin only implied. Corresponding with this central point is the *Fidèle*'s approach to Cairo—Cairo, in American literature a place of reckoning, as Huck and Jim find in the fog that commits them to their hellish downriver odyssey; in English literature, the fraudulent Eden where Dickens's Martin Chuzzlewit loses his fortune and nearly his life. In *The Confidence-Man*, the "grotesquely-shaped bluff" at Cairo known as "the Devil's Joke" is the signal for one dupe, the Missourian, to rue his encounter with the Philosophical Intelligence Officer, an avatar he sees as a sinister trickster operating "more for the love than the lucre" (978–79). Amidst narrative overtones of disease, death, and grave-digging, the Missourian's gloomy reverie ushers in the major avatar of the Confidence-Man, Frank Goodman, whose frankness and goodness are unverifiable, and who is all the more dangerous because all the more genial. His potential for this duality is remarked upon by the Missourian, the character who comes closest to seeing through him. He calls Goodman "'Diogenes masquerading as a cosmopolitan,'" invoking the name of the ancient cynic who in spite of his legendary misanthropy had the nerve to claim himself a world citizen, and who allegedly coined the word *cosmopolitan* (988). Goodman asserts his own supernatural ubiquity, "from Teheran to Natchitoches," as he ranges the world in the smiling guise of cosmopolitan and philanthropist, inspiring, undermining, and exploiting confidence (982).

Nowhere are the associations with comedy more explicitly pronounced than in this avatar: the world to him is a "Fair," and he is dressed as in a pantomime, "parti-hued," both grotesque and harlequinesque. Life, he says, "'is a pic-nic *en costume*; one must take part, assume a character, stand ready in a sensible way to play the fool'" (983). He has explicit opinions about humor and comedy, but what one reads into them is determined by the trust or suspicion in which one holds him. He deprecates irony: "'Irony is so unjust; never could abide irony; something Satanic about irony. God defend me from Irony, and Satire his bosom friend'" (986). Yet if he is indeed worthy of suspicion, then it follows that he *would* attempt to disparage those comic forms that invite suspicion. He applauds humor, which he equates with jokery; but if he is evil, then he naturally *would* approve of any joke that, he says, can redeem or disguise evil. "'Humor,'" he says, "'is, in fact, so blessed a thing, that even in the least virtuous product of the human mind, if there can be found but nine good jokes . . . those nine good jokes should redeem all the wicked thoughts, though plenty as the populace of Sodom'" (1015). This redemptive transformation is effected by what he calls, in anticipation of Huizinga, the "'catholicon and charm'" of humor; yet even he is forced to acknowledge the evil that humor might ease, or "'oil,'" into the world, "'as a pirate schooner, with colors flying, is launched into the sea on greased ways'" (1026).

The potential of both the redemptive and destructive powers of humor underlies the crucial encounter between Frank

Goodman and Charlie Noble, a second-rate confidence man. When Frank tricks Charlie into revealing himself as a fraud—" 'You played your part better than I did mine; you played it, Charlie, to the life' "—there is a satisfying sense of truth revealed through trickery (1036). But however much one might applaud the victory of a master confidence man over a presumptuous lesser rival, beneath Frank's triumph runs a disturbing implication of comedy as a demonic, exploitative ritual. He diffuses Charlie's wrath and unmasks him through an act that is at once a joke and a suggestion of the Confidence-Man's diabolical nature, echoing Melville's description of Franklin in *Israel Potter*. With "the air of a necromancer," laying ten gold pieces in a "magic ring" around Charlie, intoning a "solemn murmur of cabalistical words," Frank recreates simultaneously the charmed circle of play described by Huizinga, and a hellish snare, however farcically utilized: "Meantime, he within the magic-ring stood suddenly rapt, exhibiting every symptom of a successful charm" (1035). And if Frank can then "drop the necromancer" with the same ease of Franklin in putting on Jesus and Socrates, his demonic spell remains to infuse the play through the rest of the book. As Frank knocks off his other rival confidence men, Winsome and Egbert—the Emerson and Thoreau caricatures who preach self-reliance and miserliness at the expense of charity—one might applaud; just as one might applaud his victory in convincing the barber to remove his "NO TRUST" sign. But the Confidence-Man (both the character and the book) "increases in seriousness," not because he is any the less playful, but because the power of his play takes on such proportion as to undermine and control all who come before it. Hence the oft-quoted comparison of the Confidence-Man's original power with a great revolving light, "raying away from itself all round it—everything is lit by it, everything starts up to it" (1098).

When, making his final exit, the Confidence-Man extinguishes the light and leads away a trusting old man into the darkness, the narrator predicts, "Something further may follow of this Masquerade" (1112). At its least sinister, this might indicate Melville's plans for a sequel; but it is more likely to be interpreted otherwise. For what the reader is left to examine is not merely the possibility that Melville was predicting America's descent into the corrupt mire of the Gilded Age, or the rise of confidence men on the political or economic stages. We are left examining our own enjoyment of laughter, and whether in our willingness to dupe and be duped in an exchange of comic pleasure, we are participating in "godly gamesomeness" or something more discreditable, because deceitful. When the wooden-legged spoil-sport asks, rhetorically, "'How much money did the devil make by gulling Eve?'" (875), it is the entire concept of jokery that is placed under indictment.

CHAPTER 3

Lenny Bruce:
"I'm not a comedian"

In his lamentation, "On the Decay of the Art of Lying," Mark Twain warned, in spite of his own urges toward a brutal frankness, that "an awkward, unscientific lie is often as ineffectual as the truth." The wisdom of the ages, he said, had declared it: "Children and fools *always* speak the truth. The deduction is plain —adults and wise persons *never* speak it." Given not only his own utilization of a child's voice as a comic shield in his most famous novel, but also the dual meaning bearing upon the word *fool*, which designation he both courted and feared, Twain had already demonstrated his recognition of what had earlier caused Melville to avoid under all circumstances the temptation toward frankness. As such he was well equipped to quote the historian Francis Parkman: "'The saying is old that truth should not be spoken at all times; and those whom a sick conscience worries into habitual violation of the maxim are imbeciles and nuisances.'" The fabrication, Mark Twain, might breathe an audible sigh of relief—"None of us could *live* with an habitual truth teller; but thank goodness none of us has to"— but, as we shall later explore, he could only do so while clamping his hand over the mouth of the aging, embittered Samuel Clemens.[1]

Mark Twain does more here than foreshadow his own later violations of Parkman's maxim. He also points to the transgressions of his comedic descendant, perhaps the twentieth century's most notable example of the American comedian who would not lie when it mattered most—who, like Clemens himself, ultimately ruptured the ironic identity with the explicit betrayal of his critical intent. As a performing cabaret artist, Lenny Bruce walked a more precarious tightrope than those comedians who reach the public through print, in that the response to his comedy was more immediate. Few literary comedians have ever had cocktail glasses thrown at *them* by angry patrons; Mark Twain had been spared that even at his most disastrous public speaking engagements. But Bruce's contempt for the cumbersome demands of camouflage, his impatience with the whitewash of mitigation or ironic distance, earned for him more than the deserved impression of daring and the adulation of the rising counterculture of the 1960s. It also conferred upon him, in comedic terms at least, the kiss of death that must inevitably accompany the labels that the ironist sets out to avoid—some of which his defenders and, fatally, Bruce himself, utilized amidst the savage backlashes against him. We may recall Huizinga's litany of such labels—"apostates, heretics, innovators, prophets, conscientious objectors"—in his general category of "spoil-sports," as well as his warning of the unhappy fate that a society holds in store for them in a culture of play, with all that culture's demands of safety and untruth. In the case of Lenny Bruce— a super-hip deliverer of *"truth* truth" to the squares, an angry Jew out among the gentiles and near-gentiles, a self-proclaimed healer with the avowed mission of cutting away the cancer of hypocrisy in a sick society—revenge for his refusal to play by the rules was swift and complete. For in the end he was—as he himself declared—"not a comedian."

Hipster Trickster

Although presented and marketed as an icon, martyr, and prophet of the 1960s, spawning the posters, T-shirts, songs, stage plays, and feature films that would memorialize (and mythologize) him, Lenny Bruce belongs to a number of earlier and different contexts. He became a professional stand-up comic in the 1950s; he looked to the hip jazz world of the late 1940s for much of his aesthetic and linguistic inspiration; and behind all this lay the Jewish comedic tradition—*his* tradition—brought to America from the persecuted hamlets of eastern Europe in the late nineteenth century. He was a comedian positioned on a number of borders. Comedically, aesthetically, intellectually, ethnically, and politically, Lenny Bruce was out of step with the cultural mainstream that dictated what might be said, how and where it might be said, during his short lifetime. Yet at the same time he looked to that mainstream for inclusion and failed, however much he paved the way for his successors. He provides one of America's most important examples of a comedian straining against, and ultimately being defeated by, the limits of his contemporary comic license.

There has been a great temptation to label as "conformist" the era in which Lenny Bruce's voice was first captured on record. Images of *The Organization Man,* Eisenhower's "masterful inactivity," *Better Homes and Gardens,* Betty Crocker cake mixes, General Motors, and the constraints of the Maidenform bra dominate and threaten to define the American 1950s, as do the "stench of fear" and the "collective failure of the nerve" described by Norman Mailer in the miasma of McCarthyism—with the bleak choices of "instant death by atomic war, relatively quick death by the State as *l'univers concentrationnaire,* or with a slow death by conformity with every creative and rebellious instinct stifled."[2] James Thurber and Malcolm Muggeridge also looked ruefully over their shoulders when describing the moribund state of American comedy. Senator McCarthy's ghost was still hovering too close in 1958, Thurber lamented, to hazard any incisive political or cultural satire.[3] "When people are fearful," said Muggeridge, "they want everyone to be the same, to accept the same values, say the same things, nourish the same hopes, to wear the same clothes, look at the same television, and ride in the same motorcars." In such a society, he concluded, "there is no place for the jester. He strikes a discordant note, and therefore must be put down."[4] But America in the late 1950s was surely not without its jesters. As Hugh Dalziel Duncan noted, many of them were the millionaire chums of presidents, endorsing the products that sponsored their weekly television shows: Bob Hope, Jack Benny, Milton Berle, Red Skelton, Bing Crosby. For Duncan, these comedians demonstrated that the reigning comic ethic was far from subversive, that in popular American comedy it was the rich plutocrat, rather than the "sturdy beggar," who was more likely to appeal for public sympathy: "We hear jokes about how the income tax impoverishes, how hard it is to get Jack Benny to spend, how the government borrows from Bing Crosby. . . . The clown has become a salesman who vies with professional announcers in glorifying anything that is profitable."[5]

But there was another side to the American 1950s, energetically explored by the cultural historian William T. Lhamon in his study, *Deliberate Speed.* Beneath the strolling, golfing, middle-class decency of Eisenhower and the Pepsodent purity of Doris Day was Chuck Berry injecting double-timed sexual energy into the foundations of popular music; Little Richard emerging from the gay bars of the black South to confound America with what might be the real meaning of "Long, Tall Sally"; Kerouac and the Beats asserting that the America they crisscrossed was "an Indian thing"; Ralph Ellison's *Invisible Man* speaking on the "lower frequencies" for the dispossessed and the marginalized.[6] William Burroughs and Brion Gysin were carnivalizing the language, cutting up and reorganizing the linguistic and literary perceptions of the precious few who noticed. Sylvia Plath's early poems were already undermining the images of satisfied womanhood imposed from on high by American film, television, and advertising; and, as Alice Walker has demonstrated in the short story "1955," popular ivorizing "rebels" such as Elvis Presley were only touching the surface of alternative cultural expressions they themselves could barely identify. These were the forces rumbling beneath the sanitized crust of American culture, ignored or held at bay by the mainstream media, but soon to explode forth in a wave that would carry defiant voices into the turmoil of the 1960s. Among these voices were those of a small band of comedians learning their craft in strip joints, jazz clubs, and coffeehouses, unnoticed and thus unbridled by the censorial restraints of television, radio, and major recording houses.

Lenny Bruce was one of these invisible comedians. He could stand onstage at Strip City, or the Cobblestone Club, or any number of the obscure West Coast nightclubs, and say to an equally ignored audience: "If you've ever seen this bit before, I want you to tell me—stop me if you've seen it: I'm going to piss on you." The audience of jazz musicians, prostitutes, and their customers would laugh and applaud. Bruce could mock them for their acceptance: "Well, let me just do a few talk bits first—'No, piss on us first, and *then* you'll do the rest of it!'"[7] Had Lenny Bruce remained in the obscurity of the California jazz and drug underground, for purposes of comedic study he would only be worthy as an example of the carnivalesque voices that always accept their marginalization, that lie low and steer clear of conflict with any licensing or censorial forces. But Bruce ultimately sought wider recognition from the mainstream, and conflict with it; therefore it is important to consider not only when he came into conflict with the determinants of popular comic license but also what sources of inspiration and identification he brought to that conflict.

It is debatable, for instance, as to whether Lenny Bruce was *actually* a hipster, a "White Negro," whatever the temptation for his defenders to describe him as such. If we are to assume, as Caroline Bird did, that a hipster's main goal was to *avoid* the society that threatened "to make everyone over in its own image," then Bruce would not fit the bill; for he agitated for inclusion in, and rearrangement of, that society.[8] Mailer's overblown panegyric on the hip ethos ("one exists in the present, in that enormous present which is without past or future, memory or planned intention") also cannot apply to Bruce, since his eastern European Jewish heritage was a major source of his creativity, just as his preoccupation with the future was a block to it.[9] If, as Kenneth Tynan maintained, "Bruce was (and is) authentically, indelibly hip," it is not because he was wilfully self-destructive, "someone who had deliberately decided to kill a part of himself in order to make life bearable."[10] Not only is this a dramatic, but facile, way of describing Bruce's drug addiction; it emphasizes a dubious martyrdom at the expense of the dogged, persistent, and decidedly *un*-hip steps he took through litigation to clear his name of obscenity and narcotics charges—in Andrew Ross's words, "to 'perform' in the courts before his most legitimate audience of all."[11] If Lenny Bruce was hip, it was more than anything else a *linguistic* hipness—although, in terms of his comedy, this is no minor issue; for with words as the most significant point of contact between a stand-up comic and his audience, Bruce's appropriation of a bohemian, underground language based on black jazz parlance put him at odds with much of his later audience, as did his emphasis on verbal abstraction, improvisation, and, of course, his subject matter.

Orrin Keepnews, a record producer whose career began in the late 1940s with the flowering of bebop, said that talking with Lenny Bruce was "*so* much like conversation with a jazz musician that it was hard to remember that I wasn't talking with one."[12] To Jonathan Miller, following Bruce's act was "like reading *Finnegan's Wake* over and over." His review of Bruce's performances in 1963 at London's Establishment Club describes in musical terms a comic delivery "whose hesitant, mumbling, slipped-gear technique, full of breaks and riffs, untunes the ear of the conventional night-club audience."[13] Critical likenings such as these abound with regard to Lenny Bruce's language, for he had from the outset made his identification with the jazz player whose guiding creative principle was expressive abstraction, the testing and reordering of musical convention. He once recalled his childhood delight in confusion, which was "entertainment" for him: "a freezing blizzard that would stop all traffic and mail; toilets that would get stopped up and overflow and run down the halls; electrical failures—anything that would stop the flow and make it back up and find a new direction."[14] As a teenager in Brooklyn he was part of a street group that rubbed shoulders with jazz players and small-time cabaret artists. On Saturday nights they would gather on street corners and stage imaginary nightclub acts, trying to impress each other with exaggerations and fantasies of the previous week's sexual exploits or domestic battles. In these impromptu gatherings, Bruce practiced and honed the art of free-association and began to absorb the unconventional vocabulary bequeathed to the underworld by jazz musicians and scat-singers such as Leo Watson, Sarah Vaughan, Eddie Jefferson, and Slim Gaillard—to whom, as Kerouac wrote famously, "the world was just one big Orooni."[15] The language was comic, certainly, an energetic, ironic, alternative representation of the world from a marginalized sector upon which convention could only be imposed arbitrarily. To be fair to Mailer, it is here where his essay "The White Negro" is at its most pertinent. The language of the black jazz player of the 1940s and 1950s, he writes, is a collection of "abstract ambiguous alternatives" coming from "the cultural mentor of a people." When a man in a flash becomes a "cat," or when a narcotic or sexual awakening becomes a "turn on," the universe is in some way comedically rearranged, to the possible confusion of an untutored audience. "What makes Hip a special language is that it cannot really be taught—if one shares none of the experiences of elation and exhaustion which it is equipped to describe, then it seems merely arch or vulgar or irritating."[16] To be sure, the language of Hip would eventually become a middle-class commodity, a curiosity sold through the mock "Hepcat Dictionaries" by Cab Calloway, Steve Allen, and Gaillard himself, among others; but it could never be used among outsiders as anything other than an embarrassing indication of their squareness.

Andrew Ross's observation may well apply to Mailer and the "White Negroes" he describes: "It is easy to see how idolization of the black jazz musician by white hipsters and Beats could have been reinforced by a 'romantic version of racism' which, in Simon Frith's view, imagines 'blacks as presocial, at ease with play.'"[17] Perhaps it applies to Bruce himself; but one thing is clear—in his adoption of the language of Hip, he chose a linguistic code deliberately designed to separate a subculture from the very white, middle-class mainstream he set out at once to court and to criticize.

It was a code that accentuated difference, inscrutability, and exclusion at the expense of this dominant culture. Bruce knew this clearly, even as he rose from the obscurity of the West Coast jazz nightclubs in his bid for wider recognition. Hence his early monologue, "The Sound," in which the supposed spokesman for middle America, Lawrence Welk (who would eventually sue Bruce for libel), finds himself auditioning a saxophonist from the Hip underground. "Uhh, like hello, man. . . . A lotta cats like to put you down, Mr. Wick, but no matter what they say, man you're the best banjo player. . . . Whatever your axe is, I know you swing, you know? That's the main thing, sweetie, just swing with your axe." In this routine the uncomprehending, conventional entertainer and his audience are clearly the butts of the joke. The sax player launches into a series of musical in-jokes—"I knew Miles before he was a block. . . . I knew Basie 'fore he could count"—to which the baffled band leader can only reply, "What the hell are you talking about?" The hipster asks for "a little bread in front"; Welk says, "You're hungry? You want a sandwich?" Eventually, when all communication is broken down, it is Welk—the spokesman for middle-class convention—who finally explodes into rage and hostility: "What the hell are you talking about! What are you—a Communist?"[18]

In spite of Bruce's awareness of his exclusive alienating language (in relation to that of the popular audience), he firmly resisted the pressure to alter his approach—even when club managers repeatedly hissed from the wings that he was "working to the band" at the expense of the audience. Reviewers would complain, "All Lenny Bruce seems concerned with is making the band laugh," in reply to which Bruce would utter the mantra that most informed the avant-garde art world in postwar America, from the abstract expressionists to the Beat writers to all jazz musicians: *abstraction.* Of *course* the band was laughing, Bruce would say: "Musicians, jazz musicians especially, appreciate art forms that are *extensions* of realism, as opposed to realism in a representational form."[19] The fact that he increasingly had to make such cumbersome explanations in his early years suggests the extent to which he was bringing a challenge to American comedic convention. The challenge was not completely new; there had been for decades a small but constant presence of jazz-inspired comics in America's nightclubs. There was Harry "the Hipster" Gibson, who strutted the stage in a zoot suit singing songs like "Who Put the Benzedrine in Mrs. Murphy's Ovaltine?" and who, like Lenny Bruce, would eventually be arrested and see his songs banned. There was Slim Gaillard, the jive-talking composer of "Flat Foot Floogie with the Floy-Floy"; and Babs Gonzales, who with his band, the Three Bips and a Bop, held forth in their own New York nightspot, Babs' Insane Asylum. And there was the comedian with whom Lenny Bruce was most compared in his early days, Lord Buckley, who would also be harassed into prison, where he died quickly and suspiciously. Back in the 1930s he had been amusing nightclub patrons with his impressions of the great black jazzmen and, later, with his hip elegies of Jesus, de Sade, and "Willie the Shake" Shakespeare (whose most renowned funeral oration *actually* began, "'Hipsters, flipsters, and finger-poppin' daddies / Knock me your lobes'").[20] Yet, even though a jazz comedian like Slim Gaillard might make it to a regular spot on Frank Sinatra's prewar radio show, by the late 1950s the more daring and obscure hip comedians were still associated with the world from which they came, an underworld of drugs and potential subversion: mysterious, spooky, reflected not in the anodyne swing of Lawrence Welk or Nelson Riddle but in the incomprehensible slithering and bopping of Lester Young, Charlie Parker, and Miles Davis—musical outlaws all.

Thus did Lenny Bruce have to stand onstage at Carnegie Hall and *explain* not only what he and his jazz-inspired, improvising contemporaries were about but also his awareness of the divisions they were bringing to the audiences of American comedy. Mort Sahl, for instance, faced the same responses as Bruce did: "I hear people say, 'Ahhh, people just laugh at Mort to be smart.' No; you can't laugh at anybody to be *hip*. All laughter is involuntary, man—try to fake four laughs in an hour: *Ha Ha! Ha Heh! Ha Heh Heh!*—they'll take you away, man." Bruce's monologues frequently reflect his perception of his own audience's confusion as he confronted them with the alternative conventions of the jazz comics. Again, at Carnegie Hall he said, "Now my humor: I dig, first, recall —abstraction. I can't be ponderous. People say to me, 'Hey, how come you don't do the bits on the records?'" The reason, he explained, was that he would be like the guy at a party who tells the same funny story to every neighbor who walks in: "And by about the fifth neighbor you really get *drugged* with him, man. He tells the same story and you say, 'He's *corrupt*, man, he's not funny—*I* could tell that story now.' . . . So that's it: if you dig hearing the same thing, go by your neighbor's." With the gauntlet thus thrown down, Bruce affirmed that he would not play the game that was demanded of him by popular comedic convention, the delivery of the smooth, rehearsed bits that flowed from the mouths of the television comedians; the false impression of spontaneity in entire pages of memorized chatter. For him, abstraction was more than merely a reflection of affinity; it was literally truth itself. He spoke of having seen Bob Newhart on the Ed Sullivan show, cajoled by the host into repeating on the air an improvised bit he had done during rehearsal. To Bruce, this was Newhart's self-betrayal: "He was having fun with it, and I said, 'Ohh, boy, he's really cookin' and ad-libbin'"—and now, he went into the [rehearsed] bit, and he went into the toilet. 'Cause he wasn't happy with it. He'd said the bit so many times, it's not the truth anymore."[21]

Here again is the fundamental question: How can a comedian imprisoned in a convention that depends upon the mutual acknowledgment of *untruth* operate as though his audiences, and their policing forces, were interested in the truth? Bruce confronted America of the late 1950s and early 1960s with the same liberality of expression he had become accustomed to in the smaller clubs where comedians generally had not been monitored. One of his "New Wave" colleagues, Dick Gregory, recalled, "He just went out and said things that no one would dare say and many were scared to even listen to."[22] As late as 1959, with two centuries of American political satire firmly established in print, but with the memory of McCarthy still fresh, politics was still a taboo subject on the popular cabaret stage. Mort Sahl had broken the ice somewhat with his satiric thrusts at the HUAC ("'For a while, every time the Russians threw an American in jail, the Un-American Activities Committee would retaliate by throwing an American in jail, too'").[23] But the *truth* was: everyone knew about politicians, everyone talked about them, and everyone hated them—except in public.

When Lenny Bruce then took to satirizing Eisenhower and Nixon by name, while they were still in office, he pushed the taboo even further. Bruce's Eisenhower is a fast-talking, hip gangster hoping to have his vice president bumped off abroad, in order to divert attention away from domestic corruption. With this presentation, on the heels of the witch hunts and in the midst of the Cold War, Bruce employed the argot of the underworld hustler to deflate and subvert the majesty of the presidency. Eisenhower greets Nixon: "Hello, Nick, sweetie. Siddown, baby. Ohh, is he *cute*?— here's that black curly-haired devil. Get some of that twelve-year-old Scotch over here; a little Havana, huh, baby? Huh, sweetie?" If Eisenhower is a sinister two-face, Nixon is a nervous sap: "What's . . . goin' on here? Don't put me on, Ike." As Ike tries to bribe Nick into going to Lebanon with reminders of how "beautifully" he had done in Caracas, Bruce rubs into his audience's face the novel possibility that Americans are *not* loved every place they go. Nixon: "Are you *kidding*? They *hated* me there! They *spit* at me. Look at this suit —I never had it cleaned. . . . They spit at me, they hate me, they threw rocks at me!" In Ike's response, the standing convention is further tested: "They liked you. It's your old lady—Pat. That's it. Everybody dug you; it's *her*. She overdresses."[24]

    A generational conflict is certainly evident in this routine, not only in the fact that its prime target was the last of the country's leaders to be born in the nineteenth century. The previous generation's linguistic and comedic codes are also, implicitly, the subject of this routine and others like it, signaling that American power-wielders can no longer expect, at the worst, the saucy allegiance of their jesters. Having said this, it is by now clear that Bruce read too much significance into the generational change symbolized by Eisenhower's departure from office and the belief that with Kennedy's arrival America had gone a little more hip, a little less square. Bruce put great faith into the meaning of Kennedy's youth: "I voted for him 'cause he's dimensional, man. A president that's real—'cause for him to help me, he has to know about me; he's had to have heard the joke before." Before JFK, there had only been "grandfathers" moving into the White House: "I couldn't see President Eisenhower kissing his wife. Not on the mouth, anyway" (*MC*). But even though the new, young president and his wife might give Bruce the unique pleasure of seeing "a child born in the White House," Kennedy was still the Cold Warrior in Chief, at the helm of a nation filled with Cold Warriors. In 1961 it would be a defiant comedian who would suggest with the freedom that he took for granted backstage, "If Communism cooks for you, solid." To be sure, Bruce would first establish in his own defense that Communism *didn't* cook for him: "Communism is like one big phone company. Government control, man. And if I get too ranked with that phone company, where can I go, man? I'll end up like a *schmuck* with a Dixie Cup and a thread." Capitalism may be "the best system, man"; but with the governor of Georgia closing the schools in the faces of black children, there was little that America could teach eastern Europe about freedom. (*MC*). "The south! You know, we pissed away a million dollars on Radio Free Europe, and we never gave *them* a nickel."[25] Lenny Bruce could safely walk anywhere in eastern Europe; "But I would *shit* to walk in Mississippi with a sign on my back: 'I'm From New York, Ha Ha Ha.'"[26]

By thus injecting a sense of relativity into the Cold War debate, Bruce comedically challenged the self-righteous self-assurance of American foreign policy, which, he soon learned, had not passed away with the Eisenhower administration. After the U-2 pilot Francis Gary Powers was shot down over Russia in 1960, Americans could be heard grumbling patriotically that *they* would never spill their country's secrets to the Communists. Before long, Bruce took to deflating their bombast by constructing a comic scenario in which an alternative viewpoint is unavoidable, in which "the flag goes right down the toilet." The picture is of a captured cryptographer valiantly refusing to hand over American secrets— until a fellow prisoner is graphically threatened. "They're not gonna put that hot lead in the funnel that's in his ass, are they?— They *did*! Bullshit, here's the secrets, Jim." The moral: "If you can take the hot lead enema, then you can cast the first stone" (*WIAF*). Bruce had the similar temerity to speculate about the viewpoint of the Cuban people in their apparent regard for Fidel Castro, even as the United States was going to such terrifying and terrorizing lengths to demonize him: "If I haven't got any bread, then he's a savior. Even a promise, frig it, *something* man—then I love him; then he's right." From the stages of major venues like Carnegie Hall, Bruce was pushing into comedically uncharted territory with such scenarios as these; and he pushed even further into terra incognita when he suggested, for instance, that the Cubans might be justifiably irritated by the American presence in Guantanamo Bay, just as Americans would be if the English had withheld American territory—and just as the Seminoles and Iroquois *must* have been with the Americans who had sent them to the swamps in a nineteenth-century ethnic cleansing campaign—a "Nazi purging": "Yeah, with your *schmucky* bows and arrows—get outta here, man. Whaddya mean, *your land*? Whaddya got to show me, it's *yours*, man?" (*MC*).

In setting out comedically to disrupt the rigid, set consciousness of Cold War America on the eve of the Vietnam War, Bruce was employing the same surreal reorganizing techniques he had used among the hipsters and jazz aficionados in the small West Coast nightclubs where he had honed his craft. But when he rose from the underground, there was no certainty of even a politically sympathetic, mainstream audience appreciating *as comedy* the linguistic abstractions with which he transformed patriotic rhetoric into a senseless stream of consciousness. A monologue like "The Bomb and Political Bullshit" could puzzle even the most sophisticated listener, not because the *political* meaning behind it was inaccessible but because—according to the received convention of the recognizable plot and punchline—the *comic* meaning was lost. Backed up by a crackling recording of *Pomp and Circumstance*, Bruce would intone, like Big Brother on speed: "in these perilous times when a man-born menace, a horrible bomb, that can only disfigure and defame its creator, a horror, an evil, a bad, a lazy, a lethargic—lethargy and complacency we cannot fall into. We've got a bomb that can wipe out half the world if necessary. And we will, to keep our standards, the strength that has come from American unity, that we alone will build for better schools and churches" (*ELBP*). Even today, a monologue such as this is risky, not so much for any political daring but for its deliberate challenge to the assumption that verbal comedy must be carefully plotted, well-timed, smooth, and ultimately meaningful. And just as Bruce attempted to undermine American faith in verbal iconography, he did the same with the visual. For the American flag, he employed a debasing metaphor that may have come straight from *Better Homes and Gardens* but that was nonetheless surreal: "Because of exposure, too much exposure, [the flag] has lost all impact, definitely, for me. From being exploited, prostituted. . . . From people using it as a coffee table." The subsequent picture of American soldiers raising their "coffee table" over Iwo Jima is thus reduced from a rousing, patriotic icon to a bizarre hallucination. The damage to this revered image is already done when Bruce, in closing, discards it as a deceitful lie: "When I found out that Mount Suribachi was *posed*, I said, 'Oh, they were really—?' 'Yeah, that's right.' What a *putz* I am, right? Started to take pictures *myself*" (MC).

Bruce confronted Americans of the early 1960s with other reordered conceptions of their daily lives and *mores*—some of which are likely to appear tame to later generations comfortable with the work of George Carlin, Richard Pryor, Cheech and Chong, the Saturday Night Live crew in all its incarnations, and other comedians who have built upon the ground broken by Bruce himself. His parodies of American television commercials have mostly lost their disruptive power, such as his cigarette ads replacing tobacco with marijuana ("I don't know what the hell it is, Bill. I've been smoking this pot all day and I *still* can't get high on it"); or his rendering of the "average housewife" suffering from fatigue and iron-poor blood ("Darling, you know 'rhythm control' doesn't mean making it with every trio that plays the Blackhawk").[27] His daring prediction from the comic stage that "pot will be legal in ten years" hardly carries now the force that once engendered either cries of "Shame!" or applause ("Because in this audience probably every other one of you knows a law student that smokes pot, who will become a senator, who will legalize it to protect himself") (*ELBP*).

But one can appreciate even today the challenge he offered his audience with the stark accusation: "Now, you're all taking pills. Everybody here doesn't *think* you're all taking pills; but anyone who's got stock in Squibb, or Park Lilly, or Smith Klein French *knows* they're dropping 'em by the thousands." After all, at this point, Bruce was no longer talking to a loyal coterie of hip followers: he was accusing middle America itself. "This generation is strung out. What's Middletown? Whaddya, kidding—what's Middletown? Sedate *knacher*—*zzhlungk!* Serpicil, deximil, percodan: they're all outta their kug!" A middle-class audience's suspicions of Bruce's own drug abuse would not necessarily forestall the guilty glances they might exchange with one another during a monologue such as this: "The women are strung out. 'Yeah, my "difficult day" is getting longer and longer and longer—my period is a *semi-colon* now. And now, with no punctuation, I'm just *knached* out all the time for pain.' 'Once every four hours, once every two and one hour'—*blah*." For the men, too, there would be no quarter; for Bruce would fling into the face of the virile, two-fisted drinker an equation designed to taunt and to sting: "'That guy can really bolt 'em, man!' 'Goddamn right, he can jigger 'em back, he can stand up toe to toe—' and that's a man, and that's a man; and all of a sudden that's *not* a man. You know, the style's changed. He takes *pills* now, that's what he does. He's a JUNKIE!" (*MC*). Admittedly, it takes an awareness of the historical moment in order to appreciate the revolutionary impact of such monologues. Most Americans had never before heard anything like this coming from their comic stages.

However, of all Bruce's deconstructions of his contemporaries' social pretensions, those regarding sexuality and the human body merit the greatest attention, even now, for they were to cause him the most trouble in his confrontations with the terms of the comic license he had inherited. Sex and scatology were by no means novel subjects in the earliest history of comedy, as Gershon Legman has shown in his monumental study;[28] but they were the subjects that would return to hound Lenny Bruce to his demise when a vindictive society had determined that he had tested comedic convention enough. Again, the issue lies in *where* he chose to stage his confrontations with the repressed American libido, as much as when and how. The centrality of "the lower bodily stratum" in subversive jokelore has been well explored by Bakhtin, Freud, Legman, and others, just as it was demonstrated by Chaucer, Cervantes, Rabelais, and Swift before them. In Lenny Bruce's time, the raunchiest stages in America were still those in the neglected quarters where he began his career—the music clubs where carnality, either verbal or physical, was as much a self-assertion as a pleasure. Moreover, these may have been the only quasi-legitimate centers of alternative sexual representation, where outlaws could generally operate freely in a carnivalesque defiance and parody of American sexual propriety, barring the odd, cynical raid by the vice squad.

Of course, even in mainstream American comedy, as Bruce noticed, there had always been a homosexual undercurrent; but no one had the honesty to admit it. His job was to rub the truth in their faces: "How do people in these towns know about faggots? How? Well, 'cause of comedians. Like, who are the transvestite comedians? Milton Berle, *heavyweight* transvestite humor. Yeah, Berle's the one who *schlepped* the faggot outta the Krafft-Ebing cellar." But beyond noticing and spotlighting this undercurrent, Bruce damned it as a hypocritical, macho attempt to ward off the scrutiny of precariously erected sexual conventions. Milton Berle might try a bit *too* hard to impose a burlesque stigma of menace on his queer— " 'Ooh, I sweah I'll *kiw* you!' "—and still get a hearty laugh for it from the nervous of both sexes. But Bruce noticed something else about Joe and Jane Average: "They're not hip to dykes. 'Huh?' Idiomatic for *lesbian*. How come they don't do any dyke jokes?' " There was a *slim* chance that "the comic of that generation was not hip to butches"; but the more likely reason was plain old fear: " 'Cause maybe dykes are *shtarkers*, that's why. 'I'll close the butch bar—' *Pow!* So consequently, in *these* towns, lesbians get away with murder." Middletowners were not aware of lesbians because they were afraid to be: "The top comment you'll hear: 'There's a chick with a *severe* Mary Astor hairdo, right?' " (*MC*).

Bruce was determined to redirect scrutiny back onto the veneer of sexual convention and the hypocrisies surrounding it, goading his unsettled audiences—especially the males—with the possibility of their own sexual "perversions." He was certainly more direct than Milton Berle: " 'Cause dig: homosexual. I would assume 'homosexual' is anybody who's ever been involved in any homosexual act. That's a beautiful generalization, you know, 'cause I assume that you're all faggots, then. Yeah, 'cause the old cliché— 'there's no such thing as being a little pregnant'—that's it, man" (*MC*). Bruce would make it clear that he was not talking about the solitary outcasts straying out of the underworld, or the prison, or the grotesque "freak show" of Hubert's Museum on Forty-second Street, where "an old faggot closet queen" masqueraded as a hermaphroditic "scientific marvel" for twenty-five cents (*WIAF*). On the contrary, he was talking about Main Street: "I don't care if you were five years old, I haven't asked you. Your scoutmaster, or a gym coach—'Hey, yeah, ya got nice legs, sonny.' *Uh huh.*" No one in the hometown was untempted or untouched, men or women; there was no proprietal veneer behind which to hide: "I assume that every chick here has been involved with a pervert. *Whew*, boy—semantic, that's a heavy word, *purr-vert*. 'Were you ever with a *purr-vert*, you, Mrs. Knopfko?' Well, you got that uncle when you were eleven years old . . ." (*MC*).

It was inevitable that when a defiant comedian, contemptuous of the comic rules to which his predecessors had subscribed, brought such challenges into the American limelight, he would face retribution. The worst was to come from the law; yet other forces within the establishment also responded with whatever vindictiveness they could muster. For *Time* magazine, that filter of truth that nestled alongside the householder's glossies on most Middletown coffee tables, revenge came with the label "Sick Comic." Bruce fought desperately against this label. His defenders, such as Jonathan Miller, denied its applicability, usually with the clarification that sick humor was merely a juvenile, exploitative response to physical or mental deformity, and nothing more. If so, then actually Bruce was not wholly innocent, at least in his earliest work. But more important, there is more to what convention dismisses as sick humor, in terms of the questions such humor raises about legitimacy and the pieties surrounding it. Miller, for instance, offers a classic sick joke as an example—"'Mommy, why do I keep running around in circles?' 'Shut up or I'll nail your other foot to the floor'"—which in fact may be less a cynical response to child abuse than to the supposed sanctity of motherhood. For a comedian of Bruce's carnivalizing intent, it might not have been a bad thing to admit the label of "Sick Comic," since, as Mary Douglas notes, sick humor "plays with a reversal of the values of social life; the hearer is left uncertain which is the man and which is the machine, who is the good and who the bad, or where is the legitimate pattern of control."[29] But what Bruce objected to was the hypocrisy of the accusation: *he* was sick, while establishment comedians were *healthy*? Milton Berle, with his "sometimes-fun fag"? Jerry Lewis, with his racist stereotype capturing "all the subtleties of the Japanese physiognomy"—the buck teeth and Coke-bottle-bottom eyeglasses? Henny Youngman and his Ugly Girl routines?—" 'Her nose was so big that every time she sneezed. . . . ' 'She was so bow-legged that every time. . . . ' 'One leg was shorter than the other. . . . ' " And on top of this, the "sicknik" label came from *Time*, in which the mockery of "physical shortcomings" was "editorial policy": " 'Shelley Berman has a face like a hastily sculptured hamburger.' "[30] However much he protested against the label of "sick comic," Bruce was stuck with it. The best he could do was to appropriate it facetiously in the title of one of his albums (*The Sick Humor of Lenny Bruce*); but it would not be so easy for him to utilize the other stigmatizing weapons that were to be used against him for his transgressions, most notably the law.

As we have seen, the terms of reference that Bruce brought to the subject of political, sexual, and linguistic hypocrisy from the lower stratum—in both the bodily and the social senses—might have caused him no pain had he remained on the neglected, relatively unpoliced stages of his early career. His troubles began when he started to show himself in the more popular, middle-class clubs and concert halls, and from those stages, point to the repressed activities and terms *of* that class. He envisaged sneaking into Yankee Stadium one day—"just before Ronald Reagan sings another tune"—and commandeering the microphone, to bare his soul in fellowship with the other silent millions who could not, in spite of their own honest urgings, admit to having committed *the* ultimate act of perversity: "So we can both be saved, listen to me, sinner! Is there one *other* pervert that, one time in your life—just *one* time in your life—you did piss in the sink?" He never made it to Yankee Stadium, but he did play Carnegie Hall; and from that and other stages like it he embarked on a highly visible crusade to remind the dwellers on Main Street, Middletown, U.S.A., that they could run the water as loud as they wished, but that they couldn't hide: "When they're running the water that's what they're doing— they're pissing in the sink." He would even point to the absurdity of the extremes to which they went in avoiding or camouflaging the truth: "You're really complex when you run the water *and* flush the toilet and *still* piss in the sink. That's really insane" (*WIAF*).

As he soon learned, he had reason to regret his crusade, as more and more policemen began to line the walls of the clubs where he played. He would set out to taunt the policemen with four-letter words in a presumed solidarity with his audience; this was how he first upped the ante in his war of resistance. But what he apparently didn't realize, until it was too late, was that the police were representative of the majority *of* his audience. As Andrew Ross notes, "These cops knew that he was offending *their* plebian codes of decency. The sophisticates in the audience could take abuse; it was what they had paid for. But the humor was often at the expense of the redneck straights, like these policemen, who were just too damn dumb to get the jokes"—or so Bruce seemed to think. This was perhaps one of his greatest tactical errors: the assumption that his crusade was a popular one. Even when attacking the middle-class codes of decency in the name of which he was being monitored, he was not "playing to the gallery. On the contrary, he was more likely to be vilifying the taste of those who were 'in the gallery,' or else policing their own class; in other words, those who could not afford to be anything but serious about their taste." This seriousness extended to the *comic* taste as well as to any other, hitherto at rest upon the foundation of polite fiction and a willing self-censorship. In rejecting the rules of play already extant in the bourgeois sphere into which he had risen, Bruce—like any of Huizinga's spoil-sports—could only find himself isolated, a position he courted even as he begged for inclusion in the more popular comic fellowship. As the next section shows, there was another dimension to his isolation, separate from that of the would-be "White Negro" but nonetheless complementing it: in Ross's words, it was the "Jewish version of the hip outlaw."[31] In terms of this version, Bruce was no less resistant to identifiable rules of the comic convention that he had inherited, and no more immune to the consequences of breaking them.

Jews in Goyland

Lenny Bruce often described the feeling of being alone onstage in a town somewhere *out there* in the vast American heartland. Maybe it was Milwaukee, Wisconsin; maybe it was Lima, Ohio—wherever it was, it was usually the *starting* point for a Gray Line bus tour. The women were all blue-rinsed stereotypes with drooping armpits, the men were either Shriners or Elks or belonged to some other "dopey" fraternal order. Diversions in these towns were few: you could go to the park and look at the cannon; or to the public library, stocked with "two Fanny Hurst novels and one Pearl Buck." Other major pastimes were waiting for the Jell-O to set, or going to the Zirconi gas station to spin the display racks for a while.

Somehow these towns just didn't *swing*: *"Peyton Place* is a dirty lie" (*LBA*). What was worse, when he went onstage these people just didn't have the capacity to understand him: "I'm out there for about fifteen minutes and people are staring at me in disbelief." When the shock had worn off, they'd start whispering to each other: "'What is he? What's "schmuck"? He keeps saying "schmuck" and "pootz," "pout," "poots," "parts" . . . and, and "bread," "cool," "dig," "schmooz," "grap," "pup," "schluph," "murgh"—'" He was so otherworldly that people were afraid to walk in front of him, even on the way to the toilet: "'Yeah, but everybody's walking out. And he's still up there—"poots," "brootz," "mugrup," "blog"—he's up there.'" No music, no singing, no band, nothing—just garble: "'He's crazy. He's a weirdo. He's on the dope. Yeah. He's on it now. Oh yeah. He's right on it now. Cloud seven.'"[32] Of course, the problem was always with *their* powers of comprehension rather than *his* powers of communication.

It is not that these middle Americans had never seen a Jewish comedian. In the early 1960s American comedy was virtually monopolized by Jews—Milton Berle, Phyllis Diller, Sid Caesar, Jack Benny, Steve Allen, Sophie Tucker, Joey Bishop. Enter the newcomer: Leonard Alfred Schneider, masquerading as Lenny Bruce, son of an English-born Jew of eastern European descent and a struggling Jewish comedienne in New York. Thanks especially to his grandmother, he had absorbed a deep awareness of his family's Yiddish and Ashkenazy traditions.[33] Unlike most of his older competitors on the comic stage, he had not chosen to hide or neglect these traditions. If Lenny Bruce was indeed a "White Negro," he was a Yiddish-speaking one, which gave his unprepared audiences yet another linguistic dimension to cope with; for while the popular Jewish comedians on television and the cabaret stages had assimilated into a smooth English that could be broadcast coast-to-coast from Hollywood or Rockefeller Center, Lenny Bruce was closer, linguistically, to the Yiddish theaters and burlesque houses on New York's Lower East Side, which had all but vanished by the late 1930s. Most Jewish comedians gave their audiences comedy routines; Lenny Bruce *shpritzed* them.

His Jewish identity is important in a number of ways. Out of the deep ambivalence he felt toward Judaism came tensions that set him apart from both the Jewish minority in America and the non-Jewish majority, not only in terms of his language but also in terms of his subject matter. Moreover, there is particular significance in the Jewish comedic tradition he inherited—distinctive, for historical and cultural reasons, in its complexities and contradictions, an engine for both subversion and adaptation, alienation and incorporation. Lenny Bruce's adherence to this tradition is as noteworthy as his departures from it.

No matter the degree to which Bruce would appeal to the sense of the immediate, the hip, the now (one of his most frequent adjectives was "contemporary"), even he would have to admit that the inspirational source into which he so often tapped was rooted far back in history. For each of his appeals to *rachmunas* (compassion) or *emmis* (truth); for each *schmuck* or *putz* or *fresser* or *shtupper*; for each twitch of his antennae in the face of persecution—his own or anyone else's—Bruce was utilizing what had been bequeathed to him by a community of refugees running from the butcheries of the Crusades and the pogroms of eastern Europe: a language and a particular humor. The two cannot be separated, for while there could be no Jewish humor as it exists without the alternative language in which it was fostered, the language itself could not have developed without the comic sensibility of the oppressed in which so many of its words and phrases were obviously coined. The Yiddish that Bruce used, along with the argot of the hipster, to carnivalize—to subvert and deflate the formality of the English language—had always been a vulgar language in the Latin sense, common and informal. Like the humor with which it was entwined, it was an expression of the *shtetl* (village), the street, the marketplace, the kitchen, a folk alternative to both the sacred, rigid Talmudic Hebrew of the rabbi's study and the official language of whatever community that happened to be persecuting the Jews at the time—Russian, German, or Polish. Yiddish was a language made for parody; in fact parody was intrinsic to it, it having developed as a gleefully scavenging dialect accepting, rejecting, and reordering the characteristics of numerous languages encountered on the refugee trail. Obviously, it was a language of cultural affirmation and resistance to both persecution and assimilation. One could secretly mock the czar or the local administrator in Yiddish while nodding and smiling in Russian, just as the community would cohere through the language no matter how many borders were crossed in the diaspora.

But Bruce's use of Yiddish on the American nightclub stage was as much a weapon against other Jews, and organized Judaism itself, as against a bigoted Christianity or a homogenizing, secular American culture. He knew that the Yiddish that had flooded into New York and other American cities after the 1880s had once nurtured a thriving alternative humor; in the vaudeville and burlesque houses of the Lower East Side, Yiddish comedians could actively combat the stock Shylocks and hook-nosed tailors whining about on the gentile stages. He would also have known of the manner in which Jewish comedians had been transformed, in Sarah Blacher Cohen's phrase, "from *Yidn* to Yankees" in the assimilating process, with the prewar Yiddishisms of Eddie Cantor, George Jessel, Fanny Brice, Sophie Tucker, and Al Jolson disappearing in the conspicuous "de-Semitization of the arts" on the eve of World War II. There was ample evidence that, even as war was waged against Hitler, to be noticed as a Jew on an American street could be an uncomfortable experience; and in their bid for stardom during the war and after, Jewish-American comedians jettisoned the hyphenation and projected themselves solely as Americans. By the 1950s not many of their fellow citizens would notice that Jerry Lewis or the Marx Brothers or Jack Benny were Jewish. To be sure, there would come the ethnic revival of the late 1950s and early 1960s, with a particularly Jewish comic sensibility dominating American fiction in the work of Saul Bellow, Bernard Malamud, and Philip Roth. But if, as Cohen suggests, "a belated pride in the founding of the state of Israel," as well as the memory of the Holocaust, galvanized performing comedians into reasserting their Jewishness, it was a pride that Bruce would ridicule.[34] Not only was he no Zionist, he would see such "belated pride" as hypocritical and exploitative, coming as it did so soon on the heels of a frantic attempt to disguise one's origins and to forget one's Yiddish. The fact that this ridicule came from the mouth of Lenny Bruce rather than Lenny Schneider suggests the ambivalence with which he viewed the entire process of acculturation reflected in the history of Jewish-American comedy.

In the early 1960s Bruce would say, "Today there's no problem being Jewish, at all, man, because it's *in*." Never mind that only a few years before, the only college that would accept Jews was C.C.N.Y.—"Circumcised Citizens of New York"; or that an innocent request for the time of day could bring the hypersensitive retort, "*Yeah*, I'm Jewish!" It was an exhausting journey, an endless process in which one pose was exchanged for another: "Hey, you go through all the stages of being Jewish, you know?" You can be defensive; or you can be "*drugged* being Jewish, man. . . . 'What nationali—?' '*American!*' You go through that; and then you go through the dopey thing of, you know, 'Jewish is a *religion*' and your crap rationalization." Then the next stage: "'I'm glad I'm a

Jew—' Aw, shit, forget it, man! Who can be *glad*? Some masochist, that's all, who loves to be *schlepped* around." The ultimate lie would be pride: "You can say, 'I'm *proud*,' which means, 'I've made a good adjustment'—but that's all." Bruce had an endless supply of vitriol for Jews who had made such good "adjustments" as to become, in his estimation, cardboard cutouts of Jews. His contempt did not stop with his fellow comedians who meekly accepted cultural erasure by working entirely in English; reformed rabbis were "*so* reformed, they're ashamed they're Jewish." They sounded like Ivy League graduates preaching to a congregation of golden-haired, all-American WASPs: " 'Is yonder Is-roy-el? Out quench yon flaming *yortzeit* candle, Is-roy-el! That is the Is-roy-el of *chabelyon* David and Ruth—and Cherylanne and Joy" (*MC*).

Jews who chose to live in Goyland deserved what they got. If even *they* couldn't understand Bruce's hip, Yiddish *shpritzing*, it was because they had willfully forgotten who they were in the process of becoming American. Hence his ridicule of a Jewish family in Lima, Ohio, who in nostalgia seize on him with "a searching hope" in their eyes as the first Jew they've seen in years. " 'You're Jewish? What are you doing in a place like this?' " Bruce's savage reply: " 'I'm *passing*.' " The family drag him on a nightmare tour of their typically middle-American house—with the linen closet (" 'I, uh, like the way the towels are folded, there. . . . '") and the piano that nobody plays, upon which rests a framed picture of their son Morty in the army. They try to match him with their diet-crazed daughter, looking "like a hockey-stick with hair" and "lipstick on her teeth." But their worst crime is in their having adopted wholesale the conventional, ill-informed prejudices of the American majority: " 'You were in Hollywood, right? That's true about Liberace?' " In his mischief, Bruce tells them that two of the most beloved Jewish performing icons, Eddie Fisher and George Jessel, are in reality "big fruits"; moreover, " 'That's where the B'nai Brith money went' " (*LBA*).

Bruce suggested that assimilation was in fact an obsession for Jews who overcompensated for the insecurity they felt in the midst of an intolerant Christian majority. In the process they became twisted, possessed by the mania of proving themselves 100-percent American when they in fact were in a unique position, through their historical victimization, to act as an alternative to the bigotry and corruption that seemed to pass for Americanism and Christian virtue. If Joe McCarthy was a 100-percent American and a good Christian—as he indeed projected himself—then *perhaps* it was better to be a diluted American and a Jew. Bruce offered Jack Ruby as a Jew who had tried too hard: "Ruby came from Texas. And a Jew in Texas is a tailor. What went on in his mind, I'm sure, is that, 'If I kill the guy that killed the *President*, the Christians will go, "*Whew!* Boy, what balls *he* had. We always thought the Jews were chickenshit, but look at that!"'" Still, it was only a pathetic pose, as anyone could see: "Even the *shot* was Jewish. The way he held the gun, it was a dopey Jewish way. . . . He probably went '*Nach!*' too—that means 'There!' in Jewish—like, '*Nach! Nach!*'"[35]

Bruce attempted to highlight the potential that Jews had in injecting a rich source of diversity into what he saw as a bland cultural homogeneity dictated by the gentile majority: they might call it "American," but beside every white picket fence was a white clapboard church. Judaism—or more properly, Jewish*ness*—was a force for cultural transformation. The distinctions Bruce made between Jewish and *goyish*, or gentile, were strictly secular and cultural. They had to do with geography: "To me, if you live in New York or any other big city, you are Jewish. It doesn't matter even if you are Catholic; if you live in New York, you're Jewish. If you live in Butte, Montana, you're going to be goyish even if you're Jewish." They had to do with what Americans consumed, whether or not it was processed: "Evaporated milk is goyish even if the Jews invented it. Chocolate is Jewish and fudge is goyish. Spam is goyish and rye bread is Jewish." They had to do with how rich one's cultural heritage was, or how much one's people had suffered: "Negroes are all Jews. Italians are all Jews. Irishmen who have rejected their religion are Jews." And it had to do with how people got their kicks: "Mouths are very Jewish. And bosoms. Baton-twirling is very goyish."[36] Ray Charles and Count Basie were Jewish; Eddie Cantor, though a Jew, was *goyish*. B'nai Brith, the uptight Jewish men's society, was *goyish*, while Hadassah, the women's society, was Jewish. The United States Marines: "heavy *goyim*, dangerous" (56).

But Bruce eventually found that, in spite of his cultural identification with the Jewish heritage, some of his greatest troubles were to come from other Jews. Of the columnists and reviewers who panned him, many were Jewish; of the comedians and other performers who publicly labeled him a disgrace to the American stage, likewise; of the judges who threw the book at him, they were either old "*farbissener*" (grouches) or "junkyard Jews" with last names ending in "-witz." Bruce may have thought that, after black Americans, Jews had the greatest potential to be hip, given the percentage of young, liberal, postcollegiate Jews who were such a large part of his audience. Certainly, there were enough Jewish names among the signers of the petitions in his defense and among those intellectuals and artists called to testify in court on his behalf; but for a number of reasons—not least his mockery of assimilating Jews —by the time he died Bruce had alienated a considerable number of Jews along with the gentiles. This had as much to do with his *own* departures from the conventions of the Jewish comic tradition as with his accusations about other Jews' departures from *their* traditions.

For one thing, there was the nature of Jewish humor as an inherently *self*-critical expression. As Freud noticed, the majority of jokes and humorous stories emanating from the east European *shtetls* were "directed against Jewish characteristics" in times of persecution.[37] It was, as Sarah Blacher Cohen writes, as though the Jews were telling their oppressors, "'You don't have to injure us. We'll take charge of our own persecution.'"[38] Bruce certainly directed his humor against Jewish characteristics; but they were always someone *else's* Jewish characteristics, and never his own. Second, when directed against the oppressive majority, Jewish humor was a particularly private humor, a cautious mechanism for bolstering and protecting a community under constant threat or siege. If any hearts were to be unpacked, it took place under one's breath, in the storeroom, or the kitchen, or otherwise in "the religious, cultural, and socio-political frameworks of the Jewish community."[39] It wasn't to be blabbed from the stage of Carnegie Hall or the Gate of Horn in Chicago: Jews had enough trouble already. Third—again, as Cohen notes—Jewish humor traditionally refused "to ennoble suffering." Born itself out of intense suffering, its model was not the tragic hero but "*dos kleine menschele*, the little man who takes suffering in his stride"—the *schlemiel*.[40] Lenny Bruce, in contrast, did little to discourage the impression that he was a martyr to the American Constitution, especially when, as in his final appearances, his "comedy" was to consist of pained, verbatim readings of his court transcripts.

Moreover, the subject matter of Jewish humor traditionally had its limits. God, for one, may not have been absent from Jewish humor. In many jokes he was a character, with a divine sense of irony and some witty lines; but they always reflected upon his compassion, his *rachmunas*. However he was drawn, it was always with respect—whether in the *shtetls* of eastern Europe or in the reform synagogues of California. But Bruce dared to suggest that the "faceless" Jewish God ran an embarrassing second to his Christian counterpart, who was promoted with Madison Avenue efficiency: "Our god has no mother, no father, no manger in the five and ten, on cereal boxes and on television shows. The Jewish god, what's his face? Moses? Ah, he's a friend of god's: 'I dunno. Moses, he's, I dunno, his uncle, I dunno'" (58). Jewish humor certainly had no tradition of turning the God of Abraham into an item of choice in a consumer's market: "He's any kind of god you want him to be, god, that's what he is." He could be a "god who'll make me burn in hell for my sins and blaspheming"; he could be "a god that you can exploit and make work for you, and get you respect in the community." If you chose that god, you could even be Catholic, "and get St. Jude working for you"; or you might be Jewish: "Eddie Cantor, *putz-o* exploiter, Georgie Jessel and Kiss-it-off Santas." It didn't matter, because in America God was up for grabs along with any variety of sliced bread. He *may* even be a compassionate God, sorrowing over the bigotry of a society that martyred its citizens, including comedians it didn't like: "Yeah, he's a god that'll look at this culture and say, '*Whew!* What were they *doing*, man? They've got people in prison for thirty-five years!'" (257–58). Whatever God he was, Bruce's God certainly did not come from the Jewish comedic tradition; he was completely novel.

When Bruce took to the comic stage, one other subject was still off limits. He knew this himself, as he revealed in his equation, "satire is tragedy plus time. You give it enough time, the public, the reviewers, will allow you to satirize it." This was "rather ridiculous, when you think about it," but it was still a factor to consider: "And I know, probably 500 years from today, someone will do a satire on Adolph Hitler, maybe even showing him as a hero, and everyone will laugh" (204). But in the end, in spite of his awareness, Bruce didn't wait that long. A mere fifteen years after the liberation of the death camps, he was onstage with his satire of Hitler—with no shortage of Jews over the age of thirty in his audience. What was worse, his Hitler was no monster; he was a victim, a pawn—in the tradition of *shtetl* humor, a *schlemiel*, a poor sap at the mercy of manipulative forces larger than himself. This was the closest thing to a hero that Jewish humor allowed; and here was Lenny Bruce conferring that right upon *Hitler*, as though he were a mere human being. His Hitler is just a *schlub* with a goofy name, Adolph Schickelgruber, painting the walls of the talent agency, M.C.A. ("Mein Campf Arises"), who happens to be spotted by two agents looking for a dictator-type for their next project. His first name, they tell him, is fine; the "Schickelgruber" has to go: "'See, we should have something that's gonna really *hit* the people—*Hit* . . . *Hit*-ler. Adolph *Hit*-ler. I like that—Adolph Hitler. . . . Let's see, A-d-o-l-p-h, H-i-t-l-e-r—yeah, five and five for the marquee. Beautiful. *Ja!* '" (*SHLB*). Presenting Hitler in this way, as *dos kleine menschele*—this was taking *rachmunas* too far. So was having the nerve, in 1961, to speak of another Nazi with compassion and to have the temerity to question Jewish justice: "Eichmann really figured, you know, 'The Jews—the most liberal people in the world—they'll give me a fair shake.' Fair? *Certainly*. 'Rabbi' means lawyer. He'll get the best trial in the world. Eichmann. Ha! They were shaving his leg while he was giving his appeal!" (50).

Nevertheless, Bruce was a Jew; and when he turned to point his finger at the *goyim*, it was a Jewish finger. When he did this, he was out of bounds, violating the Jewish comic tradition of caution, and the general social taboo of criticizing a group from the outside. It was one thing to suggest that, all right, maybe the Jews *did* kill Christ—"I dunno . . . it was one of those parties, got out of hand"; or, "We killed him because he didn't want to become a doctor"; or, "I found a note in my basement. It said: 'We killed him. Signed, Morty.'" But the ice became very thin when the confession read as a preamble to the charge of Christian hypocrisy: "We killed him at his own request, because he knew that people would exploit his name. . . . In Christ's name they would exploit the flag, the Bible, and—*whew!*" (54–55). True, in the Jewish tradition, humor was a vehicle for rabbinical moralizing; but it went on *within* the enclosed Jewish community. When, from the exposed position of the mainstream cabaret stage, Bruce took on the Christian majority— and in particular, Catholicism, his most conspicuous target—his comedic transgressions were those of an interloper.

Ironically, as regards humor, the Jews and Catholics probably shared more similarities than differences. Catholics had faced their own victimization amidst Protestant majorities, in America and elsewhere. Like the Jews, Catholics were considered otherworldly: their holy men and women wore strange garb; their sexuality was peculiar by its enforced absence; they celebrated mass in an odd, foreign tongue; they were accused of plots to convert the populace and overthrow the government in the service of their foreign masters. With the history of anti-Catholicism as visible as that of anti-Semitism, it should come as no surprise that there is such a thing as Catholic humor; that such humor, like its Jewish counterpart, should have grown out of the community itself; and that it should be directed at the community from within. Just as the carnival rituals of the Middle Ages demonstrated a particularly Catholic sense of humor when Catholics were in the majority, there followed no shortage of jokes at the expense of their own customs and their very selves on the lips of *minority* Catholic peoples—as the surfeit of humorous stories about bishops, priests, nuns, and failed celibates will testify.[41]

Bruce himself may have felt a special kinship with Catholics. Certainly one of the great comic pastimes for Jews and Catholics is to challenge each other over who can lay down the heaviest guilt trip—the Jewish or Catholic mother. Perhaps less significantly, Bruce's first arrest was the result of his masquerading as a Catholic priest, soliciting donations for a fake charity in Florida. But whatever affinity he may have felt, there was little chance that, as a Jew, he should have emerged unscathed from his trysts with the organized Catholic church. When a Jewish comedian stands onstage in a major American city to announce, "I've been really interested in Catholicism lately," you can almost hear a collective breath being drawn—especially when the announcement is followed by the debasing, carnivalizing equation of the Roman Catholic church with a slick restaurant franchise: "They have one government, and when you buy the Howard Johnson franchise you can apply it to the geography—whatever's cool for that area—and then you, you know, pay the bread to the main office" (15). The *logic* of the comparison works, of course, just as it does in Bruce's ironic assertion that, if pot smoking necessarily begets "a strung out junkie," then gambling and murder necessarily begin with "bingo in the Catholic church" (*ELBP*).

Such renderings might be harmless enough; they might, at the worst, put Bruce on probation. But when he allied Christ with Moses in a modern Judeo-Christian morality tale about the degeneracy of all organized religions, it was still the Roman Catholic church, because of its conspicuous wealth and symbolism, that bore the brunt of his satire. As Bruce fashioned his images of Christ and Moses in vernacular terms, emphasizing their wisdom, humility and compassion, he may well have been acting—as Frank Kofsky suggests—in the tradition of the eastern European *maggidim*, the itinerant Jewish lay preachers who mixed humorous stories and parables with religious and moral instruction for the benefit of the villagers alienated by the formality and distance of the educated rabbis.[42] But if so, the *maggidim* directed their attention to what could be improved in the Jewish *shtetl*—not St. Patrick's Cathedral in New York, where Bruce's Christ and Moses end their inspection tour of the world. It is the rare *maggid* who would stand on a public stage and accuse a Catholic cardinal, amidst other Catholics, of the hypocrisy of preaching "love and giving" in such opulent surroundings: "Christ would be confused, 'cause *their* route took 'em through Spanish Harlem. And they would wonder what forty Puerto Ricans were doing living in one room—and *this* guy had on a ring that was worth eight grand!" It is the rare *maggid* who would depict Cardinal Spellman and Bishop Sheen as two panicking gangsters, caught by Christ and Moses with their hands in the till, complaining to the Pope in Rome, "'Look, what are we paying protection for?'" (*MC*).

After his arrest at Chicago's Gate of Horn Theatre in 1963, Bruce suggested that he was a victim of organized Catholic persecution. It is true that the arresting officer, his voice captured on tape, had obviously and unconstitutionally used the authority of his badge to redress his private religious outrage. This man Lenny Bruce, he threatened the owner, "'mocks the Pope—and I'm speaking as a Catholic—I'm here to tell you your license is in danger.'" Bruce maintained that, of the fifty people from whom the jury of his "peers" was selected, forty-seven were Catholic, and that they were not chosen at random but were hand-picked according to their seating—"*and they kept changing seats!*" All the major players, barring the defense, he said, were Catholic, in a sinister image of an Ash Wednesday *auto-da-fé*: "I could never conjure up a more bizarre satire than the reality of a judge, two prosecutors and twelve jurors, each with a spot of ash on his forehead." And he quoted Brendan Behan's reaction: "'That scares *me*—and I'm Catholic!'"[43] Possibly this scenario is merely an indication of the fact that, at the time, Chicago boasted the largest Catholic population of any American archdiocese; possibly it is a true representation of the terrifying lengths to which a scandalized community would go in avenging their violated institutions. But it is certain that it is a reflection of the hazards Lenny Bruce faced in his attempt to reorder the unwritten, though instinctively defended, comedic conventions of his time and place.

It is not that Bruce was a Jew who had it in for Catholics alone; in his monologues, millionaire Protestant evangelists are also transformed into gangsters, as are rabbis. The whole of Western organized religion is in a conspiracy—"Religions, Inc."—to defraud the people of their wherewithal: "'The graph here tells the story. That's about it: for the first time in twelve years, Catholicism is up nine points. Judaism is up fifteen. The Big P—the Pentecostal—is startin' to move.'" Is Oral Roberts dumb because he can't seem to find the Kingdom of Heaven? "'Yes, I'm dumb. I got two Lincoln Continentals, that's how goddamn dumb *I* am!'" What should they *do* with the Kingdom of Heaven if they ever did find it? Rabbi Stephen Weiss: "'I tink ve should subdivide.'" How should the Pope be marketed? "'We got an eight-page layout with *Viceroy*: "The New Pope Is a Thinking Man."'" As the Protestants complain on the phone to the Pope, the business is beset with irritations because the people want their religious leaders to *say* things—about integration: "'They're buggin' us. . . . They're gettin' hip! . . . No, they don't *want* no more quotations from the Bible. . . . They want us to say *Let Them Go To School With Them!*'" Or about war: "'Yeah, they keep saying "Thou Shalt Not Kill" *means* that, not "Amend Section A". . . . Yes, they *don't* want the bomb. . . . *Sure* they're commies.'" In the end, the denominational distinctions don't even matter, as Oral Roberts assures the Pope: "'No, nobody knows you're Jewish'" (*SHLB*).

In the real world, with comedic deception (and *reception*) as serious an issue as it is—witness the cases of comedians as varied as Molière, Lenny Bruce, and Salman Rushdie—not only do denominational distinctions matter a great deal in the world of joke telling, so does the standpoint of the comedian the moment the joke is told. One takes a chance of alienating from within as well as from without, as Bruce discovered to his increasing puzzlement before his audiences of both Jews and gentiles. What had he done except tell the truth?

After his death, numerous defenders generally seized upon that one word in their attempts to explain the reason for the hostilities Bruce faced. In the November 1972 issue of *Gallery*, James Walsh's profile was titled, "A Stand-Up Jewish Comic Who Wasn't Very Funny Because He Always Told the Truth." Paul Simon wrote and sang that he had "learned the truth from Lenny Bruce," while Ingmar Bergman proclaimed that Bruce's only crime was in his daring to tell the truth. Lenny Bruce was well read, but he never read Huizinga; or if he did, he refused to heed his warnings about transgressing the rules of play. With the lessons of *Homo Ludens* fully absorbed, Bruce would have considered that he was the heir to a comedic tradition, whether Jewish or gentile, in which "*truth* truth" was the one thing to avoid, it being the weapon of the spoil-sport— the social critic in earnest. What Bruce needed, and what he refused to cultivate, was "*false* truth," the weapon of the false player—the ironist; the cheat. Even in his most surreal or absurd renderings, he deliberately withheld the promise, or the lie, that he was "only kidding," with its implied recognition of the bounds he was to respect. The question isn't really about whether or not Bruce actually told the truth—*that* question can be debated forever. The issue is that, both implicitly and explicitly—and from the very comedic stage on which he stood—he established that truth telling was indeed his aim. He might have thrown up the smokescreen that Kurt Vonnegut described as that of the ironist who "always crossed his fingers when he was kidding."[44] But Bruce refused, and in so doing he indeed widened the cage in which succeeding American stand-up comics were still obliged to perform. That they could perform in a freer space only over his dead body raises the next question to be addressed, namely, whether Lenny Bruce—as a deliberate spoilsport—was in fact a martyr to the truth or the most foolish of fools.

"I'm not a comedian, and I'm not sick"

In 1961, from the stage of a San Francisco nightclub, Bruce recalled his first performance in the area a few years before, at another club across the street. He had asked his agent what the audience would be like, what kind of show it was supposed to be. The reply, as Bruce repeated it: " 'They're a bunch of cocksuckers, that's all. A damn fag show' " (*WIAF*). With this, Bruce became the first comedian in American history to be arrested for using an eleven-letter word onstage. At his trial, one of the defense witnesses was called upon to support Bruce's contention of his artistic responsibility to recreate life with "phonographic accuracy." Dr. Lou Gottlieb maintained that if the defendant's intent had been to reproduce " 'the actual speech verbatim with the same intonation and the same attitudes and everything else that would be characteristic of, let's say, a talent agent of some kind,' " then the offending word was indispensable. Another more " 'genteel' " term would not have worked: " 'It wouldn't be phonographically accurate. It would lose its real feel; there would be almost no point.' " He accepted that there *was* an element of make-believe in the scenarios Bruce created, a " 'generally fantastic frame of reference' " in which " 'normal dimensions . . . are transmuted into a grotesque panorama of contemporary society' "—but the offending word itself was categorically *not* part of the fantasy. Rather, it was an *accuracy*, which, when inserted into the fantastic context, created the desired comic effect.[45]

Although Bruce was acquitted at this trial, in one sense this testimony might have done more harm than good. It established that, however Bruce was otherwise prepared to make believe, to fantasize, to lie, he would not be prepared to do so simply to avoid the selection of taboo words. Bruce himself said as much: "I'll never use four-letter words for shock value, for a laugh; but if it *fits* the character, then I want to swing with it and say it."[46] His appeal to "phonographic accuracy" never once did him any favors in the courtroom. Even when his Chicago obscenity conviction of 1963 was overturned by the United States Supreme Court, it was clear that his choice of truthful words was not what impressed the justices. They explained that what had saved the defendant's hide was their grudging recognition that some of his material was "'of social importance'"; but they scoffed at his claim to the right to be "accurate" under the protection of the First Amendment. They would not, they said, "'have thought that constitutional guarantees would necessitate the subjection of society to the gradual deterioration of its moral fabric which this type of presentation promotes.'" In other words, as Bruce said, "They're really saying that they're only sorry the crummy Constitution won't permit them to convict me, but if they had *their* choice. . . ."[47] He may have been right; but if so, it would have been for his defiant insistence on "phonographic accuracy."

As the charges of obscenity against him became more frequent, Bruce resorted to some fairly torturous justifications for his use of profanity. He would say, for instance, that he was out to distinguish "between the *moral* differences of words and their connotations."[48] He referred to himself—mistakenly, as it turned out— as a "neologist," one who "either invents new words or discovers new meanings for old ones."[49] When charged that he had used the term "Eat it" in a lewd context, he argued that he had actually said "Kiss it," that between "kissing my mother goodbye and eating my mother goodbye, there is a quantity of difference"—wholly side-stepping the issue of context.[50] But it was precisely this issue that was the most important. The question was never exclusively about *accuracy* or *truth*; it was always about the social context in which he tried to tell it. In maintaining, as he did, that there was no such thing as a "dirty word," he may as well have said outright that there was no such thing as social, linguistic, or comedic convention, or that the rules of the game were just too dumb to play by. In his monologue about the "dirty toilet jokes" he was always accused of telling, he dismissed the entire concept of obscenity: it was a mere "human manifestation" (as though language itself and all the conventions surrounding it were not). He could spell it out as "logically" as he pleased, reduce the entire convention to the absurdity that it was, attempt to divest a word of the "obscenity" arbitrarily imposed upon it until it became an inert *thing*, like a real toilet: "This toilet has no central nervous system. No level of consciousness. It is not aware. It is a *dumb toilet*. It cannot be obscene." He could point as much as he wanted to the insane capriciousness of the taboo: "If it could be obscene, it could be cranky. It could be a Communist toilet, a traitorous toilet—it can do none of these things. It's a *dopey toilet*, Jim" (*WIAF*). But he had already seen the reality in which arbitrary charges like "Communist" and "traitor" were flung down from the mountaintop and absurdly stuck to all kinds of targets; so it was with all words and the other "human manifestations"—the taboos—surrounding them. He could have adopted no crusade more doomed in his lifetime than that of convincing an intolerant society of the absurdity of their taboos about language, however much he had to teach them about the rights of free speech.

In his dismissal of the obscene context in which his society had irrationally placed certain four-letter combinations, Bruce never admitted that he was guilty of the same charge that he frequently leveled at those critics who persisted in isolating *his* "obscenities" from the contexts in which he had used them. He recreated the process imaginatively in a number of his monologues, without ever apparently realizing that he was presenting a mirror image of his own futile attempts to separate words from the meanings conventionally imposed upon them. For instance, he would describe the police officer assigned to monitor his performances and repeat them verbatim in court: "'Um . . . "shit," and, uh, "Catholic," and . . . "*schmuck*," "shit," uh, and . . . uh, "*schmuck*," and "stick in your *schmuck*," uh, and . . . "Catholic," and, "asshole" . . . "Lyndon Johnson" and "*schmuck*," and, "shit" . . . "shit." . . .'" The judge would ask, incredulously, if this was the *entire* performance. "'Uh, no, he said "shit" a lot more times.'" As Bruce himself accepted, what *could* a jury say after watching an act like this, except, "'That *stinks!*'" Stripped of the context in which the words were intended, they lost the meaning they were chosen to reflect. Consequently, when the policeman finished being Lenny Bruce for the court, Bruce would "get busted—on *his* act!" Moreover: "I gotta go to court and defend *him!*" (*LBOA*).

Yet Bruce himself would fall into the quixotic trap of separating words from context—or connotations—in his attempt to prove that the meanings his society had already imposed on words did not matter anymore, or could easily be altered on his say-so. "'*Schmuck*' doesn't mean '*schmuck*' anymore"; or "'Goddamn you' don't mean 'God damn you' anymore—I didn't *curse* you, I didn't *damn* you" (*MC*). If President Kennedy were to announce on the air, "'I'm considering appointing two or three of the top niggers in the country to my Cabinet,' in six months 'nigger' wouldn't mean any more than 'goodnight,' 'God bless you,' or 'I promise to tell the truth, the whole truth and nothing but the truth so help me God.'"[51] Similarly, "to" is *only* a preposition, and "come" is *only* a verb; and if those two little words in combination "really make you feel uncomfortable; if you think I'm rank for saying it to you, and you the beholder gets ranked from listening to it," then that's *your* problem: "You probably can't come" (*WIAF*). Or, if a person can "prostitute" his art, then no one should be upset with the vulgar word "hooker" because "the word 'prostitute' doesn't mean anymore what the word 'hooker' does. If a man were to send out for a $100 prostitute, a writer with a beard might show up."[52] All these various attempts, comedic and otherwise, to rationalize away the arbitrary stigmas attached to words were in effect denials of the powers socially conferred upon language according to rules that had been established long before Lenny Bruce took to the stage. His genuine astonishment at the persistence with which those rules would be defended and, if transgressed, avenged is an indication of his failure to realize how serious the game could be. The rules of play mattered much more than accuracy or truth.

What Bruce did not admit out loud, but which he and other carnivalizing satirists had aptly demonstrated, was that the taboo word was indeed a potent critical force. As Hugh Dalziel Duncan noted, obscenity can "rob evil and malign powers of their majesty."[53] The powers need not even be so sinister; merely exalted, as Mikhail Bakhtin showed in his analyses of Rabelais and the carnival parodies that brought medieval clergy and aristocracy down to the lowest bodily levels.[54] Obscenity increases the proximity of the subject to the satirist, reduces the artificial distance imposed through such conventions as "decency" or "manners" or "good, clean humor." Kurt Vonnegut once imaginatively surmised why the Victorians would have erected such an elaborate system of manners in order to prevent the distance from being reduced: "What would Queen Victoria really feel in the presence of what she had declared to be obscenities? That her power to intimidate was being attacked ever so slightly, far, far from its center." Hence the

Victorian conventions of decency, the remnants of which were still holding their own in Bruce's time, with their origins in the fear of proximity: "She created arbitrary rules for that outermost edge to warn her of the approach of anyone so crude, so rash as to bring to her attention the suffering of the Irish, or the cruelties of the factory system, or the privileges of the nobility, or the approach of a world war, and on and on." Thus, Victoria's conventions must be protected from the smallest breach: "If she would not even acknowledge that human beings sometimes farted, how could she be expected to hear without swooning of these other things?"[55]

In placing responsibility for Victorian manners squarely at the door of this solitary monarch, Vonnegut is being less faithful to historical fact than to the defensive inspiration for any system of manners, particularly with regard to the distance it creates. The double entendre was one of many polite comedic devices instituted to maintain such distance, to block the threat of obscenity; and it was one of the first devices to be explicitly rejected by Lenny Bruce, to the consternation of many in his audiences. If an offended patron stormed out, Bruce would appear genuinely puzzled: "What kind of humor is his humor? Is his humor the Joe E. Louis, the Sophie Tucker, the double entendre, the naughty-but-nice, the spicy ha-ha-you-know-what-that means?" He did not hide his contempt for the comedians who persisted with "wedding night jokes, motel jokes, Rusty Warren, Johnny got a zero, Dwight Fisk, Mr. Yo-Yo can't get his yo-yo up, he's got the biggest dinghy in the navy"; for such jokes appeared to him a catalogue of craven evasions (206). But Bruce's surprise is almost incredible, not only because he himself had ample evidence of some bizarre attempts at legal persecution—such as the charges by a Jewish undercover detective that Bruce's Yiddish was actually a cover for profanity (as though the double entendre were not)—but also because in some of his monologues he demonstrated perfectly well his recognition of the irrational tenacity of linguistic convention and the importance of cultural specificity, or context.

His parody of linguistic hypocrisy in Las Vegas is a case in point. Even if they had a passion play, a Monet exhibition, and the New York City Ballet, everyone *knew* that there was only one big attraction in Vegas: "Tits and Ass!" Why not be honest and put it on the marquee? "Because it's dirty and vulgar, that's why not." It might be "a little better" to change it to Yiddish: "*Tuchases* and *Naynays!*" If you didn't object, "you're not anti-Semitic idiomatic, you're [only] anti-Anglo-Saxon idiomatic." If you were still offended, you might try Latin: *"Gluteus Maximus, Pectoralis Majoris!"*—except that even if it were "clean to you" it would be "dirty to the Latins" (*WIAF*). Eventually it would be *"La Nouvelle Vague! La Parisienne Folies!"* That would be different: *"French* tits and ass: that's art, and they'll buy that" (*MC*). But in order to parody a rule, as Umberto Eco notes, one first has to be aware of it, to have the capacity to respect it ("Carnival comic, the moment of transgression, can exist only if a background of unquestioned observance exists").[56] In this case, to whatever absurdity the convention is ultimately reduced—in the end "they'll just have a big nipple up on the marquee and guys will be playing it like Harpo Marx, *Honk! Honk!"*—the convention itself remains intact. The *English* words "Tits and Ass" do not go up on the marquee. The double entendre triumphs in the scenario, though of course not in Bruce's delivery of it.

But what is perhaps even more revealing is Bruce's own appeal to the "rule" and the conventions of his contemporary society whenever he felt, justifiably, that he was being victimized. As he argued, it was absurd for him to be convicted of obscenity after the *Ulysses* verdict had already established that "obscene" must apply "to contemporary community standards"—"you know, recognizing the fact that maybe a judge seventy years old doesn't get out much, doesn't *get* much" (*LBOA*). A number of his monologues eulogize the sanctity of rules and laws. He would often attempt to relate their origins: "When we first started the tribe we needed some kind of rule. And the guy said, 'Let's make some real simple rules. . . . Let's see, we'll sleep in Area A, and we'll eat in Area B, we'll throw a crap in Area C.'" Eventually the rule would be transgressed: "And they all went to sleep; and a guy woke up and he got a face full of crap, *Pow!* . . . And he goes, 'What's the deal here? We had a rule.' And they tell him it's a religious holiday. And the guy says, 'Bull *shit.* You know, that's no kind of rule, then. I'll separate the church and state right *now'"* (*LBOA*). Most pathetically, Bruce envisaged one day waking up from the nightmare of his obscenity trials to a big party thrown in his honor because he had never lost his faith in the Constitution, the Supreme Law of the land. But, as it turned out, he was dead before his final obscenity conviction could be overturned according to the rule of law.

Bruce apparently misjudged a number of things about his society and its rules—at least as they stood in his lifetime. For one thing, he found out too late the abiding fact that the narrator of Vonnegut's *Hocus Pocus* notices, "that profanity and obscenity entitle people who don't want unpleasant information to close their ears and eyes to you."[57] He appears to have been wrong in assuming that the First Amendment as it was *then* interpreted was not concerned "with anybody saying 'shit,'" but rather with "the information, that there's no bar to the communication system" (*LBOA*). For although the Supreme Court had overturned a particular conviction against him, that did not prevent his subsequent arrests and convictions for obscenity, which caught him completely off guard—especially in New York, which he had always assumed was "the most sophisticated city" in America. "This is where they play Genet's *The Balcony*. If anyone is the first person to be found obscene in New York, he must feel utterly depraved."[58] He certainly had no idea of the determination with which the authorities would at least see to his gagging, if not something worse. After his death, one of the guilt-ridden prosecutors admitted, "'We drove him into poverty and bankruptcy and then murdered him. We all knew what we were doing. We used the law to kill him.'" Another lawyer on the New York district attorney's staff who refused to participate in the prosecution confessed, "'I'm glad I don't have Bruce on my conscience.'"[59]

It is also apparent that Bruce was wrong in his assumptions about how "contemporary" his society was—not only the people who made and enforced the rules but the ones who came to his shows. Only the timid old-timers, he said, needed to maintain such conventional shields as the double entendre ("'Ha, ha, you know what *that* means, don't you?'"); but not a comedian before a "contemporary" audience. "My generation knows—and accepts— what *that* means, so there is no need for humor in that whoopee-cushion vein."[60] Bruce felt secure in his conviction that "the comedy of today has more of a liberal viewpoint" (219). If people couldn't appreciate it, it was because they were, as he frequently sniffed, "uncontemporary." One obvious problem was that not everyone in his audiences was *of* his generation, however much he might fantasize about it. "I'm gonna have the thing where nobody over forty's allowed to come in to see me. . . . 'How old are you?' 'I'm, uh . . . thirty nine!' 'I'll have to see an I.D.'" His scenario is too wistful to be true, an audience composed solely of hip, young liberals between twenty and forty, who won't turn his performances into a "whatzit mean" game: "The whole thing, 'What's it mean? What's *putz* mean what's *bread* mean what's *cool* mean whatzit mean whatzit mean?'" If only he didn't have to play by the old rules, he could *really* cook: "Man, I will take on fifty

Berles, fifty Mort Sahls, eight Shelley Bermans *and* a Bob Newhart, and I'll put 'em here, here, and *there*. I'll cut *anybody* in that area" (*MC*).

Such comedic apartheid was out of the question, and Bruce knew it. There would always be some "*schlub*" in the audience who would whine, "'I don't unnerstan it.'" There would be violence: "So dig, she takes this old-fashioned glass and starts winging it, man, *vvvooom!*" And there might always be a husband there to defend his generation's outraged morality, as well as his wife's glass-slinging response: "'What else would a lady have done?'" (Bruce's reply: "'Faint!'") (204–5). Such things did happen, in America and abroad, as Jonathan Miller described memorably in his review of Bruce's act at London's Establishment Club in 1963, where the comedian stood onstage amidst a hail of coins, ice cubes, and cocktail glasses: "It was like a seance; and Bruce himself seemed dazed, like a medium, in a trance, creating effects, cries and levitations, beyond his and the audience's control."[61]

But such a terrifying outcome might not be merely the result of an audience's inability to "unnerstan," which was the usual reason Bruce gave for their resistance—that, or the fact that they just hadn't been exposed to the hipness of his delivery. That was always possible, as we have seen; but he also must have known that the "failure to *enjoy* a joke [my italics] . . . does not usually imply failure to understand it," that "a prudish person may fully comprehend jokes about sex [for instance] although they may cause him to feel embarrassment or disgust."[62] He surely knew enough to be able to re-create the nervous introductions with which club owners felt obliged to soften up their audiences: "'Uh, folks, before we bring our star out, uh, I want you to know, what the hell, a joke's a joke, right? And, uh, I mean, he kids a lot about religion, you know, and, uh, lesbians and dope, and, uh, politics, but what the hell . . . he was in the service for three years.'" If, as Bruce suggests, this introduction alone "loses forty people," then obviously their failure to understand a joke is not even an issue, for they will have walked out before having heard one (*MC*). Remove the comic characterization, and you have the actual, stumbling introduction by the master of ceremonies at Bruce's Carnegie Hall performance: "Perhaps as a short explanation to the people who don't understand what he does, it is not that Lenny Bruce *per se* is a sick comedian, but that Lenny Bruce comments, reflects, holds up the mirror, so to speak. . . ." Thus would an audience be told, in all seriousness, that they were not primarily in for a good time, for a bit of fun; they had paid their money to be told about "the sick elements in our society that should be reflected upon and that should be spoken about" (*MC*).

A conceivable, if uncharitable, response to this might be, "We didn't come to see an anthropologist; we came to see a comedian." At least one writer, Stephanie Koziski, has suggested that a stand-up comedian might in fact have much in common with an anthropologist. Both, she says, are "sensitive to the common pattern of things"; both are public witnesses to "socially enacted behavior"; and both, in isolating objects of scrutiny to fit into "a theoretical model of the studied society," create a sort of "artifice from a social reality."[63] Bruce would indeed couch some of his monologues in anthropological contexts: he would talk about "reflecting the culture" or "the tribe." He would recreate scenarios in primitive societies, such as when describing the origins of civil authority: "A lot of the missionaries who sort of gave religious instruction to the savages never really were definite with the people about it—that they weren't God, and that they were constructed like they were: just *people*." As he explained, "And the savages would go, 'Are you God?' And they'd go, 'Well, I'm not *God*, but . . . heh heh'" (LBOA). He would attempt to emphasize the fickle, transitory nature of cultural *mores*—that if someone or something is wrong, it is "just wrong for that minute." His model might be Roman society: "Now, there's one group in this Roman society that isn't correct, and this group is against everything that's 'good.' And this group are called *Christians*. Now, what do we do with the Christians? Only one thing that is correct and moral to do with them: throw them to the lions" (*MC*). Or it might be his own society, presented from the point of view of an objective ethnologist: "This is the typical white person's concept of how we relax colored people at parties" (*LBA*). He would describe the predatory sexual customs of American men: "They can go through plate-glass windows, fifty people laying dead on the highway—and on the way to the hospital in the ambulance, the guy makes a play for the nurse" (*LBA*). In these and other presentations, Bruce demonstrated to a degree the affinity described by Koziski, not only in terms of subject matter but in her comparison between the stand-up comedian who "shares his views of reality with an audience" and the anthropologist in a lecture hall. But she makes one crucial distinction, none the less so because of its obviousness: "The comedian's basic thrust as he or she stands before an audience, however, is to be entertaining rather than to elucidate culture theory."[64]

This is where Lenny Bruce most seriously misjudged the charity of his audience and the expectations under which he performed. *He* was not on a mission to entertain. With no little sense of martyrdom he proclaimed that comedians of his generation had "a cross to bear" unlike those of any previous day. It was the *old-timers*, the *nafkes* (prostitutes), who were only kidding, folks: "A comedian of the older generation did an 'act' and he told the audience, 'This is my act.' Today's comic is not doing an act. The audience assumes he's telling the truth." And of the new breed of comedic martyrs, none had a heavier cross to bear than Bruce himself: "When I'm interested in a truth, it's really a *truth* truth. And that's a terrible truth to be interested in" (200). *Emmis*, as Bruce would frequently say. This Yiddish mantra that punctuated so many of his monologues is, as Sanford Pinsker notes, "akin to '*Selah*' or 'Omayn' [or] *quod erat demonstrandum* ('which was to be demonstrated'). Either way, Bruce hath spoken."[65] There is no telling how many of the world's comedians have privately believed that their errand was to tell the truth: only Lenny Bruce would admit it with no accessible trace of irony or self-effacement. He did it many times, and in so doing explicitly rejected the comic mask, the lie that was demanded of him: "'I'm not a comedian. And I'm not sick. The world is sick and I'm the doctor.'" It was a thankless task, but someone had to do it: "'I'm a surgeon with a scalpel for false values. I don't have an act. I just talk. I'm just Lenny Bruce.'"[66] Toward the end of his career he was actually closing his acts—the precious few that remained to him—with the nightly apology to his dwindling audiences, "'I'm sorry I haven't been very funny, but you see I'm not a comedian; I'm Lenny Bruce.'"[67] Thus did he tell his audience, effectively, that the ironic identity was not for him— that he just didn't want to play anymore.

Of course Bruce's inability to keep up with the masquerade was at its greatest toward the end of his life, when the strains of arrest, litigation, and drug abuse took their toll along with the increasing ugliness he identified in his society. The theater critic Clive Barnes remembered the playfulness, the "almost boyish charm," with which Bruce had performed in his early days. By the end he had become "an incompetent, foul-mouthed loudmouth"—an irritable spoil-sport. "When I saw Bruce, white and ferret-faced, caught in the spotlight of notoriety and trying to face the horror, the guy wasn't very funny." As Barnes recalled, "the boyishness had been replaced with the snapping vitality of a cornered animal."[68] Malcolm Muggeridge also remembered the last time he saw Bruce onstage: "He looked very nervous and shaky; chain-smoked all the time. I suppose he might have been high, but more, I thought, wretched, broken; if a manic-depressive, then decidedly depressive." The comedian was nowhere to be seen, the presentation "a meandering monologue of distaste, with a certain number of old fashioned digs at the American Establishment; not particularly arresting, certainly not funny in the ha!-ha! sense." At best, Muggeridge could detect a trace of piquancy amidst the incoherent mumblings and the sketchy remains of old monologues with which Bruce buttressed the recitals of court transcripts and personal grievances. It was possibly the aborted comic promise that gave rise to Muggeridge's funereal comparison between Bruce and two former, doomed confidence men—Jay Gatsby and his creator: "You thought of Dorothy Parker, who, when she saw Scott Fitzgerald's sodden and too youthful corpse, murmured: 'The poor son of a bitch!'"[69]

It is difficult to say *what* Bruce thought he was trying to be, if not a comedian. Possibly, as he said, a kind of social surgeon; or, as Frank Kofsky thought, a hip Jewish preacher, a *maggid*. Albert Goldman got considerable mileage out of his estimations of Bruce as a modern-day shaman, the tribal exorcist who knowingly and obsessively destroyed himself in the act of healing. In 1964 he described the rapid transformation Bruce underwent as he approached his outright dismissal of the comic mask. Only a few years before, Bruce would appear onstage dressed as a conventional nightclub comic in an expensive Italian suit, depending entirely on impressions and linguistic communication. By the end, he had done away with the standard trappings of the comedy stage, slouching in a rumpled black raincoat, unshaven, disheveled, and gaunt-faced, almost satanic. Rather than depending on words, he now placed more emphasis on dramatic devices—bits of pseudo-voodoo magic, flashing lights, beating on drums, wailing and howling aboriginal-sounding chants and poems, screaming out of the darkness and hiding from the audience, jumping onto furniture and throwing things, opening and slamming doors in what appeared to be a ritual. It was theatrical enough, perhaps even somewhat ironic; but the last thing Bruce seemed interested in arousing was laughter. He would pick up a chair and menace a patron, and if the audience laughed he would scold them for their sadism with the accusation that, had he gone so far as to kill the patron, they would even have accepted *that* for the sake of a laugh.[70]

But one need not look only to the end of Bruce's career for evidence of his unease with the ludic expectations that his audiences had inherited and—to him—obstinately advanced. Even in the 1950s he could be heard rejecting with scorn and sarcasm the complaints that he wasn't *funny* enough: "'A comedian should get a laugh every 25 seconds for a period of not less than 45 minutes and accomplish this feat with consistency 18 out of 20 shows.'"[71] As Sanford Pinsker notes, throughout Bruce's career it would always be possible that the patron who expected a punchline might very well get a sermon instead. And even in his earliest performances, one could detect a tendency in Bruce to distance himself from those comedians who willingly—and in his estimation, timidly and dishonestly—satisfied the expectations of the traditional nightclub patron. He was always critical of other comedians who had made fortunes by "doing an act," sneering at their onstage masquerades while onstage himself, trying his hardest to improvise himself away from any comparison with set routine performers. It was as though he were trying to put himself as far as possible from the contemporary comic stage while still remaining on it. A number of his monologues reveal precisely the contempt he felt for the requirement of arousing laughter. His portrayal of the New York comedian booked at the Palladium in London—whom Bruce admits is "naturally, part me"—presents a lonely figure crucified at the hands of an audience sitting stonily like "Mount Rushmore," as animated as "an oil painting." After going "straight into the toilet" with each act for two consecutive nights, he loses his cool, calls his audience "Limey assholes," and taunts them with images of the I.R.A. They destroy the place trying to get at him, as amidst the debris he tries and fails to convince them that he was "only kidding" (*IANN*).

In other instances he would present comedians as social parasites—as though he had set out to update Plato or St. Augustine, if not Melville. One of his earliest characterizations was the Shingle Man, a figure associated with New York comedy since the 1940s, based on the real-life confidence men who traveled from slum to slum, softening up homeowners with deft patter and impromptu comedy before swindling them out of monstrous deposits for the roofing and aluminum siding they would never receive. The connections between comedy, confidence games, and disrepute were inseparable; and out of such characterizing came all sorts of figures preying on the gullible and confident. Any of the world's corrupt power wielders—television preachers, Mafioso popes, conniving presidents, smart-ass comedians—could be reduced to a common, fast-talking shingle man in Bruce's monologues. This included Bruce himself. "I'm a hustler," he admitted. "As long as they give, I'll grab." He envisaged being hauled up before a tribunal along with a host of other performers—Frankie Laine, Sophie Tucker, Sammy Davis, Jr.—to answer for the crime of earning more in one week than what a schoolteacher earned in a year. "We'll have to answer, I'm sure of that. I'm just waiting for the day. I'm saving some money to give back—'I know I was stealing! I didn't *mean* to take it—they *gave* it to me!'" (*IANN*). Likewise, in another monologue the Lone Ranger is told that he will never again hear the famous radio signature cry, *Thank you, Masked Man!* "'The Messiah has returned. You see, men like yourself and Lenny Bruce—you thrive upon the continuance of segregation, violence, and disease. Now that all is pure, *you're* in the shithouse'" (*LBOA*). Bruce described himself as "a comedian who has thrived both economically and egotistically upon the corruption and cruelty he condemns with humor . . . a parasite whose whole structure of success depended on despair."[72] Paradoxically, in spite of his admission that he was just another confidence man, he would also liken himself to Jonas Salk or any other "people who hold that superior moral position of serving humanity." Thus public servants—corrupt or otherwise—life-saving physicians, moralizing comedians, all will have become aware on Judgment Day that "their very existence, creative ability, and symbolic status had depended wholly on intellectual dishonesty."[73]

   More than anything, these autobiographical passages reflect the greatest danger in which Bruce placed himself as a comedian. In Pinsker's words, "Bruce, the entertainer, was in danger of being taken seriously as Bruce, the prophet, as Bruce, the discerning social commentator." One might argue that, in his lifetime, Bruce was in fact considered none of these things by many of those who were in a position to give him the most trouble—judges, detectives, hostile reviewers, and bored audiences. But Pinsker is correct in asserting, "Even more important, Bruce was in danger of taking *himself* seriously, of becoming that saddest of all tricksters—the con man conned."[74] If this is the case, then out the window must go any conception of Lenny Bruce as a martyr to the truth, however much we willingly grant that he was a martyr to the cause of free speech. Eric Bogosian surmises that "the Lenny-as-martyr mythology" was mostly a product of the mid-1970s, resting in the minds of a self-consciously bohemian generation with a "real commitment to non-commitment" and an unfocused "*idea* of the '60s" as an alternative to the course marked out by the Vietnam carnage and the cynical corruptions of Watergate. Bogosian suggests a reconsideration of

Bruce's place "without the mystification and blurriness that come with the passing down of legend."[75] Andrew Ross offers just such a reconsideration, arguing that it would be "probably unfair to say that Bruce actively courted the storm of police harassment and persecution that descended upon him in the early sixties." It was not until this systematic harassment was well under way that Bruce began to make his unhelpfully ostentatious claims to truth-telling in his defense. Yet, as Ross notes, it was the issue of free speech, and not truth versus untruth, that kept Bruce from serving "a proper prison sentence" (as opposed to his frequent arrests), and which led to the posthumous overturning of his final New York obscenity conviction.[76]

The question as to whether Lenny Bruce died a martyr must lead, then, to two conclusions: no and yes. As a comedian, his presumption to tell the truth, and then to advertise the intention and hope to get sympathy for it, was a criminal act. *Comedians do not tell the truth.* Whether guilty of frankness or merely attempted frankness, the comedian in him was in any case guilty, and deserved to have the book thrown at him. As a critic with the right and the responsibility to observe, analyze, and speak frankly about his own culture under the protection of a Constitution that explicitly guarantees the right and implicitly affirms the responsibility, Lenny Bruce was indeed crucified. The record of relentless hounding reads like a conspiracy, with law officers looking for any motive to get him off the stage, frequently embarrassing themselves in the process. 1961: arrested for narcotics possession in Philadelphia, case dismissed. 1961: arrested for obscenity in San Francisco and acquitted. 1962: banned from performing in Australia. 1962: arrested for narcotics possession in Los Angeles—convicted, but the sentence is overturned when the arresting officer, who had allegedly seen Bruce drop a packet of heroin into the gutter, is himself convicted of perjury, smuggling, and possession of heroin. 1962: arrested for obscenity in Hollywood, acquitted. 1963: arrested for obscenity in Chicago—convicted, with the verdict upheld by Illinois State Supreme Court, only to be overturned two years later by the U.S. Supreme Court. 1963: arrested for narcotics possession in Los Angeles, certified (and stigmatized) as an addict in need of confined treatment . . . the list goes on.

With all his attention to these cases and the subsequent appeals, Bruce was virtually finished as an ironist and artist, driven until his death to master the proceedings and the language of the courtroom. Moreover, the continued arrests had the desired effect of forcing nightclub owners across the country into viewing Bruce as a liability; for whether or not he was criminally convicted, say, for narcotics possession, the fact of his being a certified drug addict frightened even the most sympathetic club owners into boycotting him. The stigma did not stop at the American border, either: in addition to being banned in Australia, Bruce was barred in April 1963 from performing in, or even visiting, Great Britain. Any remaining professional resilience he might have had was finally smashed by his last arrest for obscenity, at New York's Cafe Au Go-Go in April 1964. The New York Criminal Court convicted him, sentenced him to three four-month terms in the workhouse, and banned him from performing in New York. The case went to appeal, but the stigma remained, along with the fear of the district attorney's office on the part of New York's nightclub owners, who permanently cut Bruce off from his most sympathetic audience. He died a legal pauper before the decision was reversed, and before the prosecuting attorneys admitted that they had believed him innocent of violating any law.

Thus, whether or not the legal conspiracy unleashed on Lenny Bruce caused him to jab a needle into his arm just once too often, he indeed earned his martyrdom to the American Constitution. As Andrew Ross notes, "This, more than anything, was the lesson of Bruce's hipsterism."[77] But again, it was not as a comedian that Bruce earned the right to that sanctified role, for on the comic stage he never argued in terms of free speech as much as he argued for "accuracy"—for "truth." Moreover, if it is Lenny Bruce of whom Don McLean sings in "American Pie"—the enigmatic ode to the rock-and-roll years in which the jester steals the king's "thorny crown"—if it *is* Bruce (and this is by no means certain), then it is an honor to which the comedian in him is not entitled. For even before his death, he had ended his career by repudiating the ironic identity outright, being perhaps the first recognized comedian in American history to excommunicate himself verbally—and seriously—from the profession. Rather than focusing his attention on the delivery of playful untruths from the cabaret stage, his final energies were devoted to the anti-ironic, deadly literal discourse of the courtroom. Lenny Bruce died a spoil-sport; but in so doing he paved the way for a rewriting of the rules of play.

CHAPTER 4

Bill Hicks:
"Bob, they're just jokes"

In 1995, the updated publication of Bill Carter's *The Late Shift* appeared to reviewers as a Shakespearean tale of intrigue, passion, ambition, and betrayal in the "network battle for the night" between David Letterman and Jay Leno.[1] Even if not agreeing with the inflated comparison, one can accept that, like any of Shakespeare's tragedies, Carter's book is littered with a variety of seemingly inconsequential victims and minor pawns in the power struggle. Yet, as Tom Stoppard showed with his Rosencrantz and Guildenstern, there are no such things as minor characters, only perspectives. Another point of view, then, will reveal the importance of a character who was missed entirely in Carter's reportage of the struggle. In November 1993, John Lahr published a profile in the "Annals of Comedy" section of the *New Yorker*. It began: "On October 1st, the comedian Bill Hicks, after doing his twelfth gig on the David Letterman show, became the first comedy act to be censored at CBS's Ed Sullivan Theatre, where Letterman is now in residence, and where Elvis Presley was famously censored in 1956." There was a significant difference between the two: "Presley was not allowed to be shown from the waist down. Hicks was not allowed to be shown at all."[2] Four months after this profile appeared, Bill Hicks was dead from pancreatic cancer, leaving Lahr to recall his importance: "He was really an ass-kicking comedian—the best kind. The only kind that matters—when jokes are meant to kill."[3]

The death of this Texan comedian at the age of thirty-two attracted nowhere near the media attention devoted the following month to his fellow southerner, Lewis Grizzard—at least, not in America. In Britain, where Hicks had been lionized, the quality dailies carried illustrated obituaries, documentary tributes were broadcast on network television, and on the first anniversary of his death, appreciations appeared in newspapers and on television. In America, Hicks had never gained the popular following of the sentimental, conservative Grizzard; he was rather, in Mike Sager's words, the "best-known unknown in the business. The comics' comic. The critics' comic."[4] But on the other hand, Lewis Grizzard never had the honor (no irony intended) of being banned by American network television. In accomplishing this feat, Bill Hicks demonstrated why, in the long run, he is more worthy of notice, at least in a study such as this. Few American comedians since George Carlin have brought any significant challenges to the most powerful and censorial medium of communication, network television; and perhaps no other recent career raises such disturbing implications about the successful taming and silencing of the satiric voice by the commercial interests in that medium—especially in an era of reactionary tendencies on the left and right; an era of political correctness and "family values" in which Catherine MacKinnon and Jesse Helms could conceivably be allies against freedom of expression; a bizarre era in which the most influential American ironist is arguably the quasi-comedian and self-conscious demagogue, Rush Limbaugh.

Bill Hicks was a progressive and a civil libertarian, a complex figure in which the paradoxes of his cultural and political milieu came to light. On the libertarian side, his routines dwelt on such issues as the legalization of drugs, sexual openness, freedom of all and any expression (including the pornographic), abortion, and the rights of smokers. He was defiantly politically incorrect. As a progressive, he reserved his most scathing attacks for the arms trade, the domestic gun lobby, the Christian fundamentalist-Republican axis, the anti-abortion movement, and American militarism at home and abroad. His intellectual hero was Noam Chomsky (he enjoyed being called "Chomsky with dick jokes"). In the months before he died, he was invited to write for the *Nation*, America's venerable progressive weekly. Had he lived, he would have joined the ranks of such contributors as Chomsky, Gore Vidal, Molly Ivins, Kurt Vonnegut, Calvin Trillin, and Alice Walker. His "caustic observations," in *Nation* editor Katrina vanden Heuvel's words, would have been similar to those already enjoyed by readers of the satirical British magazine *Scallywag*, to which Hicks had been a regular contributor before *that* thorn in the side of the Tory establishment was brought down by none other than the prime minister himself.[5]

The savagery of Bill Hicks as a satirist brought comparisons not only to Lenny Bruce but also to Jonathan Swift and "the devil's lexicographer," Ambrose Bierce—the latter of whom Hicks recalled in his signature outfit of all-black and in the satanic imagery of his routines, which earned him the appellation of "the Prince of Darkness" among colleagues and critics. At the same time, few American comedians in the past two decades have made such frequent and explicit appeals to the unfashionable 1960s ideals of love and peace. For our purposes, though, the most important contradiction in the case of Bill Hicks—as with Lenny Bruce before him—lies, as ever, in the conflict between the urge to tell the truth and the comedic requirement of the playful untruth. That Hicks was aware of this requirement, there is no doubt. True, he once took the potentially fatal, Brucian step of admitting that he was a "preacher"—but that was only to his mother (*IJR*). Otherwise, he could tell the most playfully violent lies in the name of "truth," a paradox that was the source of his supreme irony and the cause of his greatest outrage, censorship at the hands of American commercial interests.

Recalling Swift and the Either/Or of Irony

In order to appreciate why Bill Hicks might have been used by the producers of a late-night talk show to enhance the impression of their own subversive daring, and why he would be ultimately discarded by them in their subsequent retreat from that very impression, consider the interplay between Hicks and one of his live audiences. Picture him onstage, stopping his narrative in midflow in order to offer a modest proposal: "By the way, if anyone here is in advertising or marketing—kill yourself." Imagine the audience's stunned laughter, followed by the comedian's protest: "No, really. There's no rationalization for what you do, and you are Satan's little helpers. O.K.? Kill yourselves—seriously. You are the ruiner of all things good—seriously." The more he protests his earnestness, the louder the audience laughs; the louder they laugh, the more he protests: "This is not a joke. You're going, 'There's gonna be a joke coming —' There is no fucking joke coming. You are Satan's spawn, filling the world with bile and garbage; you are fucked and you're fucking us: *kill yourself*. It's the only way to save your fucking soul."[6] The comedian is drowned out in laughter and applause; short of pulling out a gun and committing the act himself, there is nothing left for him to do. Of course, even the advertising and marketing people are laughing—and a few weeks later, to Hicks's amazement, one thick-skinned adman will actually approach him with the request to endorse his client's orange drink product. (Hicks will refuse with derision.) It is a routine that, in its pacing and dynamics, shows an experienced ironist, in John Lahr's estimation, "easy—at ease, *masterful* with an audience" (*IJR*). With a little taming, a little cleaning-up of the old demon F-word, one can see why he might be David Letterman's prize catch.

This very routine, I believe, encapsulates both the ironist's victory and his dilemma—the same victory and dilemma faced by Swift with his "modest proposal" to cure the tragedy of starvation and infanticide in Ireland by fattening up the children as "prime dainties" for sale to cannibals. H. D. Rankin believes that *that* joke relies on the likelihood that Swift really felt that his proposal "would be better than the contemporary practice of starving and drowning, etc."[7] Perhaps Bill Hicks felt the same about *his* proposal; certainly the interpretation of his routine is akin to that required by Swift. In D. C. Muecke's words, it "is not a process that entails discarding the literal meaning; it is still there in all its plausibility."[8] Logically, the case Swift makes for "the utilization of poor Irish infants is watertight in every particular."[9] The same can be said for Hicks's proposals—with regard not only to the elimination of advertisers' detritus but also to the utilization of "terminally ill people as stunt men in pictures." Cruel? "You know what I think cruel is? Leaving your loved ones to die in some sterile hospital room, surrounded by strangers. Fuck that. Put 'em in the movies." Inhuman? "Do you want your grandmother dying like a little bird in some hospital room, her translucent skin so thin you can see her last heartbeat work its way down her blue veins? Or do you want her to meet *Chuck Norris!*"[10] Hicks's kinship with Swift is again evident. Rankin notes that "the outrageous suggestion in 'A Modest Proposal' that children in Ireland should be fattened for food is well known to be no more absurd and outrageous than the accepted treatment of children in that country at that time."[11] The same may well be said of Hicks's observations about the treatment of the aged and the terminally ill in modern America.

But however plausible their proposals, and however heartfelt the anger that inspires them, could either Swift or Bill Hicks be taken seriously? For this to happen, they would have failed in their ironic endeavor just as much as if they had *not* been taken seriously. Gilbert Highet noted that "the Nazis fiendishly misunderstood Swift, for their 'final solution to the Jewish problem' followed lines not dissimilar to the *Proposal*, without, however, confining attention to the children."[12] Such is the danger of the literal interpretation; but on the other hand, "readers of *Mein Kampf* who thought that Hitler must have meant something different from what he said were making a risky mistake."[13] Such is the danger of assuming a joke. It is the either/or that Kierkegaard described as part of the ironic problem; and even Bill Hicks's competitors for the comic ear of America—Limbaugh, or Gordon Liddy's "G-Man"—must shudder to think of the part their mock-hysterical cries about rescuing American "hostages" from federal captivity *may* have played in the 1995 Oklahoma City bombing. The thought to them would be as unbearable (one hopes) as if they had not been heeded at all. But this is the dual risk of irony, which carries with it both the danger of credence and the license to dismiss an utterance at one's peril. And, as we shall see, it is precisely the potential canceling out of the two sides—the "negativity" also identified by Kierkegaard—that could make an accomplished ironist like Bill Hicks such a valuable booking for David Letterman, himself looking at once to be edgy and safe. Hicks professed astonishment at the possibility that he could ever have been considered a threat to Letterman's audience or his commercial sponsors, given that all he had offered was one man's ironic voice. His modest self-assessment marked a great contrast not only to the monumental expectations that Lenny Bruce held for *his* voice but also, admittedly, to the conflicting opinions Hicks otherwise uttered about the destructive potential of comedy. Like Keillor, Bill Hicks knew when to throw out a smokescreen in order to disguise his critical intent; and if he could not quite play the winsome, shy Keillor to Lenny Bruce's Carol Kennicott, he at least learned something about strategy from the trials of his predecessor. What makes his story sad is that even the most compromising strategy was not enough to avoid the gag of the censor. What makes it shameful is that, in 1993, in the United States of America, such a strategy should have been necessary in the first place.

Shiva the Destroyer

Like Lenny Bruce, Bill Hicks often infused his irony with explicit appeals to the "truth" in a variety of contexts, most notably with regard to censorship, media disinformation, advertising, and artistic integrity. But at the same time, unlike Bruce, he neither proclaimed nor implied that he was anything but a comedian. In the climate of conservative backlash in which he performed, he may still have been considered a threat by those who would—to use Vonnegut's image—dress up in a suit of armor to attack a hotfudge sundae. After all, Hicks stood squarely in opposition to an ascendant right wing culturally presided over by Limbaugh and tacitly or otherwise supported by a host of popular comedians. This in itself makes him noteworthy, along with a handful of colleagues such as Sandra Bernhard, Eric Bogosian, Will Durst, the "def jam" comics, and—on the unfettered comic stage as opposed to their network shows—Brett Butler and Roseanne. Otherwise, Limbaugh's "dittoheads" could conceivably applaud the law-and-order diatribes of Dennis Miller (however appalling Miller himself might find it), the dramatized racism and sexism of Andrew Dice Clay, or the homophobia of Eddie Murphy and Sam Kinison. Any patron of any Rush Room across America could also feel comfortably unchallenged by the deliberate lack of critical engagement characterizing *Seinfeld*—a sitcom priding itself on being "a show about nothing"; or the *Cosby* show's apparent self-satisfaction; or the static "rhetorical spleen attacks" of Denis Leary; or the right-leaning libertarianism of Howard Stern.[14] Even the challenges held out by Comedy Central's *Politically Incorrect* were lost to the reruns of old shows like *Soap*, which consistently carried higher ratings up until the time of Hicks's death.[15] If, as it appears, the political consensus in America had removed popular satire from the grasp of left populism and placed it firmly in the hands of Limbaugh and his imitators—a conferment enabled by the default of any viable opposition—then Bill Hicks's comedic stance was rare for its political moment: "To me, the comic is the guy who says 'Wait a minute' as the consensus forms. . . . He's the antithesis of the mob mentality." Hicks suggested that, like "Shiva the Destroyer," his job as a comic was to topple idols, "no matter what they are"; and while part of his importance to this discussion lies in the necessity imposed upon him to detract from just such an impression of destructive capacity, it may at least be asked what idols there were to be toppled in 1993 —the election of Clinton notwithstanding—other than those thrown up or maintained by a conservative consensus and left virtually un-challenged by the progressives in their disarray.[16]

Hicks's stance as an anticonsensus comedian must be one among a number of factors accounting for the high regard in which critics and his fellow comedians appear to have held him. In 1991, while yet a relative unknown, he received the Edinburgh Festival Critics Award for comedy. In 1993—the year of the Letterman banning—*Rolling Stone* named Hicks their "Hot Stand-up Comic" of the year; he was then also nominated for his third American Comedy Award. Len Belzer, the "dean of syndicated comedy radio," called Hicks "the hippest, most intelligent cutting-edge comic of our day."[17] Edith Sorenson wrote, "If imitation is the sincerest form of flattery, then half the comics working are genuflecting before him."[18] (Most commentators on the subject have pointed in particular to Denis Leary's "flattery" of his old New Year's Eve booking-companion, Bill Hicks, in terms of both mannerism and material—an observation made credible by a comparison of the content and dates of their first comedy albums and videos.)[19]

Less speculative are the recollections of Hicks's colleagues, such as those contributed to a British documentary made shortly after his death. Richard Belzer recalled how Hicks had "challenged not only his audience but . . . other comedians." Richard Jeni said, "He was the type of guy that, you'd watch him as a comedian, and you'd kind of feel bad. You'd go, 'You know, I really should be doing more of this kind of thing. I really should be telling the truth more often.'" Jeni mused on Hicks's integrity as a stand-up comic in particular: "With Bill you'd always get the impression that stand-up was an end in itself. To many people in the stand-up business it's just a stepping-stone. You know, it's 'Hey, I'll get a sitcom, I'll have a wacky neighbor, and the next thing I know I'll be chatting with Regis.' And it shows. Bill Hicks wasn't just out there to get some laughs and collect a check." The British comic Sean Hughes envied "his *bravery*" and wrote for him a moving elegy, while Eric Bogosian described him in the shamanistic terms that, a generation before, had been reserved solely for Lenny Bruce: "He was taking fully the role of the witch-doctor in front of the audience . . . like a big, giant exorcism of all the evil shit that's inside of us, that poisons us day to day. Talk shows aren't gonna help it, the news isn't. . . . You just need a guy to get up there, take you by the lapels and shake the shit out of you." To Bogosian, Hicks personified a welcome contempt for the slickness that had still defined American stand-up comedy in spite of a resilient alternative scene:

"He wasn't like the guy who just comes up and stands at a mike and lays out one-liners, but rather, there's this sort of tornado moving around the stage and cycling around and throwing all this energy out at you" (*IJR*). Dennis Miller called him "the Waylon Jennings of Comedy—the Texas Outlaw" while Steve Wright, Robert Klein, Eddie Izzard, and John Cleese all sang praises for both his comic artistry and his critical incisiveness.[20]

The question remains as to why, if Americans had a comedian of such apparent reckoning in their midst, they were denied the opportunity to hear him. Anonymity can indeed be deserved on the grounds of a lack of talent or substance; but in Britain, Hicks could sell out a 2,500-seat concert hall for a twenty-three-night run, get mobbed in the streets by fans, and see his specials broadcast unexpurgated on prime-time television. In America—well, as he said in his last performance, "I've loved *every* moment of the sixteen years I've been doing it in total anonymity in the country I love. . . . Playing the Comedy Pouch in Possum Ridge, Arkansas, every three months—it was *my* treat."[21] If he indeed deserved anonymity, what was there about him that would have made him so attractive to Jay Leno, for whom he had first opened at a Houston comedy club in 1983? It was Leno who handed him over to Letterman because he was "still too far off the wall for the *Tonight Show*." Why would Letterman have wanted Hicks "to come on and just blow the roof off the place" eleven times in the late 1980s and early 1990s (*IJR*)? It could only be for the same reason that he was invited for a twelfth appearance, the first on Letterman's new CBS show, the battle for which was documented in Bill Carter's book. It must have been for his peculiar sharpening of what Linda Hutcheon has called "irony's edge"—the edge that always threatened to draw blood but never could; the edge that nonetheless got him censored.

Gag Artistry

Bill Hicks would have added an important dimension to Carter's *The Late Shift*, for with all the author's scrupulous attention to the ratings war, demographics, corporate interests, and the advertising dollar, he makes at least one highly debatable assertion: "As the weeks went on and Letterman turned in classy show after classy show [in the new CBS time slot], even members of his own staff marveled at his skill in modifying his comedy just

enough to broaden out his audience base. . . . Yet he was not alienating those who had come to view him as a subversive, nonmainstream comic."[22] If this were indeed so—if the new, "modified"
Letterman show had still kept the "subversive, nonmainstream"
edge that it had maintained on NBC through the booking of comedians *like* Bill Hicks—why, then, would Hicks end up on the cut-
ting-room floor with his first appearance on the CBS show? The
answer appears to lie in the old dilemma admitted by Melville to
Hawthorne: "What I feel most moved to write, that is banned—it
will not pay. Yet, altogether, write the *other* way I cannot."[23] The
banning of Bill Hicks raises the same questions that Melville implied: To what extent is the dollar the leverage between the voice
of the subversive critic and the safe comedian? What is the actual
price of "truth," or at least of "frankness"? These questions are
what make the editing of Hicks's mere seven minutes so significant and unsettling. Letterman's coproducer, Robert Morton, had
said of Hicks, "We always pushed the envelope by seeing, 'O.K.,
just how much of a fuck-you attitude can you have without going
over the line on network television?' And that was always the
thrill of presenting him" (*IJR*). This was in reference to the old
show, where—no surprise—the commercial stakes were significantly lower. On the new show, where, by having jumped one
hour earlier, Letterman could go from drawing $18,000 for a
thirty-second advertising spot to twice that amount for the same
thirty seconds, Morton's "line" was considerably farther from the
edge, and the cost of the "thrill" was conclusively higher—too
high, in fact, for Hicks to be heard at all.[24]

As I will argue, there is more to the case of Bill Hicks's
censoring than the raw economic lure, important as it is. His
colleague on the comic stage, Thea Vidale, had a theory: "Bill
said a lot of things that were so true, that they just couldn't deal
with. . . . You know, a spoonful of sugar makes the medicine go
down. But there wasn't no spoonful of sugar with Bill" (*IJR*).
With respect to Vidale, I would of course disagree with her final
sentence. There was indeed a "spoonful of sugar" with Hicks—
there *had* to be, just as there must be with her own work and that
of any comedian with something critical to say. The "spoonful of
sugar" is inherent in the comic discourse; it is the trick that turns
an earnest social critic into a comedian—it is what prevents his
remaining a mere polemicist. Hicks knew this and demonstrated
it in his art; in fact his art, inasmuch as he *was* a comedian, consisted largely of knowing how to measure the spoonful. Brett

Butler observed why, in Hicks's case, it was all the more indispensable: "For all the talk about Bill being like Hendrix, or Dylan, or Jim Morrison, or Lenny Bruce, it was *Jesus* Bill wanted to be. . . . He wanted to be Christ at his angriest" (*IJR*). With such an *angry* critical motivation, the comedian's measuring needs to be especially accurate. Bill Hicks, like any "ass-kicking comedian," must necessarily place himself exquisitely close to the margin between pure sugar and unadulterated medicine. Not to cross the margin must entail at least *some* compromise of the "truth" (Vidale's and Jeni's observations notwithstanding).

But what makes the case of Bill Hicks and Letterman especially disturbing is the extent to which Hicks had *already* compromised in order to get his voice heard on network television in the first place—even before his banned appearance. At the very least, there was his profanity. It was *true*, for instance, that the F-word was a regular feature of his speech, as it was with many his age and younger. It was *true* that the word hardly meant anything anymore among the people who used it. It had become, in linguistician Lewis Allen's words, "just an intensifier . . . like shucks and golly and darn." Ending in *-ing*, it had become "simply a substitute for 'very.'"[25] The real taboos were racial slurs, which Hicks despised anyway. Still, it was no problem for him to jettison the F-word if required. He could easily compromise over *that* little bit of truth; in fact, he had read Vonnegut's *Hocus Pocus* and concurred with the observation about profanity offering a convenient excuse for one's ideas to be ignored. His language on television was always clean, while on the live stage—thanks to the rewriting of the rules by Lenny Bruce, George Carlin, Redd Foxx, and others—profanity was no longer even an issue (as I trust it will not be in this chapter).

No, the most significant compromises that Hicks made in order to get on television had nothing to do with the F-word; they involved something more fundamentally restrictive. As Jay Leno recalled, a subtle taming process had begun with the first meeting between Hicks and the Letterman staff in the mid-1980s: "I remember bringing him down, and Morty [Robert Morton] and the producers would hear him and go, 'Bill this is good, but can you change this?' And he'd go into these fits of rage—'No, I can't! It's the essence of the bit!' And we'd have these arguments, and I'd say, 'Look, just *get on TV*, will you?'" (*IJR*). In the early days, it may well have seemed to Hicks like an intriguing puzzle—in his words, "a challenge to write material that I still believe in, and maintain a sort of integrity. . . . Network TV doesn't really like people with opinions."[26] By his twelfth performance, however, it had become a process of outright self-betrayal, as Hicks told Howard Stern after the banning: "No one has ever come up to me after any of the other eleven times and said, 'Boy, I saw you on *Letterman* and it was great.' You know why? Because it wasn't me. I'd been so declawed by the censors, that I went on as this perfunctory little joke-blower, and it wasn't me."[27] The process was in fact disarmingly insidious, as the CBS program *48 Hours* demonstrated in a segment on Hicks the night before one of his earlier *Letterman* appearances on NBC. It is a jokey portrayal of Hicks making the rounds of the New York comedy stages under the policing eye of a *Letterman* producer, Frank Gannon, whose job, he says, is often to "fight" with the comedian: "I will say that it's my judgment that a joke will not work with our audience. . . . I've never been wrong."[28] Ultimately, it was a gagging by whatever name, as Hicks remarked more than two years *before* his banning: "David's been great to me, but his show is still network TV, so they tape your hands behind your back, tape your ankles, put tape over your mouth and then tell you to go out there and be yourself."[29] Even more insidious, Hicks implied, was the normalization of the gagging process to the extent that it could not be recognized, let alone admitted, for what it was. In a letter to John Lahr, he recalled making the rounds of the comedy clubs before another *Letterman* taping: "During the course of the night, Mr. Morton decided I should drop a few of the bits from my set because they weren't 'right for our audience.' The next morning I did a radio show, and the interviewer asked me if it was difficult to translate my club act to television. I responded by telling her of the previous night's activities. That afternoon, when I showed up at the Letterman studio, Robert Morton ran up to me and said, 'Hey, Hicks, why were you dissing us on the air today? . . . You were saying we edit your stuff for T.V. We've never done that!'"[30] After the banning, which caused Hicks to vow he would never attempt a return to American network television, he marveled at both his capacity to have submitted to the taming process for so long, and the irony of the fact that what had attracted the *Letterman* producers in the first place was precisely what they were afraid of showing: "I've finally realized something. I've been, for the last however-many times I've done it, in an abusive relationship, and I've kept going back for more. 'Bill, we love you because you're so edgy and hip—but when you come on our show, could you not be that way?' And I made the mistake of doing it, thinking, 'Oh, well, I'll rewrite everything so it fits.' And now I have no interest in doing that whatsoever."[31]

What, then, was a great American television network afraid of, after it had already "declawed" one of its favorite comedians on the rise? I use the term "network" loosely; for another question remains as to who, precisely, was responsible for banning a set that had already been approved *twice* by the show's producers. As Lahr's *New Yorker* profile documents, Hicks was told by Morton that it was not the producers but rather the CBS "Standards and Practices" officers who had deemed the set "unsuitable" for broadcast. Yet that very office denied any part of the censoring when pressed by an outraged viewer: "The decision was solely that of the producers of the program who decided to substitute his performance with that of another comedian. Therefore, your criticism that CBS censored the program is totally without foundation."[32] In the wake of the press storm caused by the *New Yorker* exposé, the last word came in a dubious statement from a *Letterman* spokesperson to the effect that "there exist broadcast standards that the show is obliged to follow every night. As entertaining as Bill Hicks is, the show's producers and CBS felt that Hicks' set didn't follow those standards."[33] Again: never mind that the banned set had already been softened and doubly approved by the producers—word for word—presumably to satisfy the very "broadcast standards" referred to. In their separate urges to avoid the brand of the hated word, *censor*, the producers and the network's Standards and Practices officers, after first pointing their fingers at each other ultimately agreed to share the responsibility—at least in public. And though David Letterman, visibly ill at ease, shifts in front of the documentary camera and admits his "personal sense of regret" about "mistakes that were made," Hicks went to his grave convinced that he had been betrayed at the eleventh hour by Letterman himself and his producers (*IJR*).

Of course, it doesn't matter which person or persons were responsible for ensuring that Bill Hicks's seven minutes would never appear on the contraption he came to call "Lucifer's Dream Box." But is it conceivable that one comedian's little jokes could send the CBS corporate structure into paroxysms of fear for their ratings or their commercial sponsorships? This was the most astounding part of it, according to Hicks. His first response to Morton upon learning that his taped set had been cut that afternoon was: "Bob, they're just jokes. . . . Why are people so afraid of jokes?"[34] Later in the day, as he discussed it with his manager, Colleen McGarr, his bewilderment turned to rage: "'They're just jokes, they're just jokes, they're just jokes. . . . What are they so afraid of?' I yelled."[35] Finally, Hicks could write to Lahr upon calm reflection: "Jokes, John, this is what America now fears—one man with a point of view, speaking out unafraid of our vaunted institutions, or the loathsome superstitions the CBS hierarchy feels the masses (the herd) use as their religion."[36]

Ah. Not "just jokes" but jokes "with a point of view." Hicks had finally come to the crux, identifying not only the double-bind of all ironists who wish for the "point of view" behind their irony to be apprehended but something even more distressing: nearly three decades after the death of Lenny Bruce, critically minded jokesters who presumed to challenge the consensus were still considered a threat in America. To his credit, Hicks never took the step taken by Lenny Bruce, denying the comedian in him; on the contrary, in the few months left to him following the *Letterman* banning he brought the excised set to his remaining comedy club audiences, confronting them not only with the points of view that the network had denied them but also with the safety factor of his jokery. As he explained, "I'm going to play it for many, many people and show them the exact set that was canceled, and see if you, the audience, were so offended—that you felt so threatened by my little skit—that you went out of your fucking minds."[37] In order to recognize the strategic compromises Hicks had thus made, let alone those that were, apparently, further expected in order for him to be heard on network television *without* an advertising budget behind him, a reproduction of the banned set is helpful. (In defense of free expression and as a gesture of contempt for American censorship, it is obligatory.) It also acts as a springboard for a discussion of one of the most prominent concerns of Bill Hicks's comedy: the relationship between artistry, truth, the media, and the advertising dollar.

The Censored Seven Minutes[38]

Good evening! I'm very excited to be here tonight! I just got some great news today. I finally got my own show on TV coming out this fall as a replacement series.

(The audience applauds)

Don't worry, it's not a talk show.

(The audience laughs)

Thank God! It's a half-hour weekly show that I will host, entitled "Let's Hunt and Kill Billy Ray Cyrus."

(The audience bursts into laughter and applause)

I think it's fairly self-explanatory: Each week we let the Hounds of Hell loose and chase that jar-head, no-talent, cracker idiot all over the globe 'til I finally catch that fruity little pony tail of his, pull him to his Chippendale knees, and put a gun in his mouth—*Pow!*

(The audience is applauding and laughing throughout this run)

Then we'll be back in '94 with "Let's Hunt and Kill Michael Bolton."

(The audience laughs and applauds)

Yeah, so you can see, with guests like this, our run will be fairly limitless.

(The audience laughs)

And we're kicking the whole series off with our M. C. Hammer/Vanilla Ice/Marky Mark Christmas Special.

(The audience whoops and applauds)

And I don't want to give away any surprises, but the first one we hunt and kill on that show is Marky Mark . . .

(Audience cheers)

. . . because his unbuttoned pants kept falling around his ankles, and he couldn't run away.

(Bill mimes a hobbling Marky Mark. The audience laughs)

Yeah, I get to crossbow him right in the abs! It's a beautiful thing. Bring the whole family. Tape it! It's definitely a show for the nineties.

(The audience applauds)

"At this point," Hicks writes, "I did a line on men dancing. But it was never mentioned as a reason for excising me from the show, so let's skip ahead to the next 'Hot Point' that was mentioned."

You know, I consider myself a fairly open-minded person, but speaking of homosexuality, something has come to my attention that has shocked even me. Have you heard about these new grade school books for children they're trying to add to the curriculum, to help children understand the gay lifestyle? One's called *Heather's Two Mommies*, the other one is called *Daddy's New Roommate*.

(Bill makes a shocked, disgusted face)

I gotta draw the line here and say this is absolutely disgusting. It is grotesque, and it is pure evil. *(Pause)* I'm talking, of course, about *Daddy's New Roommate*.

(Audience laughs)

Heather's Two Mommies is quite fetching—you know, they're hugging on page seven!

(Audience laughs)

(Lasciviously) Oooh! Go, Mommies, go! Oooh! They kiss in chapter four!

(Audience laughs)

Me and my nephew wrastle over that book every night. *(Bill mimes his little nephew jumping up and down. As nephew:)* "Uncle Bill, I've gotta do my homework!"

(Audience laughs)

Shut up and go do your Math! I'm proofreading this for you.

(Audience laughs)

You know who's really bugging me these days? These pro-lifers.

(Smattering of applause)

You ever look at their faces? "I'm pro-life! *(Here Bill makes a pinched face of hate and fear; his lips are pursed as though he's just sucked on a lemon.)* I'm pro-life!" Boy, they look it, don't they? They just exude *joie de vivre*. You just want to hang with them and play *Trivial Pursuit* all night long.

(Audience chuckles)

You know what bugs me about them? If you're so pro-life, do me a favor. Don't lock arms and block medical clinics. If you're so pro-life, lock arms and block cemeteries.

(Audience laughs)

Let's see how committed you are to this idea. *(Here Bill mimes the purse-lipped pro-lifers locking arms. As pro-lifer:)* "She can't come in!"

(Audience laughs)

(As confused member of funeral procession:) "She was ninety-eight! She was hit by a bus!"

(Audience laughs)

(As pro-lifer:) "There's options!"

(Audience laughs)

(Again, as confused funeral-procession member:) "What else can we do—have her stuffed?"

(Audience laughs)

I want to see pro-lifers with crowbars at funerals opening caskets—"Get out!" Then I'd really be impressed by their mission.

"At this point," continues Hicks, "I did a routine on smoking that was never brought up as a 'Hot Point,' so let's move ahead to the end of my routine."

I've been traveling a lot lately—I was over in Australia during Easter. It was interesting to note they celebrate Easter the same way we do—commemorating the death and resurrection of Jesus by telling our children a giant bunny rabbit . . . left chocolate eggs in the night . . .

(Audience laughs) Gee, I wonder why we're so messed up as a race. You know, I've read the Bible—can't find the words "bunny" or "chocolate" in the whole book.

(Audience laughs)

Where do we get this stuff from? And why those two things? Why not "Goldfish left Lincoln Logs in our sock drawers?" I mean, as long as we're making stuff up, let's go hog wild.

(Audience laughs and applauds)

I think it's interesting how people act on their beliefs. A lot of Christians, for instance, wear crosses around their necks. Nice sentiment, but do you think when Jesus comes back, he's really going to want to look at a cross?

(Audience laughs. Bill makes a face of pain and horror.)

Ow! Maybe that's why he hasn't shown up yet.

(Audience laughs)

(As Jesus looking down from Heaven:) "I'm not going, Dad. No, they're still wearing crosses—they totally missed the point. When they start wearing fishes, I might go back again. . . . No, I'm not going. . . . O.K., I'll tell you what—I'll go back as a BUNNY. . . ."

(Audience bursts into applause and laughter. The band kicks into "Revolution" by the Beatles.)

Thank you very much! Good night!

(Bill crosses over to the seat next to Letterman's desk.)

(Letterman:) Good set Bill! Always nice to have you drop by with an uplifting message!

(Audience and Bill laugh. We cut to a commercial.)

America saw no trace of Bill Hicks at all that evening but rather "a series of Orwellian cuts and edits that were so obvious and clumsily done, many people called to ask what had happened."[39] Hicks was never told precisely *why* any of his set was deemed "unsuitable" for the *Letterman* audience. In the rush of interviews and writings that followed the banning, he speculated on the possibility that he might have offended the odd Christian fundamentalist who couldn't see through his irony to the point of grasping his respect for an ideal meaning of Jesus, free from degrading or irrelevant associations; or he might have offended the odd gay activist who couldn't recognize that he was mocking the double standards of male voyeurism and homophobia. Hicks dismissed the importance of such possibilities: "We now live in the 'Age of Being Offended.' Get over it."[40] But there was no speculation needed about the fact that in the week of Hicks's banning, the *Letterman* show was broadcasting highly lucrative commercials for the anti-abortion lobby. Again, David Letterman himself had admitted, in the context of his switch to CBS, that "at the end of the year, everybody adds up the dollars."[41] To Ken Auletta, the logic of the switch "was inexorable: the earlier the Letterman show was broadcast, the bigger the audience; the bigger the audience, the greater the advertising revenue."[42] As far as Hicks was concerned, his banning from this new time slot meant one thing: "Same old Dave, brand new censors."[43] CBS could pontificate about the maintenance of their "broadcast standards" as much as they liked; but to Hicks there was a different message: "The fact of the matter is, this vast empire of network television called CBS are a bunch of shameless cowards who kowtow to very organized, although minority, special interest groups in America. They fear losing their corporate sponsorship, and that is the threat these special interest groups promise."[44] Hicks concluded that his entire experience with network television was based on a misunderstanding finally cleared up for him by David Letterman and CBS: "We live in the U.S.A., the United States of Advertising, and there is freedom of speech to the highest bidder."[45] He would not go back to *Letterman* or any other commercial network show, even if invited, for the advertisers' demands were too eviscerating: "What kind of material?" he asked. "How bad airline food is? Boy, 7-11's sure are expensive? Golly, Ross Perot has big ears?"[46] Letterman's embarrassed producers did in fact ask him back; so did Jay Leno in *his* continued battle for the late-night ratings. Hicks refused: "I don't know if I can learn to *juggle* that quickly—'Hi, I'm Bill Hicks. I used to have a social conscience and wanted to help the world by trying to point out how our belief systems are affecting us negatively. Now watch this—an apple!'"[47]

Lucifer's Dream Box

John Lahr concluded that the banning from the *Letterman* show only confirmed Hicks in the belief that "television worked to control the society, to keep the culture credulous, to keep it from thinking; to *enchant* it—literally, to spellbind it. And his job, as he saw it, was to break the spell" (*IJR*). Ironically, he had hoped to do so with comic enchantments of his own. "People watch T.V. *not* to think," he said; "I'd like the opportunity to stir things up once, and see what happens."[48] His charm indeed would be irony, in his view, "a trick to make you admit what you've always known."[49] Thus his strategy would be to employ the means of artistic illusion toward highly ironic ends: "You have people that want to hear comedy where they don't have to think about anything. To me they are missing the point. They say, 'I just want to escape from reality.' No you don't. You want to escape from illusion."[50] In television, people had at their fingertips a magical box with an unprecedented power to inform and illuminate; but it had fallen into the hands of accountants, demographics analysts, and marketing experts whose intent was to deceive—for money alone. In concert with them were a host of lesser, though equally satanic, deceivers. There were the critics and commentators invited on television to indulge in earnest, self-reflexive discussions *about* television: "Every few years, they cart out the old argument regarding television's role in our society. As usual, they pose the same two questions that are guaranteed to keep us divided and keep the problem unresolved, then it's back to 'business as usual.' The herd has been pacified by our charade of concern as we pose the two most idiotic questions imaginable—'Is T.V. becoming too violent?' and 'Is T.V. becoming too promiscuous?'" (Hicks offered *his* answer: "T.V. is too *stupid*. It treats us like morons. *Case closed*.")[51] There were also the talk show hosts themselves who shied away from any controversy but the most sensational and insignificant, leaving the broadcast media as playthings at the disposal of "Satan" himself, Rush Limbaugh, and his fellows (*I*). Once upon a time a lone investigative journalist named Rivera could work undercover to expose the horrors of the Willowbook asylum; but now, "Geraldo gets plastic surgery done on the air, in the name of journalism. I can't wait until he tries that Kevorkian suicide machine. *That's* the show I'm taping."[52] An even greater betrayal came from other comics who had graduated to hosting talk shows of their own, each one becoming in the process "another whore in the capitalist gang bang."[53] The pre-HBO Dennis Miller; Arsenio Hall; even Hicks's early mentor, Jay Leno—"It's amazing these young, hip guys have done their best to put on 'The Mike Douglas Show.' Who are they speaking for?"[54] Leno had been, at one time, "the number-one comic in the country." He'd had such challenging potential—now, he was reduced to "talking with Joey Lawrence from *Blossom*. I'm sure that was his ultimate comedic dream. 'So Joey, good to see you again. What are ya, sixteen? Got a license? Oh God, what have I done with my life!'"[55] Arsenio Hall was "the most dangerous one of all. . . . Jesus is gonna do that show when he comes back: 'Tonight on Arsenio: Paula Abdul, Della Reese, and Jesus of Nazareth. Let's get busy! Jesus, tell me the truth now. Mary Magdalene. Didja do her? Arf, arf, arf, arf. We'll be right back.'"[56] Comedians had virtually taken over the front line of the talk show system, only to become complicit stooges in the networks' design to misinform and divert: "What's happened with this plethora of comedy on every channel is that it's totally trivialized what comedy can do and should do."[57]

One thing Hicks felt that comedians could have done was to counter the biased viewpoints and outright fabrications that television networks purveyed under the guise of objective news reporting. He was one of the tiny handful of comedians who dared to challenge, for example, the popular impressions of the Persian Gulf War created largely by CNN and reinforced by other networks. Eric Bogosian recalled how rare it was for comedians to make such an attempt, and how some unnamed "top comedians in this country" actually admitted to him why they had avoided challenging the official and received versions of the war's progress and aftermath. "They said they wouldn't put their neck on the line. They were against the war and they wouldn't say anything, because they basically felt that they'd watch those little bags of money just fly away. It was, like, kiss your career goodbye" (*IJR*). Hicks, however, was not afraid to propose comedically that the Gulf War was virtually a media fabrication: "First of all, this needs to be said: there never *was* a war. 'How can you say that, Bill?' Well, a war is when *two* armies are fighting. So you see, right there, I think we can all agree, it wasn't exactly a *war*."[58] It was, if anything, a transparent public relations exercise carried out by the Bush administration in concert with the network news organizations: "Remember how it started? They kept talking about the Elite Republican Guard in these hushed tones, like these guys were the Bogeyman or something. 'Yeah, we're doing well now—but we have yet to face the *Elite Republican Guard*.'" The ineptitude of the attempted media con soon showed itself, however, in the changing terminology of the news reporting: "After two months of continuous carpet bombing, and not *one* reaction at all from them, they became simply 'the Republican Guard.' Not nearly as elite as we may have led you to believe. And after another month of bombing they went from 'the Elite Republican Guard' to 'the Republican Guard' to 'the Republicans Made This Shit Up About There Being Guards Out There.'" The unspoken message of the entire news campaign was: "We hope you enjoyed your fireworks show" (*RC*).

What Hicks called "the Persian Gulf Distraction" did not end with the war, however, nor with the defeat of the Republicans in 1992. The Clinton administration's launching of twenty-two cruise missiles on Baghdad in retaliation for what Hicks emphasized was "the *alleged—failed—*assassination attempt against George Bush" offered another opportunity for diversion, if not outright deception, in the highly orchestrated outrage that accompanied the reporting. "Everyone in the government and media called it a cowardly act on the Iraqis' part, because some Iraqi guy was going to drive a Toyota car bomb, and blow himself up in the process of trying to kill the President of the United States. . . .

Meanwhile, we're launching cruise missiles two hundred miles away from floating iron islands. Who are the cowards again?" ~ (Hicks proposed his own alternative: "We should have *embarrassed* the Iraqis. *We* should have assassinated Bush, and said, 'That's how you do it, Towelhead. Don't fuck with us.'") (*I*).

Hicks suggested that even comedians had the capacity ∘ ⅄ to define what was both truthful and newsworthy, given that network television generally failed in that responsibility. "If I were going to do a newscast, I'd have the most interesting people in the world I'd do stories about, and I'd just keep the camera on them, going, 'No, we're not going to leave. Look at them. They're skilled artists who are doing holy work.' But these psychos get all the news time. Man, I'm afraid to go to the post office at this point."[59] Aware of the fact of the news mogul as a controlling phenomenon, he reflected upon the negative sensationalism characterizing American news broadcasts—"You'd think if you just walk out ∘ your door, you're immediately going to be raped by some crack-addicted, AIDS-infected pit bull"—and comedically proposed it as part of a calculated corporate strategy: "Ted Turner is making this shit up. Jane Fonda won't sleep with him, he runs to a typewriter. '"By 1992 we will all die of AIDS." Read that on the air. I don't get laid, *nobody* gets laid.'" Hicks implied that the sensationalizing tendency of the news, however beneficial in the network ratings wars, acted as a bar to public engagement with important issues, in addition to its simple terrorizing: "Pretty soon we're all going to be locked inside our homes, with no one on the streets but pizza-delivery guys in armored cars, with turrets shooting pizzas through the mail slots of our front doors. And every house will glow with *American Gladiators* beamed in: 'We are free. Keep repeating. We are free'" (*REV*). Hicks's championing of Public Access television as a potential counterweight to the corporate bias of the news networks is a further indication of his ironically informing goal, if not his quixotism. Hence his decision, as he watched the buildup of the media circus at Waco, to travel to the Branch Davidian compound with his producer, Kevin Booth, to film an alternative news broadcast for Austin's Public Access station. Filmed on the seventh day of the siege, the footage shows Hicks in newscaster's pose, ruminating on the perils of religious fundamentalism, with the compound in the background: "We're out here at Mount Carmel, [with] the Branch Davidian Latter-Day-Saint Adventist Seven-Day-Church (Lutheran Yahweh Division) breakaway group. . . . It looks like Grandma's house."[60] At that time, of

course, Hicks had no idea of what would transpire on the final
day of the siege; but in the fatal storming's aftermath he risked the
inevitable charges of paranoia in order to speculate as to why none
of the network news organizations had bothered to pick up the
freely available Public Access footage of Bradley tanks apparently
shooting fire—*not* teargas—into the compound. In any event, he
maintained, the news organizations were too compliant even to
question the Clinton administration's official justification for the
military assault—child abuse: "If that's true, how come we don't
see Bradley tanks knocking down Catholic churches?" (*I*).

It was a politically incorrect proposition, to be sure, but
wholly in keeping with the brutal nature of the "attack comedy"
that characterized Hicks's battle with the American television networks.[61] Given that their objective was to anaesthetize, his objective was to shock. As he saw it, the shock would need to be
ferocious enough to cut through the passivity engineered by complicit—or at least, compliant—television programming: "Go back
to bed, America. Your government is in control again. Here—
here's *American Gladiators*. Watch this. Shut up. Here's *American
Gladiators*. Here's fifty-six *channels* of it. . . . Here you go, America:
you are free to do as we tell you" (*REV*). When Hicks looked
around for comedic assistance in his attacks on the network deceivers, he found that some of his most potent colleagues had
joined their ranks. Leno and Letterman were in fact the two greatest American gladiators, battling it out for the ratings, the advertising spoils, and the credulity of the public. Jerry Seinfeld was
about to become one of the highest-paid performers on network
television, following in the footsteps of Bill Cosby. Whoopi Goldberg, Chevy Chase, Roseanne, Brett Butler—they too had signed
contracts that implicitly required them to watch their mouths.

In *his* brief dalliance with the networks and their sponsors, Hicks had also agreed to watch his mouth: they silenced him
anyway. But it was an uncharacteristic dalliance on his part, as the
liberality and subjects of his comedy club material would demonstrate. Most of that material indicates, by contrast with the banned
set, the sacrifice he was willing to make in order to be heard on
commercial television, as well as the reasons that he might have
considered it an act of self-betrayal. Paradoxically, his live routines
also show that even at their most incisive and urgent, his various
appeals to the "truth," in whatever context, were necessarily re-
liant upon the fictions of trickery, and thus a great test of his critical integrity.

"Where's *my* commercial?": Diet Coke and the War on Drugs

It is perhaps the greatest irony of all that Bill Hicks should have been silenced on network television by, of all things, advertising interests, for no two subjects had borne so much contempt in his live comedy as the agenda of network television to mystify and the selling of the soul to advertising. It was in relation to television and advertising that nearly all of his imaginative references to "truth" were made, informing his advocacy of firsthand drug knowledge (as opposed to the manipulations of the "Just Say No" propaganda) and his scorn for artists—musicians in particular —who had sold themselves to advertisers. Inevitably, he opened himself up to accusations of irresponsibility, incitement to drug addiction, brutality (for his withering attacks on corporate rock stars), antipatriotism (for his skepticism about the reliability of the Gulf War reporting), and godlessness (for his scornful treatment of televangelists and the Christian fundamentalist media machine). His response to all such charges would be either a plea for "truth" or, at least, for the allowance of another "point of view" through which the truth might be perceived, as distinct from those biased points of view that massive funding alone had enabled. The popularity or unpopularity of a viewpoint was not an issue—consensus had nothing to do with "the truth": "Regardless of how many people go with it, a billion times zero is still zero."[62] The repercussions of such appeals came right to his doorstep: "Sometimes my dad even gets on this kick: you hate this country, you hate the government, and you hate religion. I have to tell him to step back. 'Dad, I really don't think you're watching me. I just hate being lied to.'"[63] It was a curious position to be in, attempting to combat corporate and media lying through the lies of comedy. It was also an unenviable position, because his advocacy of "truth" as the first principle put him on a collision course with generally popular social agendas, beliefs, and personages—in spite of his acknowledgment of the requirement that he *play* with the truth (which, although he could be heard to grumble about it, ultimately distinguished him from Lenny Bruce). And through the ironic play to which he had thus committed himself, Hicks embarked upon a meteoric crusade against what he saw as a host of competing liars.

His comedic attacks on the War on Drugs, for instance, were based on his belief that the campaign was not only an exercise in mendacity but the work of uninformed amateurs, whatever their expertise in advertising. His references to the War on Drugs are consistently those of an accomplished trickster out to expose the inept confidence game of lesser rivals. "They lump all drugs together: it's not gonna work. Pot *and* crack? Hey, hey, hey, dude—don't put *pot* in the drug category. It's an herb, man. Like *tea*." As far as Hicks was concerned, the incompetence of such attempted trickery was embarrassing not only to anyone with the least experience of drug use or an academic knowledge of drugs but to anyone concerned with the fine art of fooling: "George Bush says, 'We are losing the war on drugs.' You know what that implies? There's a war being fought, and people on drugs are *winning* it. Well, what does that tell you about drugs? Some smart, creative people on *that* side. They're winning a war, and *they're* fucked up. Hah!"[64] As a player highly sensitive to the requirements of artful manipulation, Hicks derided the condescending advertisements that so blatantly presumed a naive viewing public: "I knew we were in trouble with that damn egg commercial. . . . 'Here's your brain.' I've seen a lot of weird shit on drugs, but I've never, ever, ever, *ever* looked at an egg and thought it was a fuckin' brain, not once" (*RC*). Having exposed the opposition's inability to fabricate a credible version of the "truth," Hicks raised his own (double) standard of truthfulness regarding drugs. As a reformed alcoholic and drug abuser who had once feared for his own life, he made a defiant admission of a *fact* that the War on Drugs advertisers had not only failed to accommodate but, if anything, had actively set out to suppress: "I'll tell you something honestly about drugs. Honestly—and I know it's not a very popular idea. You don't hear it very often any more. But it *is* the truth: I had a great time doing drugs. *Sorry*." Again, truth had nothing to do with social agendas or conventional wisdom. "Never murdered anyone, never robbed anyone, never raped anyone, never beat anyone, never lost a job, a car, a house, a wife, or kids. Laughed my ass off, and went about my day. *Sorry*. Now, where's *my* commercial?" (*RC*). These were verities about Hicks's drug experience that could not be denied, even in spite of his own awareness that he had been in danger, and that some of his acquaintances had gone so far as to organize betting pools as to when he might die: "But I am not sorry I did the drugs. I had fun, and it changed my thinking. I stopped because I didn't want to die."[65]

Nevertheless, the possibility of his own death or anyone else's could not reduce certain truths, no matter what the surgeon general said. "Drugs have done good things for us. 'What do you *mean*, Bill?' Well, if you don't believe drugs have done good things for us, do me a favor, then. Go home tonight, take all your albums, your tapes, and your CDs, and burn 'em. Because, you know what? The musicians who made that great music that has enhanced your lives throughout the years: *real* fuckin' high on drugs." The Beatles: "They were real high, they wrote great music: drugs had a positive effect" (*RV*). Keith Richards: "You never hear the surgeon general mention Keith, do you? Oh—a little hole in the *theory* there!" The crime of the War on Drugs was that it churned out mystifying propaganda while burying points of view that were valid, however thorny: "Keith Richards is shooting heroin into his *eyeball*, and is still touring. All right? I'm getting *mixed signals*" (D). Thus, no matter its ends, the corrupt means of the campaign were suppression and disinformation at the expense of knowledge and experience: "The extent of our drug education is a slogan. 'Just Say No'—that's our drug education. To me, 'Just Say No' is very closed-minded— the opposite of open-minded, the opposite of *learning*. See, all my friends, and myself—we Just Said Yes, and I guarantee you, we learned a whole bunch about drugs."[66] Not a popular admission— *sorry*—but it *was* the truth. Moreover, it enabled a perception that might credibly challenge the status quo: "Why is the drug czar of this country a cop? Why isn't he instead someone who's been through recovery, who has had an alcohol and/or drug addiction and overcome it? . . . Putting sick people in jail—does that make sense?" (*I*).

But there was more to the War on Drugs than its "know-nothingness" and its obstinate refusal—after the fashion of propaganda—to encourage a dialogue. There was also its conspicuous selectivity, appearing in the collusion between government, media, advertising, and the tobacco and alcohol industries, in a transparent attempt to divert attention away from the harmfulness of protected drugs. "The War on Drugs is hypocrisy, man. That's why it's not gonna work: it's a fucking lie. Alcohol and cigarettes kill more people than crack, coke, and heroin combined."[67] The standard retort was predictable: " 'Oh, wait a minute, Bill. Alcohol's-an-acceptable-form-of-social-interaction-which-for-thousands-of-years-has-been-the-norm-under-which-human-beings-congregate-and-form—' 'Shut the fuck up. Your denial is beneath you. And thanks to the use of hallucinogenic drugs, I see through you'" (*RC*). The aspiring tricksters in television programming and marketing departments were shamelessly showing their hands: "All day long we see those commercials—Here's your brain, here's your brain on drugs; just say no; why do you think they call it dope?—And then the next commercial is: 'This Bud's for You.'" If anything, the selectivity of the War on Drugs made network pretensions to "broadcast standards" all the more contemptible: "Exactly what *standards* are you practicing? I've seen these commercials during 'in depth' reports on the war against drugs. At least drug dealers have enough shame to lurk on street corners and in alleyways, and not come over the tube into our homes with all the slick, glossy production values the beer-hawkers can muster."[68]

Thus, the one inescapable meaning of the War on Drugs was revealed by its artless confidence men through the brazen messages in their television commercials: "It's O.K. to *drink* your drug; we meant those *other* drugs—those *untaxed* drugs. Nicotine, alcohol: *good* drugs. Coincidentally, *taxed* drugs." Having grasped the obvious meaning behind the inept commercial charade, the intended dupes—the American public—were fully entitled to draw an uninvited conclusion: "Thank God they're taxing alcohol, man. That means we've got those good roads we can get fucked up and drive on. . . . We'd be doing donuts in a wheat field."[69] Moreover, in its discriminating protection of socially harmful drugs, the Just Say No campaign blinded the public from other possibilities that, to Hicks, were grounded in truth—and if it took a more able hypocrite, a *comedian*, to set the record straight, so be it: "If I were going to have a drug be legal, it would not be alcohol. . . . Pot is a better drug than alcohol—*fact*—and I'll prove it to you. You're at a ball game, you're at a concert, and someone's really violent, aggressive, and obnoxious: are they drunk or are they smoking pot?" The resounding "*Drunk!*" invariably shouted out by the audience would confirm Hicks in the belief that his superior trickery could release people from the spells cast by presumptuous rivals in the advertising departments. "I have *never* seen people on pot get in a fight, because it's fucking impossible." Hence, an ironic alternative to a no less hypocritical official agenda: "Not only do I think pot should be legalized, I think it should be mandatory. . . . That'd be a nice world, wouldn't it? Mellow, hungry, quiet, fucked-up people everywhere? Domino's Pizza trucks passing each other on every highway" (*RC*). The absence of tobacco commercials, too, was no indication of either government or media sincerity in the War on Drugs: "Shoot, T.V. would still be hawking cigarettes if the government hadn't stepped in. Why the government stepped in in the first place is anybody's guess. Perhaps it's because we've opened so many new overseas markets to push the number-one killer drug in the

world."[70] So, the advertising competition should have fooled no
one, as any *real* trickster could see.

Hicks did not fully expend his comic scorn on the commercial operators in television's War on Drugs; he reserved some
for the news managers. They, too, were confidence men, and sorry
specimens in their failure to hide their bias and collusion. "Did you
ever see a good drugs story on the news? Never. News is supposed
to be objective. Isn't it supposed to be *The News*? But every drugs •
story is negative. Well, hold it: I've had some killer fuckin' times on
drugs. Let's hear the whole story." The "whole story" was the only
way to the truth; but news managers were less interested in truth
than in convenient plausibility: "Same L.S.D. story every time, and
we've all heard it: 'Young man on acid. Thought he could fly.
Jumped out of a building. What a tragedy.' What a *dick*. He thought
he could fly? Why didn't he take off from the ground, and check it
out first? You don't see ducks lined up to catch elevators to fly
south" (*RV*). The "whole story" *must*—by definition—include a
positive report: "Wouldn't that be newsworthy? Just once? To base
your decision on information rather than scare tactics and superstition and lies? Just once? *I* think it would be newsworthy." And he
would offer the positive report, in the interests of "truth" rather
than advocacy: " 'Today a young man on acid realized that all matter is merely energy condensed to a slow vibration, that we are all
one consciousness experiencing itself subjectively, there is no such
thing as death, life is only a dream, and we are the imagination of
ourselves. . . . Here's Tom with the weather' " (*REV*).

In its entirety, then, the War on Drugs was to Hicks a
greater evil than the drug abuse it purported to attack, because it
was based upon censorship, misinformation, hypocrisy (without
the saving grace of irony), and the manipulation of fear rather than
the inculcation of awareness. While in one libertarian aside he
maintained, "No, it's not a War on Drugs, it's a War on Personal •
Freedom," he implied that it was much more: a War on Truth (*D*).
It was yet another advertising campaign that benefited only the advertisers or the interested parties in concert with them.

Among such parties, and bearing the brunt of Hicks's
scorn, were those high-profile rock stars whose participation in the
War on Drugs was one of many indications of their willing submis-
sion to the pressures of consensus and the enticements of corporate
sponsorship. In the hands of the new rock "heroes," the War on
Drugs—like any of the other products they endorsed—became just
another distraction intended to condition the American public into

passive consumers (of ideas and agendas) rather than responsible thinkers. Having grown through the 1960s and 1970s as a hero-worshipper of Jimi Hendrix and a host of other rebellious artists, Hicks viewed the 1980s and 1990s as decades of betrayal by the very people in whom the power to resist conformity most resided: America's rock musicians, timid and talentless now, hiding behind the facades of glamour, overproduction, and relentless marketing.

Hicks found it easy to segue from the War on Drugs into a critique of artistic prostitution and dishonesty. After invoking Hendrix, the Beatles, Keith Richards, Janis Joplin, and other musicians for whom drug experimentation proved a litmus test for the creative pursuit of an alternative viewpoint—an "altered state"—he would "extend the theory to our generation now, so it's more applicable" (*RC*). His conclusion was merciless: "These other musicians today who don't do drugs, and in fact speak out against them: boy, do they suck. What a coincidence. Ball-less, soul-less, spiritless, corporate little bitches, suckers of Satan's cock, each and every one of them." Signing up to the War on Drugs was tantamount to *masquerading* as a rock star: " 'We're Rock Stars Against Drugs because that's what the *President* wants!' Aw, suck Satan's cock. That's what we want, isn't it? Government-approved rock and roll" (*REV*). The same rock stars fighting the War on Drugs were just as likely to be selling Pepsi-Cola and Taco Bell products: there *was* a connection. Certainly, a review of the 1980s' and 1990s' most prominent rock stars suggests an advertising chumminess inconceivable in the 1960s and 1970s, when the music was synonymous with nonconformity: Michael Jackson pushing Pepsi; Phil Collins and Eric Clapton pushing Michelob; George Michael pushing Diet Coke ("Diet Coke? Even Madonna fuckin' hawked *real* Coke"); M. C. Hammer pushing Kentucky Fried Chicken; Barry Manilow pushing McDonald's; Genesis pushing Volkswagens; Pink Floyd pushing Volkswagens. (Heaven alone knows how Hicks would have handled the news that, less than two years after his death, even Keith Richards would be pushing Volkswagens.) "Everyone is hawking *products*. That's the highest thing you can achieve now, isn't it—become some barker? . . . I'm waiting to see, 'It's Jesus, for Miller! I was crucified, dead for three days, resurrected, and I've waited two thousand years to return to Earth—it's Miller Time!' " (*D*).

Brett Butler suggested that "Bill got freeze-framed in the scene where Jesus went through the temple and said, 'This is my father's house and you have turned it into a den of thieves'" (*IJR*). If she is right, Hicks was indeed "Christ at his angriest" when he confronted both his musical targets and the audiences he would scold for supporting them: "You don't see the imminent danger, do you? You're staring at me like, 'Well, they're just musicians and they're just doing their thing, and —' NO! They are *demons* set loose on the Earth to lower the standards of the perfect and holy children of God, which is what we are. Make no mistake about it" (*D*). Music was artistry and artistry (ironically) was truth, not the trick-turning of prostitution. Hence the explanation Hicks offered for those who could not apprehend the meaning of his character assassinations: "You can print this in stone, and don't you ever forget it: Any—*any* —performer that ever sells a product on television is for now and all eternity removed from the artistic world. I don't care if you shit Mona Lisas out of your ass on cue: you've made your fucking choice." The product could be either Diet Coke or the War on Drugs —it made no difference: "'Oh, come on; it's just a good product, and it's making a good—' *Suck* that big, scaly pecker down your mouth—*suck it!*" (*RV*).

Hicks maintained that he was in an "art war" between the forces of slick, commercial lies and the forces of integrity.[71] If commercialism and integrity were antithetical, then music designed solely to sell *as* a commodity was just as satanic as music that sold other commodities. This left most modern popular music open to Hicks's guns. M. C. Hammer, Vanilla Ice, George Michael, the New Kids, Debbie Gibson, Tiffany, Rick Astley, Marky Mark, Michael Bolton, Billy Ray Cyrus—all fell before his satire, all because of their blatant commercialism. They would turn Hicks into a comic demagogue onstage: "'Oh, come on, Bill—they're the New Kids. Don't pick on them. They're so good, they're so clean-cut. They're *such* a good image for the children—' *Fuck that!* When did mediocrity and banality become a good image for your children? I want *my* children to listen to people who fucking *rocked!* I don't care if they died in puddles of their own *vomit*—I want someone who plays from his fucking *heart!* . . . I want my rock stars DEAD!" (*RV*).

Given the extent of corporate backing and image-projection that Hicks's targets had behind them, they were, in his estimation, fair game for violent satire: they were hardly powerless. Thus, he could in good conscience dramatize the dismemberment of Debbie Gibson; or the shotgun murders of Kenny Rogers and George Michael; or the sexual degradation of Michael with a pair of Gibson's bloody panties—it was all part of the "art war" being fought here on "the third mall from the Sun." In the battle for truth and integrity, Debbie Gibson—"that little mall-creature"—must be chopped into little pieces of "mall-cordwood" by a raging Jimi Hendrix: the soul of America depended on it (*D*). "They're putting music to AIDS germs, putting a drum machine behind 'em in a metronome beat, and Ted Turner's colorizing 'em. These aren't even *people*, man—it's a CIA plot to make you think malls are good. Don't you *see*?" The price of losing the "art war" was nothing less than the virtual lobotomization of the world at the hands of American commercial interests: "You *do* realize that by the year 2000 all malls in the world are going to be connected. There's going to be a subculture of Mall People who have never seen daylight—born, bred, and raised in the malls—and sent out to the wafting tomb of Debbie Gibson to become *happy* consumers" (*SM*). Consumerism and infantilism went hand in hand; and through their spending, the consuming public were just as culpable for their own infantilization as the corporate "artistes" and their marketing agents: "I mean, who *buys* that shit? Is there that much babysitting money being passed around right now? . . . When did we start listening to prepubescent white girls? I must have missed *that* meeting" (*D*). For their complicity, the buying public set themselves up for the same Swiftian solutions that Hicks offered to the sold-out performers: "'I'm a *happy* consumer! And you know, I'm concerned about what my *children* consume! I'd like to consume the barrel of a twelve-gauge shotgun right now—*blam!*'" (*SM*).

Here, then, was a profusion of ironies. In his quest to be heard and to inform, Bill Hicks had to master the very hypocrisies he condemned in more inept confidence men. He wanted to sell his comedy albums: they needed to be advertised and marketed—even in malls. He didn't want to die by drugs nor see anyone else do so: yet in the interests of "the whole story" he had to advocate knowledge and experience that he admitted could prove fatal. He wanted maximum exposure: he had to court Letterman and his censors on "Lucifer's Dream Box." He wanted to tell the truth: he had to lie with the implicit grin of the comedian. Richard Belzer identified the overarching irony that so characterized Hicks's predicament: "It's very frustrating for somebody like Bill, whose antennas are always up. He lays himself open, his heart and his mind, to see all the hypocrisy and the contradictions [between] what we could really be and what we are" (*IJR*). Inevitably, "the hypocrisy and the contradictions" that Hicks saw outside of himself were often precisely those that he had to accommodate and utilize, as a comedian, within. His frustration remained until the issue was taken out of his hands altogether.

Chomsky with Dick Jokes

One of the most memorable passages in Albert Goldman's biography of Lenny Bruce is the description of the last New York appearance, performed in defiance of the ban imposed on him by the New York Criminal Court in 1964. With his cabaret card revoked and his name effectively taboo among intimidated club owners, Bruce had stormed onto the stage like "a man who had nothing to lose, a performer without hope, a show-biz kamikaze." He had become "the Jewish equivalent of James Brown, stripping down his mind to the bare bone just the way the rhythm-and-blues cats tear off their clothes and scream out their guts and finally regress to tribal totems drenched in sweat. Soul, not jazz, was Lenny's final aesthetic."[72] Yes, Bruce had been released; but he was not yet a man with "nothing to lose." By his own admission, he may no longer have been a comedian; but he still had his life. When Bill Hicks taped his last performance in November 1993, he knew that he was dying—*had* known it for five months. Only his family and closest friends shared that knowledge with him. Unlike Bruce, he was still a comedian. To view the film of that performance, however, is to witness a transformation akin to that of his predecessor. Hicks, too, is stripped down—physically, by the cancer inside him; but also in another way. No longer the chubby-faced, sleekly groomed, black-garbed "Prince of Darkness," he is more like a world-weary Rasputin—bearded, mystical, lank-haired. There is also a change in his musical aesthetic: he comes onstage to the rock tune of Hendrix and leaves to the rap tune of Rage Against the Machine. Upon first viewing, it is difficult to tell whether the film signifies a wretched degeneration or an exhilarating release. Hicks inscrutably maintained that nobody could touch him now—not Letterman and his censors; not Leno, stung and angered by the criticisms of an early protégé. If the American mainstream was forever out of his grasp, he was out of *it's* grasp just as well. "I'm at peace with myself," he said. "I don't really care anymore."[73] He told John Lahr, "As Bob Dylan said, the only way to live outside the law is to be totally honest. So I will remain lawless."[74] His banning from *Letterman* was, he said, "a badge of honor"; and following the *New Yorker* exposé, he could write to Lahr: "Somehow, people are listening in a new light. Somehow the possibilities (creatively) seem limitless."[75]

But they were not limitless; for even at the end of his life, frankness, at least, was not at Hicks's disposal. He was still a comedian, and as yet unreleased from the constraints that that identity entailed. He still had Chomsky on his mind, quoting him to Lahr: "'The responsibility of the intellectual is to tell the truth, and expose lies.' While I do not consider myself an intellectual by any stretch of the imagination, his quote, coincidentally, is the same way my parents taught me how to live. So in honor of them, I'll continue doing what I've been doing, the best way I can."[76] But Chomsky had also told him something else: "'The Emperor wears no clothes, but he doesn't like to be told.'"[77] Thus, for Hicks to continue what he had "been doing" meant to continue being less than frank; it meant being at the mercy not only of comedy's lies but of the unspoken *assurance* of comedy's lies. Richard Jeni may have felt that comedians "probably have more license to tell the truth than anybody. Most of them don't take it. Bill took it, and you have to admire that about him" (*IJR*). But it is precisely the comedian's "license" that implicitly negates the truth: Bill Hicks had no more license to tell the truth than any other comedian has. He knew this, and it could indeed gall him: "As H. L. Mencken said, America's biggest failure is its inability to take comedy seriously. Some people go: 'You're a comic. Tell me a joke.' I'm a clown to them."[78] Yet half of him—the unavoidably lying half—had been obliged to protest, "Bob, they're just jokes." Could America be blamed for its failure to take comedy seriously, when comedy gave it just that license *not* to take it seriously?

In one of his last interviews, Hicks elaborated on the conflict in which he had been placed by virtue of his particular ironic identity. Comedy, he said, was "like a mistress. It beats the hell out of me sometimes, but it's actually saved my life, too."[79] To save the life of the truth teller by removing the truth from the telling: Hicks accepted this ironic fix. Here, for instance, is one example of what he wanted to say, most likely in earnest, during the tirade of his last performance: "There ain't no battle over fucking NAFTA; that's a *fucking* charade, like our elections are a *fucking* charade; and tomorrow, ladies and gentlemen, they're selling your *fucking* life out from under you. And don't you *fucking* forget it, either." But here is what he had to promise in the next sentence: "There's dick jokes coming up. Please relax" (*I*).

On the eve of his release from everything, including comedy, Hicks said, "I've never been more happy or at peace about it. It's been a long enough road, but what is length in the context of eternity?"[80] At various points along that road, however, he had, like Lenny Bruce before him, intimated clearly enough through comedy his frustrations *with* comedy: "It's great to be here. I thank you. I've

been on the road doing comedy for ten years now, so bear with me
while I plaster on a fake smile and plow through this shit one more
time" (*IJR*). "You gotta bear with me—I'm very tired of traveling,
and very tired of doing comedy, and very tired of staring out at
your vacant faces looking back at me, wanting me to fill your
empty lives with humor you couldn't possibly think of yourselves.
Good evening!" (*RC*). "It's great to be here, it really is. I love my
job, and I love being here performing for you. . . . It's the greatest
job in the world, for one very simple reason—and it's not the sharing of laughter and all that horseshit. It's the fact that I don't have a
boss" (*RV*). Comedy was play; he had serious things to say: "You
know all that money we spend on defense and nuclear weapons
every year—trillions of dollars, correct? Instead—instead—just *play*
with *this*: if we spent that money feeding and clothing the poor of
the world . . . " (*SM*). Hicks knew that he was under an obligatory
contract to play with both his audiences and the truth. In the film of
his last performance, his contempt for that obligation is almost
palpable, although, unlike Lenny Bruce in extremis, he honors his
part of the bargain: "Folks, here's the deal. I editorialize for forty-
five minutes. The last fifteen, I pull my chute, we all pull our
chutes, and float down to Dick Joke Island together." On that island, his audience will be offered the contemptible license to dismiss all that he had wished to be heeded: "We will rest our weary
heads against the big purple-veined trunks of dick jokes, while
bouncing on our spongy-scrotum beanbag chairs, and giggle away
the night like good American comedy audiences are supposed to,
goddammit" (*I*). At this point, he is practically spitting; but he
knows he has signed his name to the contract.

    So he plays the game to which he is committed one last
time, repeating the banned *Letterman* set, reducing Rush Limbaugh
to a "scat muncher" and his followers to dittoheaded children
("What are you all looking for—a new Dad?"); hammering into the
War on Drugs, the Waco assault, the bombing of Baghdad, Christian fundamentalism, the sanctity of childbirth ("Do you mean to
tell me you think your child is special, because one out of two-hun-
dred-million sperm *connected*?"), and—with the greatest vitupera-
tion—the state of American comedy. "This is the material, by the
way, that has kept me virtually anonymous in America. . . . Meanwhile, they're draining the Pacific and putting up bench seats for
Carrot Top's next Showtime special. Carrot Top—for people who
didn't get Gallagher." Gallagher: the comedian who made his name
by "destroying good food with a sledgehammer" at the end of his

show. "Gee, I wonder why we're hated the world over. All these fat Americans on the front row—'Haw, haw, haw, haw, haw. Now, *this* is comedy. Ho ho ho. That Bill Hicks is just *bitter*. . . . Why can't *he* hit fruit with a hammer? He's just jealous *he* didn't think of it.'" Hicks is indeed bitter, at least enough to dramatize his bitterness: "Folks, I *did* think of that. I was two at the time. . . . I could have been the young Gallagher in diapers, walking around being a millionaire, franchising myself—but *no*. I had to have this weird thing about trying to illuminate the collective unconscious and help humanity. Fucking *moron*" (*I*). It is not quite the self-conscious martyrdom of Lenny Bruce.

For all his fidelity to the ironic charade, however, Bill Hicks's final gesture on the American comic stage is a dramatic act of defiance against the very demands of play to which his more popular competitors have acceded. He has finished his last performance and disappeared into the dressing room amidst the applause. Onstage there sits a watermelon on a stool, waiting for the next Gallagher to come and smash it, signifying the depths to which popular American comedy has sunk. The sound system is blaring out the music of Rage Against the Machine, with their call to "take back the power." Hicks returns to the stage for his final bows. In his hands, the mike stand becomes a sledgehammer. He raises it to *smash the watermelon*. . . . But the song being broadcast behind him —for the benefit of Letterman, his producers, and his censors; for Leno, who had said, "Look, just *get on TV*"; for the confidence men in the Standards and Practices offices and the advertising agencies; for the sellout performers; the viewers; the listeners; the consumers of infantile American comedy—for them, the song repeats the refrain: "Fuck you, I won't do what you tell me to." Hicks drops the "sledgehammer," kicks the stool over, and leaves the stage forever —not because he is giving up as a comedian, but because he is going to die. The watermelon drops to the floor, but it remains whole.

CHAPTER 5

Kurt Vonnegut:
"I had to laugh like hell"

Who can have failed to notice a pattern emerging among those confronting the ethical problems of their own ironic practices —especially those for whom the practice becomes the identity? We have seen Herman Melville troubling over the more sinister implications of the mendacity with which Franklin was so comfortable, and which he himself sought to master. We have seen Garrison Keillor tire of his own ironic obligations, expressing the wish that as he approaches old age he could "quit writing humor and just write irritation for awhile." We have seen how Lenny Bruce ultimately opted for the "*truth* truth," dismissing the comic mask outright and publicly banishing the confidence man in himself before he turned forty. And we have seen Bill Hicks, only thirty-two, washing his hands in disgust for almost all that mainstream American comedy had become. "How can I be me in the context of doing this material?" he asked aloud, given that, to him, American comedy had been "totally gutted" by comedians willingly succumbing to the self-censorship demanded by commercial television producers and their sponsors. "Do I even want to be part of it anymore? Show business or art—these are the choices."[1]

These questions and demonstrations are more or less indicative of the tendency identified by Kurt Vonnegut when he had himself reached the age of sixty-eight: once more, the tendency for American comedians to effectively stop being comedians—that is, to "become intolerably unfunny pessimists."[2] In his latest novel,

Hocus Pocus, he offers a narrator who, like Lenny Bruce, is by his own admission "not a comedian," and who faces similar persecution for betraying his unmasked, critical pessimism. Fired from his academic post, Eugene Debs Hartke wonders how his colleague, a history professor, had managed to escape persecution, given that he too had spoken just "as badly of his own country." He is willing to hazard a guess: "My guess is that he was a comedian, and I was not. He wanted students to leave his presence feeling good, not bad, so the atrocities and stupidities he described were in the distant past. There was nothing a student could do about them but laugh, laugh, laugh."[3] As Hartke ruefully acknowledges, this colleague had saved his own skin by doing what he himself could not: deflect the force of his criticism by hiding behind the masks of allegory and play. In *Fates Worse than Death*, Vonnegut describes what had happened to himself at the age of sixty-three when he briefly decided to refrain from public speaking. Having lost confidence in his comic masquerade on the lecture platform, he had carried on with it halfheartedly in print: "Since I knew how jokes worked, hooking and releasing, I could still make them, even though I no longer felt like making them."[4] This is a startling admission for a comedian to make—but in Vonnegut's case it is not surprising, since he had for decades implied the strain that threatened to enervate him, as it had threatened not only Mark Twain before him, but —as Keillor, Bruce, and Hicks demonstrate—his younger contemporaries as well. Twain, Vonnegut said, was "Quixotic . . . in his wish to please crowds without lying to them," forced into hiding his "pessimism and religious skepticism and anti-patriotism" behind his own unique disguise, that of "an utterly winsome sort of teddy bear, in need of all the love he could get." Vonnegut admitted that he, like all American comedians, had been left with the legacy of Mark Twain's curse: "Every present day comedian who says after mocking something supposedly sacred, 'But I'm only kidding, folks,' is following in the footsteps of Samuel Clemens . . . who became a world citizen while necessarily disguised as Mark Twain."[5]

Vonnegut has ostentatiously advertised his kinship with Twain, citing him and his influence in enough places to arouse suspicion as well as recognition. He has not convinced everybody of his having successfully appropriated the mind of Mark Twain, given the calculated soft focus, the reluctance to pronounce judgment, and the air of failure that characterize his work—devices that liken him more to Keillor, possibly, than to Twain, especially given the latter's savagery as he approached old age. Failed comedians and rueful confidence men populate Vonnegut's work, many of them sharing the doomed task of convincing either themselves or others that laughter and its kindred forms of play are desirable in a world where not only earnest criticism but serious action is needed. What sets Vonnegut apart from Twain is that, like Keillor, he *begins* from the standpoint of admitting the impotence of comedy. If he indeed shares anything with Twain, it is neither the faith in, nor the savagery of, his satire; it is rather the maintenance of a highly self-conscious public facade that, in Vonnegut's case, relies on the out-right admission of powerlessness. Through this facade, he avows his own defeat as a comedian, part of a contradictory stance he has taken for decades, in which he simultaneously damns and cele-brates artistic confidence games of all sorts. And in this, it is ac-tually Melville whom he echoes, rather than Twain.

As he has done with so many of his characters, Vonne-gut has called outright attention to his own public masquerade as the necessary fabrication of a tightrope walker: "I keep losing and regaining my equilibrium, which is the basic plot of all popular fic-tion. And I myself am a work of fiction."[6] But to which self is this admission to be applied—to the comic persona, or to the despairing cultural critic who makes such a show of dismissing that very per-sona? The public Vonnegut is a multiple personality, in some ways more complex than the dual personality of Samuel Clemens and Mark Twain, or Keillor's multifarious Prairie Home Companion. He once admitted the autobiographical nature of Kilgore Trout, himself a composite of multiple personalities appearing in a num-ber of Vonnegut's novels; but it may be equally helpful to consider Vonnegut's public image in the light of a number of his other fabri-cations. Robert Scholes sees a parallel in two of Vonnegut's charac-ters, "the lovely false prophet Bokonon" from *Cat's Cradle* and "the kindly, untrustworthy, honest, quadruple turncoat Howard Camp-bell of *Mother Night*."[7] To these I would add the twin masqueraders, Wilbur and Eliza Swain of *Slapstick*. As these three novels in partic-ular demonstrate, the comedian as confidence man is Vonnegut's public, self-conscious obsession, the focus of his highly visible anxi-ety about the questionable morality and efficacy of a comedian's success. In terms of this obsession, Vonnegut is once again more akin to Melville than to Twain, and *Mother Night, Cat's Cradle,* and *Slapstick* lie closer (mark the word *lie*) to Melville's *The Confidence-Man* than to any of Twain's works.

Few American comic writers, if any, have been so delib-erately public as Vonnegut in his wrestling with the paradox of the critic at warning and the comedian at play. *Cat's Cradle* focuses explicitly on what its narrator calls this "cruel paradox" of comic deception in an already dangerously benighted world—"the heartbreaking necessity of lying about reality, and the heartbreaking impossibility of lying about it."[8] In an equally stark paradox, the preface to *Mother Night* contains what Vonnegut says is his only sure moral: "We are what we pretend to be, so we must be careful about what we pretend to be." As the example behind this one certain moral, Howard Campbell refers to the duplicitous voice characterizing any comedian who seeks to *divert* attention from his critical observations, the voice of "that simple and widespread boon to modern mankind—schizophrenia." Just as Melville's focus on the schizophrenia of the generic Confidence-Man revealed a capacity for a sinister ludic duplicity, so does Vonnegut describe in the preface the vile potential that Campbell both playfully and fatally unleashes in the novel: "If I'd been born in Germany, I suppose I would have been a Nazi, bopping Jews and gypsies and Poles around, leaving boots sticking out of snowbanks, warming myself with my secretly virtuous insides."[9] There is, of course, little that is risible in the implications of this particular statement; but what is needed is the comedian's outrageous willingness to pretend that it *is* risible. One can debate, after Richard Todd, over whether Vonnegut is merely "pretending to pretend," but one then risks the mental short-circuiting that befalls any potential dupe at the mercy of the Confidence-Man.[10] If social criticism begins with the premise that "truth" is the paragon and "falsehood" is base, then the tension between goodness and evil that the comedian Bokonon seeks in *Cat's Cradle* is inherent in the comedic paradox itself: "It was the belief of Bokonon that good societies could be built only by pitting good against evil, and by keeping the tension between the two high at all times" (67). This, Bokonon proclaims, comes through living by the "harmless untruths" that make one, among other things, "happy" (6). Yet it is precisely the "harmless untruth" of ironic play that threatens to compromise the object of criticism, to the great peril of the society that willfully ignores the truth and instead solicits for its gratification an "untruth" that may not be so harmless after all. This is the debate that Vonnegut enacts most explicitly in *Slapstick, Mother Night, Cat's Cradle,* and in the construction of a public persona that purports to be comfortable with the implications of such an impasse while at the same time quixotically challenging them. There is little wonder that the strain of maintaining the facade should have taken its toll and that Vonnegut should have gone through such pains to document the process.

The Strain of *Slapstick*

On the one hand there is Vonnegut's claim that his critical observations *don't matter*: "I am as full of baloney as anybody, and . . . anybody who says for sure what life is all about might as well lecture on Santa Claus and the Easter Bunny."[11] Thus will he adopt the role of a mentor to a new generation, only to proclaim to a university graduating class, as though he were Bokonon himself, "Only in superstition is there hope. If you want to become a friend of civilization, then become an enemy of truth and a fanatic for harmless balderdash."[12] Amongst such "balderdash" may be the crucial, critical observations of Vonnegut and any comedian who is "only kidding." The strategy is to deflate the impact of the observations—but then, what are the consequences? Vonnegut implied them with reference to *Cat's Cradle*: "I myself once staged the end of the world on two pieces of paper—at a cost of less than a penny, including wear and tear on my typewriter ribbon and the seat of my pants. Compare that with the budgets of Cecil B. DeMille."[13] The combination of the throw-away voice and the import of the subject matter in comic, though critical, observations such as this exemplifies the "schizophrenia" which has become such a potent metaphor for Vonnegut with regard to the ironic identity.

Vonnegut has been most articulate about the adoption of roles, or poses, in his discussions over the conflict between the critic at warning and the comedian at play. On the one hand, his task is to awaken and to alarm: "Writers are specialized cells doing whatever we do, and we're expressions of the entire society—just as the sensory cells on the surface of your body are in the service of your body as a whole. And when a society is in great danger, we're likely to sound the alarms." In this, he likens the critic to a canary in a coal mine, aware of self-destructive possibilities that accompany the role: "You know, coal miners used to take birds down into the mines with them to detect gas before the men got sick. The artists certainly did that in the case of Vietnam. They chirped and keeled over."[14] Vonnegut has himself come close to this fate, given such bitter reactions to his work as William F. Buckley's claim that he "had made a career of despising America" and the decision by certain school boards across America not only to ban his books but publicly to burn them as well.[15]

What Vonnegut here offers with one hand, however, he ostentatiously retracts with the other. The social alarm device—the canary in the coal mine—has its opposite in the comic anesthetist who sets out to desensitize rather than to awaken. Vonnegut has seen comedy as "an analgesic for the temporary relief of existential pain," and more often than not his public statements on the role of comedy have centered on the notion of providing comfort and diversion for both comedian and audience. Hence his eulogies of the great radio comedians of the Depression, among his earliest comic influences. The 1930s were, he said, "a great time for comedians," with people all across America gathering around their radios for their "little dose of humor every day. . . . It got everybody through three more days of Depression."[16] That comic desensitization is a valuable defensive strategy he readily admits. Given his German name at the end of World War II, and in spite of his Purple Heart and imprisonment at Dresden, he admits to having stumbled on the "good idea . . . to tell a joke as soon as possible." This tactic he shared with many Germans in America after the war: "They, too, became screamingly funny as soon as possible." And, here as elsewhere, Vonnegut emphasizes his fellowship with Mark Twain, who, he recalls, "had served in the Confederacy briefly, after all, in the bloodiest war in American history, and later faced paying audiences of, among others, Union veterans and their wives."[17] Having highlighted the defensive nature of a comic strategy, Vonnegut will take pains to camouflage any offensive capacity—he will dismiss it, diminish it, and emphasize the modesty of his intentions. For him, laughter is merely "a response to frustration, just as tears are, and it solves nothing, just as tears solve nothing. Laughter or crying is what a human being does when there's nothing else he can do."[18] With such deprecating admissions, Vonnegut sets out to divert attention from precisely what the critic in him wants people to heed. By submitting to the demands of comic license, with the implicit assurance that he is at play, he, like all comedians, must do great violence to that which motivates him. This has serious repercussions for both the comedian and the society he serves by providing it with the comic anesthesia it craves and that threatens to blind it. The implications for both sides in the masquerade are the subject of *Mother Night*, *Cat's Cradle*, and particular points in all his successive books.

But they are raised most immediately in *Slapstick*, wherein Vonnegut is hardly coy in attempting to describe what life as a comedian *"feels* like" for him, being under the implicit and potentially intolerable injunction to speak as a buffoon, however prescient and incisive his observations might be from behind the mask. *Slapstick* is, he says, "the closest I will ever come to writing an autobiography."[19] It is a grim book, depicting its comedic protagonists as seeming idiots with a hidden capacity for critical genius that, once revealed, destroys them both. Wilbur and Eliza Swain are a pair of freakish, dizygotic twins—"neanderthaloids" banished by their parents to an isolated family mansion. They cultivate idiocy, Wilbur explains, because "all the information we received about the planet we were on indicated that idiots were lovely things to be" (29). Their intelligence and critical awareness is known only to themselves: on the outside, they are harmless, babbling, amusing clowns. In private, they put their extraordinary minds to work, criticizing Darwin's evolutionary theory and, implicitly, social Darwinism "on the grounds the creatures would become terribly vulnerable while attempting to improve themselves." They compose "a precocious critique" of the American Constitution: "We argued that it was as good a scheme for misery as any, since its success in keeping the common people reasonably happy and proud depended on the strength of the people themselves—and yet it described no practical machinery which would tend to make the people, as opposed to their elected representatives, strong" (37). However, mindful of their protected status as idiots in their own ludic "Paradise," they keep their criticism to themselves: "We did not itch to display our intelligence in public. We did not think of intelligence as being useful or attractive in any way" (30). But when their mother pleads for "the faintest sign of intelligence" on their part, they dispense with their masquerade and announce, "WE CAN NEVER BE PRETTY BUT WE CAN BE AS SMART OR AS DUMB AS THE WORLD REALLY WANTS US TO BE" (49, 50). In thus switching from "false players" to effective "spoil-sports," Wilber and Eliza find themselves in a situation of "intolerable tragedy"—culpable for their observations and offensive to others in "asking for respect" (53). In the face of contempt from those around them, they attempt in their naïveté to make a "return to the consolations of idiocy"; but it is too late (61). For revealing the workings of their confidence game and dismissing it outright, they are both banished, ejected from what had been a Fool's Paradise. The question in *Slapstick*—as in *The Confidence-Man*—remains as to who precisely the fools are: the comedians who play the game, the earnest critics who presume to do without it, or the dupes who are oblivious to the dangers ameliorated through the mask of ironic play.

The first of Vonnegut's works, however, to continue explicitly the explorations about comic mendacity initiated by Melville in *The Confidence-Man* are *Mother Night* and *Cat's Cradle*. The earlier of these focuses on the telling of ostensibly playful lies in the service of social evil, and the latter upon lies told in the service of social good; but in each respect it is the comedian as confidence man who bears Vonnegut's scrutiny. At one point in *Mother Night*, Howard W. Campbell faces the same challenge as any comedian who hovers on the border of acceptance or resentment. "'I don't know if you're kidding me or not,'" a policeman tells him, in the midst of this story of a comedian whose life, and that of many others, is destroyed by his failure to convince the public that he is kidding (153). *Mother Night* and its immediate successor, *Cat's Cradle*, are Vonnegut's earliest cost-benefit analyses of comic deception for both the comedian and his audience. They both present play as deadly, although in different respects: in *Mother Night* the comedian is damned because his confidence game is too convincing, without the accompanying acknowledgment of play, while in *Cat's Cradle* the comedian's game is deadly in *spite* of the open admission of play. Together, these two novels seem to cast Vonnegut into at least one unsought association with Mark Twain, whose Huck Finn concludes that in doing a social good and a social evil, "the wages is just the same."[20] In the cases of Howard Campbell, Bokonon, and the willing subjects of their deceptions, the wages are culpability and death for all players—in spite of Campbell's apparent fabrication of evil, and Bokonon's of good.

Mother Night: Something Satanic about Irony

We might begin with Howard Campbell's early Jewish jokes, World War II vintage, the ones that have made him famous: "'There are No Atheists in Foxholes.' I should like to expand this theme a little and tell you that, even through this is a war inspired by the Jews, a war that only the Jews can win, there are no Jews in foxholes, either" (115). There is his cartoon, "a caricature of a cigar-smoking Jew" to be used as a target for rifle practice: "The Jew was standing on broken crosses and little naked women. In one hand the Jew held a bag of money labeled 'International Banking.' In the other hand he held a Russian flag" (99). And there is his idea for bringing comic theater to life, his blue-and-gold uniformed, Nazi-loving, Free American Corps: "It was to be a volunteer organiza-tion. . . . Only three American P.O.W.s joined" (61–62). They may not be funny, but we know these are jokes because Campbell says so, long after the fact. Of his wartime Jew-baiting radio broadcasts: "All I can say is that I didn't believe them, that I knew full well what ignorant, destructive, obscenely jocular things I was saying" (116). Of his cartoon target he says, "I overdrew it, with an effect that would have been ludicrous anywhere but in Germany" (99); and his Free American Corps he dismisses as a mere "Nazi day-dream" (61). In all his Nazi posing, he says, he had hoped "to be merely ludicrous" (102).

The other factor establishing Campbell as a comedian at deadly play—in addition to his belated admissions of jokery—is the fact of his role as an American agent throughout the war, broad-casting coded messages to the Allies in the guise of Nazi radio propaganda. The English-speaking world knows him as a traitor as well as "a shrewd and loathsome anti-Semite" (8). Only three peo-ple know that he is a radio comedian broadcasting "truth" under the cover of untruths: an American intelligence officer, an American general, and the president—as Campbell is told, " 'The man you called Franklin Delano Rosenfeld. . . . He used to listen to you glee-fully every night'" (124). In Campbell, Vonnegut offers a comedian who must live and—if he is to be believed—die by the conse-quences of his jokes. In accepting the terms of play, he must accept the fate of the "false player" whose falsehood is never discovered and is, ultimately, unverifiable. Campbell is told when he is re-cruited as an agent that, for national security reasons, he must be prepared to play the game forever—that the truth will never come out, and the end of the game never signaled: " 'There will be no magic time when you will be cleared, when America will call you out of hiding with a cheerful: Olly-olly-ox-in-free'" (31).

That it is the pure love of the confidence game that moti-vates Campbell's comedy, there is no doubt (if, indeed, this book offers any certainties); and this emphasizes the connections Vonne-gut has always made between creativity (comic or otherwise), ma-nipulations of confidence, social inaction, and the potentially dire consequences of all. "Everybody is supposed to play games for mental health," Campbell admits, especially under the disagreeable circumstances of rising Fascism in a world on the brink of madness (30). His prewar life is devoted to creative games: he is a playwright, churning out "medieval romances, about as political as chocolate *éclairs*" (23). He is not at all a part of the real world, neither a fighter nor a political activist. Like the laughter and tears he arouses in his plays, he himself is about as effectual as a chocolate *éclair*. "'I am an artist,'" he tells the American intelligence officer who wants to recruit him; "'If war comes, I won't do anything to help it along. If war comes, it'll find me still working at my peaceful trade'" (26). Confronted with the fact of "'things going on in Germany . . . Hitler and the Jews and all that,'" Campbell replies, "'It isn't anything I can control . . . so I don't think about it'" (24). Instead, his thoughts revolve around his fantasy-in-progress, a comic romance: "It was going to be about the love my wife and I had for each other. I was going to show how a pair of lovers in a world gone mad could survive by being loyal only to a nation composed of themselves—a nation of two" (23). It is only fitting, then, that the American intelligence officer, with his eye on the coming war as well as on Campbell's fatal weakness for a masquerade, finally hooks him by presenting a seductive plot of his own, "'a pretty good spy story'" about "'this young American, see, who's been in Germany so long he's practically a German himself'" (25). This, Campbell admits, is his downfall, as the "ham" in him rises to the bait: "As a spy of the sort he described, I would have an opportunity for some pretty grand acting. I would fool everyone with my brilliant interpretation of a Nazi, inside and out" (27). As he is forced to conclude, his private joke is too convincing: "I *did* fool everybody. I began to strut like Hitler's right-hand man, and nobody saw the honest me I hid so deep inside" (27).

Campbell justifies his acting in the role of Nazi propagandist with a view to the same "uncritical love" solicited by any comedian out to please an audience. Whether from his wife, the actress for whom he writes, or from the high-ranking Nazi officials who flock around them both, this is what motivates Campbell along with the love of the masquerade itself: "People used to tell us that we cheered them up, made them want to go on. . . . My Helga believed I meant the things I said about the races of man and the machines of history—and I was grateful. No matter what I was really, no matter what I really meant, uncritical love was what I needed" (29). Eventually, Campbell admits that such love had been a "narcotic" strong enough to blind him to the evil of the people whose approval he had courted. The Nazis, he says, were "a big enthusiastic part" of his audience: "I knew them too well as people, worked too hard in my time for their trust and applause" (25).

But Campbell's convincing comic play throws him into an inescapable double-bind. He cannot admit to the Nazis that he is only joking, for fear of death, nor can he admit it after the war to the American public, who are out for his blood because, as far as they know, he had been serious. Neither side accepts the license to laugh at him or dismiss his play, because they are not offered the convention, even implicitly. This does not diminish the playful nature of Campbell's masquerade; it only makes it more dangerous for both the comedian and his audiences. Campbell reaps the rewards of his ostentatious performance when he is flushed from hiding after the war: "I was high on the list of war criminals, largely because my offenses were so obscenely public" (18). The effectiveness of his masquerade strikes him in all its varied force: war veterans vilify him because they think he believed the lies he told, so to them he is "'absolutely pure evil . . . the pure thing . . . the Devil,'" deserving public scourging and death (163). On the other hand, American Nazis and neo-Nazis crawl out from under their rocks to praise him "'for having the courage to tell the truth during the war . . . when everybody else was telling lies'" (55). But, most chillingly, there are those who are even willing to surmise that Campbell *was* playing and that the play didn't matter. One Nazi accepts that he was probably a spy but dismisses it because he was such a good *actor*—"'Because you could never have served the enemy as well as you served us. . . . Almost all the ideas that I hold now, that make me unashamed of anything I may have felt or done as a Nazi, came not from Hitler, not from Goebbels, not from Himmler—but from you'" (65). Altogether, these three audiences partially demonstrate the truth of Campbell's rueful conclusion that "this is a hard world to be ludicrous in, with so many human beings so reluctant to laugh, so incapable of thought, so eager to believe and snarl and hate" (102–3). But for Campbell, the problem is not so much that laughter is beyond people in general but that he is unable to establish what precisely should be laughed at. With only three people admitted to the convention, his knowing audience is too select.

For this reason, Campbell must conclude that, as an unacknowledged comedian, he is—dangerously—all things to all people. He is an American patriot, a spy who in spite of his patriotism has managed to give aid and comfort to his enemies, and—as even the American intelligence officer admits—a de facto Nazi, "'one of the most vicious sons of bitches who ever lived'" (121). The fact that he was "only kidding" does not prevent the government of Israel from considering him "as much a murderer as Heydrick,

Eichmann, Himmler, or any of the gruesome rest" (102). The fact that Campbell considers his Nazi superiors "ignorant and insane" and himself "neither ignorant nor insane" does not alter what his play ultimately makes him: a Nazi (47). "'How else could a responsible historian classify you?'" he is asked (121). Eventually this knowledge forces Campbell to accept his culpability in playing into the hands of his several audiences, who in their unwitting participation in his jokery are made all the more vile, whether as Nazis, as self-righteous American nationalists, or as hypocrites who blandly encourage his duality for their own purposes.

As a comedian and player of creative games, Campbell finds himself thrust into the company of "'confidence men, prostitutes, and other disturbers of the peace'" (71). As both a comic artist and an American spy, he associates himself with Mata Hari, to whom he initially dedicates his memoirs: "She whored in the interest of espionage, and so did I" (xi). Although Campbell's particular brand of prostitution is avowedly comedic (if only to himself and three others), it is enough to cast him into the vilest fellowship, that of other artists and game players, some comic and some not. Rudolf Hoess, commandant of Auschwitz, proposes a collaboration with him; Adolph Eichmann sees him as a colleague, in terms of not only writing but comedy and Nazism as well: "Eichmann made a joke. 'Listen—' he said, 'about those six million. . . . I can spare you a few for your book. . . . I don't think I really need them all'" (107). Perhaps the most damning association is with the character who is the most bonded to Campbell through the combination of artistry, deceit, and play, the painter George Kraft: "Kraft and I played at least three games a day, every day for a year. And we built up between ourselves a pathetic sort of domesticity that we both felt need of" (37). In this new ludic and creative nation of two, Kraft impresses upon Campbell the extent to which his playful artistry—however appalling—must define him: "'Howard'—he said to me, 'future civilizations . . . are going to judge all men by the extent to which they've been artists. You and I . . . will be judged by the quality of our creations. Nothing else about us will matter'" (38). What Kraft does not know is that the great creation by which Campbell is to be judged is not his dramatic oeuvre but his playful, convincing image as a Nazi.

Eventually, Campbell concludes that his comedic deception has made him a dupe as well as a guilty confidence man: "I committed high treason, crimes against humanity, and crimes against my own conscience" (20). He has allowed himself to be manipulated just as he has manipulated others, and both crimes are equal in his estimation. He is the victim of an entire school of confidence tricksters—Kraft, his best friend, who turns out to be a Russian agent out to expose Campbell as an example of American softness toward war criminals; Resi Noth, also a Russian agent, so effective as to convince Campbell that she is his dead wife, Helga; and the entire American intelligence apparatus, who allowed him to broadcast without his knowledge the disappearance of his wife: "It represented . . . a wider separation of my several selves than even I can bear to think about." With this last scam, Campbell's duality comes back to him as anything but playful, however the result of an initially comic premise: "I would have liked to mourn as an agonized soul, indivisible. But no. One part of me told the world of the tragedy in code. The rest of me did not even know that the announcement was being made" (119). The play of other manipulators thus becomes Campbell's nemesis, dissolving the hubris with which he had initially set out to charm the entire world with his own comic expertise. He finds himself " 'like a pig that's been taken apart, who's had experts find a use for every part. By God—I think they even found a use for my squeal! The part of me that wanted to tell the truth got turned into an expert liar! . . . The artist in me got turned into ugliness such as the world has rarely seen before" (133).

Ultimately, Campbell damns himself for his own willing participation in a monstrous comedy spawned of his own willingness to do to others what—in the end—he finds done to himself. Even as a victim, he is in his own estimation more guilty than Eichmann, deserving brutal "punishments by fair, just men" instead of the psychiatric treatment he feels Eichmann deserves: "My case is different. I always know when I tell a lie, am capable of imagining the cruel consequences of anybody's believing my lies, know cruelty is wrong. I could no more lie without noticing it than I could unknowingly pass a kidney stone" (106). Thus when the American intelligence officer who had recruited him finally admits to the world that Campbell had been in fact " 'one of the most effective agents of the Second World War,' " the comedian's guilt cannot be expiated, and Campbell resolves to "hang Howard W. Campbell, Jr., for crimes against himself" (175). But whether or not Campbell intends this self-inflicted fate, it may be the book's closing joke, not only by virtue of the ham acting with which he bids farewell—"Goodbye, cruel world!"—but also the fact that he has already cried wolf (176). As the rescuing American spymaster asks him, " 'How could I ever trust a man who's been as good a spy as you have?'" (135). Campbell has been too effective a spy; too convincing an actor; and in his mastery of the role, a doomed comedian because of the crucial code he has failed to broadcast until it is too late —the admission of play.

Cat's Cradle: Dangerous, Not Serious

There is one other noteworthy comic deception at work in *Mother Night*: the ostensible editor, signed "Kurt Vonnegut, Jr.," whose duties, it is *claimed*, "are in no sense polemic. They are simply to pass on, in the most satisfactory style, the confessions of Campbell" (ix). It is an old literary device; what counts is precisely the "polemic" the editorial note purports to hide. Campbell—like all critically minded comedians—is guilty of both "informing" and "deceiving," with the conventional demands upon him "enough to make him lie, and to lie without seeing any harm in it" (ix). On the one hand, Campbell's crime—"the crime of his times"—is to have "served evil too openly and good too secretly" (xi). I believe that Vonnegut is not satisfied with so stark a division as his "editor" and namesake here describes—the clear-cut division between good and evil. After all, he has put into the mouth of Campbell, his co-median, the observation that "virtues and vices, pleasures and pains cross boundaries at will" (86). He also suggests this in the fate of his next comedians—Bokonon in *Cat's Cradle*, and his lesser auxiliaries—most of whom, in contrast with Campbell, set out to serve good openly but who end up serving evil either secretly or indirectly. Like Campbell, they are doomed and damned by their play, that is, for their part in hiding or ameliorating the awful truth that any good comic anesthetist wishes to transform into the stuff of comedy.

Cat's Cradle demonstrates what Howard Campbell both justifies and expresses in *Mother Night*: "Say what you will about the sweet miracle of unquestioning faith, I consider a capacity for it terrifying and absolutely vile" (103). In *Cat's Cradle*, however, rather than putting their faith in what turns out to be an undiscovered lie, the dupes of the Bokononist confidence game put their faith in what is openly admitted as a lie. "Nothing in this book is true," the epigraph proclaims, above the injunction to "Live by the *foma* [harmless untruths] that make you brave and kind and healthy and happy" (6). The narrator warns us at the outset that his book will be a Bokononist book, that—just as in *The Books of Bokonon*—the "true things" he relates will all be "shameless lies" (9). On one hand, this is a mere repetition of the ancient argument about comedy holding up a mirror to truth, that—in the words of *Mother Night*'s "Editor" —"lies told for the sake of artistic effect . . . can be, in a higher sense, the most beguiling forms of truth" (ix). But on the other hand, it is the comedian's dare to accept the promise of play for what it ostensibly is, that is, harmless—a dare that the book itself shows to be fatal. Thus, while *Mother Night* warns against a "terrifying and absolutely vile" capacity for "unquestioning faith" in what is offered as true, *Cat's Cradle* warns against faith in what is openly offered as playful falsehood—even as it offers no alternative.

In the world of *Cat's Cradle*, it is pranksters and game players who determine the entire course of events, from the narrator relating the tale, to the actors he describes, to the grinning You Know Who presiding over the joke of Creation. The narrator is a player: "Call me Jonah," he urges, even though his name is John. He is an artist and a liar, a writer who has given up writing "factual" books for "the bittersweet lies" he has learned to tell, and admits telling in an opening gambit (7). His story is about how games, and their appeal, destroy the world, just as they had destroyed Hiroshima in 1945. The end of the world is set in motion by the apparent playfulness of a "seeming Christmas elf," Dr. Felix Hoenikker, the Father of the Atom Bomb (75). As his son, Newt, describes him, " 'He was one of the best-protected human beings who ever lived,' " his protection being that " 'he just wasn't interested in people' "—only in games (14). While Hoenikker's superiors eulogize him for his relentless pursuit of "truth" and "pure knowledge," they fail to appreciate the extent to which it is the charms of play that blind him to the truth of what he wreaks upon the world. As Newt relates, during the days before the successful nuclear test at Alamogordo, Hoenikker " 'just came to work . . . and looked for things to play with and think about, and everything there was to play with and think about had something to do with the bomb' " (16). The end of the world is spawned in a laboratory that looks like a cheap toy shop: "There was a paper kite with a broken spine. There was a toy gyroscope, wound with string, ready to whirr and balance itself. There was a top. . . . There were numerous pieces of conventional laboratory equipment, too, of course, but they seemed drab accessories to the cheap, gay toys" (39). Given that his pursuit of knowledge is actually the pursuit of play, after the test at Alamogordo, Hoenikker can remain at once as merry as one of Santa's elves and as questionably guiltless as Pilate washing his hands. "'Science has now known sin,'" he is told; "'What is sin?'" he asks in reply (17). To Hoenikker, there can be nothing sinful in games.

Thus, with the innocent puzzle of nuclear destruction solved, Hoenikker turns to another game. As his supervisor, Asa Breed, recalls: "'In his playful way, and *all* his ways were playful, Felix suggested that there might be a single grain of something— even a microscopic grain . . . '" (32). This is the birth of *ice-nine*, the seemingly innocent compound that ultimately freezes and destroys the earth; but it is still only a puzzle with which Hoenikker playfully teases his children: "'Come on now, stretch your minds a little. I've told you that its melting point is a hundred and fourteen point four degrees Fahrenheit . . . '" (154). Finally, it is through careless fun that the compound gets into the hands of the children and, through them, into the earth's ecosystem: "Before he sat down in his wicker chair and died, the old man played puddly games in the kitchen with water and pots and pans and *ice-nine*" (155). But play in *Cat's Cradle* is a source of evil, and deadly in its appeal. As Dr. Breed says of Hoenikker and his relentless refusal to see the universe as anything but a playground, "'The man was a force of nature no mortal could possibly control'" (19). And as Breed's disaffected brother asks of such a game player, "'How the hell innocent is a man who helps make a thing like an atomic bomb?'"—let alone *ice-nine* (47).

It is through Felix Hoenniker that Vonnegut extends the paradox of deadly play from science into other realms with the metaphor of the cat's cradle—art, religion, country, comedy: all are damned as deception while simultaneously offered as a saving placebo. The cat's cradle that Newt Hoenikker first describes is the game his father plays before the backdrop of Hiroshima's destruction. Normally, his father has no use for games as other people know them—"'Why should I bother with made-up games when there are so many real ones going on?'"—but on August 6, 1945, he plays his first made-up game with Newt: "'He went down on his knees on the carpet next to me, and he showed me his teeth, and he waved that tangle of string in my face. "See? See? See?" he asked. Cat's cradle. See the cat's cradle? See where the nice pussycat sleeps?'" (13). To Newt, this harmless game comes to stand for everything that is deceitful and sinister: "'For maybe a hundred thousand years or more, grownups have been waving tangles of string in their children's faces. . . . No wonder kids grow up crazy. A cat's cradle is nothing but a bunch of X's between somebody's hands, and little kids look and look and look at all those X's.'" But it is a sick joke—a despicable confidence game: "'No damn cat, and no damn cradle'" (105). For every lie that Newt hears afterwards, his cynical response is, "'See the cat? See the cradle?'" (113, 115). Newt's obsession with the lies of the cat's cradle transform him, at once, into an artist and a ghoulish clown in the effort of painting on canvas the sinister allure of the confidence game: "He put his black, painty hands to his mouth and chin, leaving black smears there. He rubbed his eyes and made black smears around them, too"; and what he offers in the "small and black and warty" painting is equally chilling to Jonah: "It consisted of scratches made in a black, gummy impasto. The scratches formed a sort of spider's web, and I wondered if they might not be the sticky nets of human futility hung up on a moonless night to dry" (105). But it is the embittered doctor, Julian Castle, who interprets the painting of the game most confidently and directly: to him, it is simply "hell" (106).

Julian Castle is perhaps the most complex character participating in the book's comic exchanges, precisely for what he reflects about the incompatibility between social activism and comic pleasure. On the one hand he illustrates Vonnegut's contention that comedy is "merely a response to frustration" intended to divert attention *away* from an unbearable reality; it is Castle, if anybody, who demonstrates Bokonon's claim that "'Maturity . . . is a bitter disappointment for which no remedy exists, unless laughter can be said to remedy anything'" (125). Castle is at once "saintly" in his deeds and "satanic" in his jokery, giggling at the sight of the "stacks of dead" he had valiantly tried to save in a plague epidemic. Yet in spite of his appeal to the saving lies of comedy—as if there could be anything funny in a hospital that "looked like Auschwitz or Buchenwald"—the lies of art mean nothing to him (102). "'Garbage—like everything else,'" he declares, before throwing Newt's painting into a waterfall (107). In Castle one most sees the paradox of the critic at work and the comedian at play; he considers Newt's painting worthless inasmuch as it is art but valuable in another form, drying in the sun along a squalid riverbank: "'This is a poor country—in case you haven't noticed. . . . Four square feet of gummy canvas, the four milled and mitered sticks of the stretcher, some tacks, too. . . . All in all, a pretty nice catch for some poor, poor man'" (112). Yet at the same time, it is the mirage of comedy that enables Castle to cope with his failures in the face of overwhelming odds, just as he recognizes the saving graces of Bokononist fiction: "'I'm grateful for things that work. Not many things *do* work, you know'" (108).

It is fitting that Castle is the man through whom Jonah learns most about the comic duplicity of Bokonon, sensitive as Castle is to the simultaneous combination of play with both cynicism and philanthropy. He describes how Bokonon, upon taking over the "miserable country" in which the book is set, had "cynically and playfully" invented a desensitizing religion intended to divert attention from insurmountable social and economic ills. "'Truth was the enemy of the people, because the truth was so terrible, so Bokonon made it his business to provide the people with better and better lies'" (109). Bokonon's appeal to diversion has its intended effect. In setting himself up as an outlawed holy man, and with his co-conspirator, McCabe, playing the role of the country's dictator, Bokonon ensures that life in San Lorenzo becomes "'a work of art.'" Castle notes the "truth"—that life for the people is "'as short and brutish and mean as ever'"—but, doctor that he is, he can also see the placebo effect of the Bokonon/McCabe masquerade: "'As the living legend of the cruel tyrant in the city and the gentle holy man in the jungle grew, so, too, did the happiness of the people grow. They were all employed full time as actors in a play they understood, that any human being anywhere could understand and applaud'" (110).

But the people of San Lorenzo are *aware* that they are participating in a confidence game. Unlike the victims of Howard Campbell's masquerade, they know that they are involved in an elaborate joke at the hands of a pair of sophisticated manipulators —their bible tells them so. One of the "Calypsos" in *The Books of Bokonon* establishes the comic convention outright: "I wanted all things / To seem to make some sense, / So we all could be happy, yes, / Instead of tense. / And I made up lies / So that they all fit nice, / and I made this sad world / A par-a-dise" (82–83). Their bible itself is a joke, and admits itself as such, warning each reader on the first page, "Don't be a fool! Close this book at once! It is nothing but *foma*!" (165). As Castle tells Jonah, the pressures of maintaining the comic deception take their toll on the "'two main actors, McCabe and Bokonon. . . . [who] paid a terrible price in agony for the happiness of the people—McCabe knowing the agony of the tyrant and Bokonon knowing the agony of the saint. They both became, for practical purposes, insane'" (110–11).

What Castle never learns before his death is that the people of San Lorenzo *also* pay—with their lives—for the pleasures of succumbing to Bokonon's deceptions. The comedian as saint becomes the comedian as Satan, with Bokonon transformed into an evil manipulator along the lines of Jim Jones, compelling the mass suicide of his surviving followers after the freezing of the earth through the legacy of Hoenikker's play, *ice-nine*. Even in this act, the comedian acknowledges himself as such, leaving a note at the death site: "These people made a captive of the spurious holy man named Bokonon. . . . The mountebank told them that God was surely trying to kill them, possibly because He was through with them, and that they should have the good manners to die. This, as you can see, they did" (170). Thus, in taking the joke to its fullest possible extent, all the willing players in Bokonon's comedy are destroyed.

There is one other comedian at play in *Cat's Cradle*, the cynical Prankster who seems to preside over life and death as though they are part of a joke with which he has long ago grown tired. The creation of man appears the listless diversion of an all-powerful entity with an eternity on his hands, at least in *The Books of Bokonon*: "In the beginning, God created the earth, and he looked upon it in His cosmic loneliness." This lonely deity needs both playthings and an adoring audience: "And God said, 'Let Us make living creatures out of mud, so the mud can see what We have done." Bokonon's God gets bored easily, declining to play long enough to confer any purpose upon his creation; it *all* appears an idle game: "And He went away" (165–66). Bokonon himself plans to get the last laugh, as he writes in the final sentence of his holy book, wherein he follows his flock into ingesting *ice-nine*: "I would make a statue of myself, lying on my back, grinning horribly, and thumbing my nose at You Know Who" (179). But it is the Great Comedian who remains, serenely acknowledging his practical joke and, apparently, quite pleased with his comic mastery, as the Bokononist "Calypso" has it: "Someday, someday, this crazy world will have to end, / And our God will take things back that He to us did lend. / And if, on that sad day, you want to scold our God, / Why, go right ahead and scold Him. He'll just smile and nod" (168).

Thus, *Cat's Cradle* and *Mother Night* together depict two sides of the ironic coin: the risks of taking ironic play at face value and the risks of not doing so. It is a recipe for crisis, not only with regard to the negativity or "nothingness" left in irony's wake (as described by Kierkegaard) but also to the insoluble plurality—the schizophrenia—that Vonnegut went on to demonstrate in his successive writings. Nothingness and schizophrenia seem to have posed the most extreme threats to the longevity of the comic masquerade as Vonnegut has explored it and are the preoccupation of many characters following on the heels of Howard Campbell and Bokonon—including one variously named "I," "me," and "the author of this book."

Toward *Breakfast of Champions*: A Crisis of Confidence

When Joseph Heller published *Closing Time*, his sequel to *Catch-22*, in October 1994, the reviewer for the *New Yorker* noted the absence of one particular comic voice from the World War II generation: "Kurt Vonnegut seems to have had his say," he wrote.[21] Vonnegut had already signaled this playfully in the American edition of *Bluebeard* (1987) when, having listed all his fifteen published titles on the opening page, he exclaimed, "Enough, enough!" As he explained elsewhere, this game of being continually funny was "tiring"; but then he went on to offer his next novel, *Hocus Pocus* (1990), and his third "autobiographical collage," *Fates Worse than Death* (1991).[22] It may have been too early to propose in late 1994 that Vonnegut had finally given up the game; but one could be forgiven, since so much of Vonnegut's writing had already documented the struggles of an American comic voice to survive the premise that ironic play can be a substitute for earnest criticism. About the time he published *Breakfast of Champions* (1973), Vonnegut lied in a *Playboy* interview, "As I get older, I get more didactic. I say what I really think. I don't hide ideas like Easter eggs for people to find. Now, if I have an idea, when something becomes clear to me, I don't embed it in a novel; I simply write it out in an essay as clearly as I can."[23] Perhaps "lie" is too strong an accusation; it might be more fair to say that Vonnegut was indulging in wishful thinking, expressing at a particularly difficult time in his life his exasperation with the demands of comic deceit. He was fifty years old, having reached what he calls in *Breakfast of Champions* his "spiritual crossroads." But many critics, as well as Vonnegut himself, have seen that point more as a nadir than as "the spine of a roof" from which Vonnegut describes his descent into old age.[24]

Lawrence Broer divides his chronological study, *Sanity Plea: Schizophrenia in the Novels of Kurt Vonnegut*, into two telling sections: the first part, entitled "The Struggle," begins with the first novel, *Player Piano* (1952), and culminates in *Breakfast of Champions*.

Thenceforth comes "Resolution: The Second Fifty Years"—as though from *Breakfast of Champions* there was no direction Vonnegut could go except up. The importance of this novel cannot be overemphasized, showing as it does the comedian on the edge, stretching the limits of his confidence game to a breaking point at which both he and the game itself are ravaged. The comedian may be Kilgore Trout, or he may be the fictive Vonnegut who steps into the action as a duplicitous, ironic deus ex machina; in either case he is on the brink of madness, tormented by the relentless demands of play. Broer reports that in a personal letter on the subject of his book—Vonnegut's renderings of schizophrenia—Vonnegut expressed the hope that no one would think *he* was crazy. "'I haven't ever hallucinated, or been hospitalized or incapacitated for mental illness of any sort. I have been profoundly depressed, but have always been able to keep working somehow.'"[25] It would be truly irresponsible to confuse the living Vonnegut with any of his characters, including the paradoxical, highly self-conscious public persona that he has constructed for himself over the decades. While leaving the historical Vonnegut in the peace he deserves, it *is* possible to suggest that the public persona does in itself suggest a "schizophrenic episode," artistic rather than clinical, encapsulated in the two-faced identity of a literary comedian, a serious critic apparently at play.

As Broer notes, pretense is "the main schizophrenic game," one that Vonnegut has repeatedly illustrated as taking its toll upon the players.[26] In spite of admitting the artful construction of his own "theatrical stances," he warned early in his career about the capacity for games to divert attention from social realities, in places other than the pages of *Mother Night* and *Cat's Cradle*. Of games, he has said, "Parker Bros. has one for every gathering . . . and there's a game for every season—ice hockey, basketball, baseball, football. Life soon appears to be a game, and it isn't."[27] The ironic paradox of warning against play through a playful stance signifies the artistic schizophrenia to which I refer above: creativity is a game in the world of affairs, but it is nonetheless potentially deadly, whether in the hands of scientists, politicians, artists, or the public who subscribe to their diversions (as both *Mother Night* and *Cat's Cradle* show). But the psychic toll on the artist of perpetuating the game against his own will or inclination, and the consequences of being trapped in an ironic double-bind, extend beyond the "crimes against himself" described by Howard Campbell.

Vonnegut has in fact explored this artistic entrapment to some degree in all his works and has gone far to demonstrate why a confidence man may ultimately want to escape from the identifying role he has created. Referring in one instance to Jackson Pollock, he lamented that "people are doomed to be the sorts of artists they are." Pollock, he said, "lacked maneuverability, because he was in fact trapped both by society and by his own particular talent into doing what he did. . . . Pollock killed himself—because he thought, Christ, I'm going to have to keep doing this for the rest of my life."[28] The longing for the release from an entrapping role that has in fact become an identity, and which Vonnegut ascribes to Pollock, is akin to that which motivates Howard Campbell toward his own "death worshipping." As Campbell admits: "I, hiding from many people who might want to hurt or kill me, often longed for someone to give that cry for me, to end my endless game of hide-and-seek with a sweet and mournful—'Olly-olly-ox-in-free'" (16). Campbell promises to escape from the psychic consequences of his play with the aid of a hangman's noose; but Vonnegut does not offer that route for all his other characters who likewise find themselves entrapped in play worlds of their own making. For most of them, there are two possibilities: madness or withdrawal from the game. A comedian, through his play, wishes like Campbell to "hide from many people who might want to hurt" him (if not kill him) for the implications behind his jokes. In this respect, Vonnegut's many tormented characters are allegorical renderings of comedians who are trapped in a similarly intolerable game of hide-and-seek.

What Leonard Mustazza says about *Cat's Cradle* applies to all such renderings, which explore "the problematical relationship between human creativity and destructiveness"; in these cases, the creativity is comic, and the destructiveness just as likely to be the threat of self-destruction.[29] Tony Tanner's observations about *Cat's Cradle* may also be expanded to include all of Vonnegut's comedians who are threatened by "the ambiguities of man's disposition to play and invent"; and the threat shows itself in the many novels following *Mother Night* and *Cat's Cradle*.[30] It shows itself in the story of Eliot Rosewater, the protagonist in a comedy he tries to bring to the lives of the dispossessed and neglected in *God Bless You, Mr. Rosewater* (1965). "'I'm going to be an artist,'" he declares, "'I'm going to love these discarded Americans, even though they're useless and unattractive. *That* is going to be my work of art'"—and for his pains in attempting to bestow "uncritical love" upon them, he is made to fight for his sanity amidst "the straightjacket, the shock treatments, the suicide attempts" that are the price of his impossible play.[31] When Rosewater steps from his own novel into *Slaughterhouse-Five* (1969), it is as a mental patient sharing a room with a fellow would-be comedian, Billy Pilgrim. Both of them, having "found life meaningless, partly because of what they had seen in war," attempt "to re-invent themselves and their universe" through the mendacious consolations of comic science-fiction. As Rosewater tells a psychiatrist, " 'I think you guys are going to have to come up with a lot of wonderful *new* lies, or people just aren't going to want to go on living.' " For Billy, the lie through which he tries to divert his attention from the genocide he has witnessed is the construction of a comic fantasy set on the planet Tralfamadore, populated by outlandish creatures, "two feet high, and green, and shaped like plumber's friends."[32] In Billy's fantasy there is neither chronological time nor death; thus genocide is an impossibility. But not only are his comedic self-deceptions powerless to protect him from recurrent mental collapse, hysteria, and death-wish; they may in fact be the actual cause if not the symptoms. Both Rosewater and Billy Pilgrim demonstrate the strain of maintaining a comic outlook in the face of tragic reality.

Two more threatened comedians flounder in the wake of *Mother Night* and *Cat's Cradle*. The first is Kilgore Trout, the neglected writer whose bizarre stories are fittingly reduced to pornographic pulp, given that—as comedy—they share with pornography "fantasies of an impossibly hospitable world." In *God Bless You, Mr. Rosewater*, Trout is likened to "a frightened, ageing Jesus, whose sentence to crucifixion had been commuted to imprisonment for life"—and who, although he "had never tried to tell anything but the truth," is at the same time "an ultimately dishonest man."[33] Although Trout does not appear in *Slaughterhouse-Five*, his stories do, poisoning the minds of Rosewater and Billy Pilgrim with the sort of comic inspiration that turns them into inept liars about their own "impossibly hospitable world." *Slaughterhouse-Five* also introduces the last of the comedians sentenced to "imprisonment for life" in a mendacious role: this is the "I," the "me," the "author of this book"—the "old fart with his memories and Pall Malls" who dares to affect with Billy Pilgrim a serenity in the face of assassinations and massacres: "So it goes."[34] These latter two comedians— Kilgore Trout and the fictive "I"—are, of all Vonnegut's characters, the two who threaten to come closest to the Jackson Pollock described above: literally "doomed" in being the kinds of artists they are, overwhelmingly depressed, and seemingly without the maneuverability to escape from their ironic identities, short of their own extinction. Their perilous encounter constitutes the nadir of Vonnegut's career-long disquisition on the comedian as confidence man: they meet in *Breakfast of Champions*, in the company of one other noteworthy confidence man, Rabo Karabekian, the artist-trickster figure important enough to return as the subject of *Bluebeard*. Together, these three comedians demonstrate the crisis point to which Vonnegut had apparently brought himself in the struggle to negotiate the conflicting demands of the critic at warning and the comedian at play.

In *Breakfast of Champions*, Vonnegut is most explicit in confronting the possibility of suicide as a means of escaping from the entrapping irony, and the finished book is offered as his promise that he is beyond such a solution. Before his having written it, he suggested, suicide had come to seem "a perfectly reasonable way" of avoiding any number of confrontations, including the delivery of comic lectures and books to deadlines; "I think I'll blow my brains out" might have been the answer to the simplest of problems.[35] One indication of this crisis point is the startling narrative interruption in *Breakfast of Champions*, wherein the fictive Vonnegut tells himself, "'This is a very bad book you're writing. . . . You're afraid you'll kill yourself the way your mother did'" (193). The threat appears always to hang in the background until the action is completed, by which time the renderings of Trout, Karabekian, and the duplicitous "Vonnegut" himself are shown as the exorcisms—however temporary—of contempt for the practice of comic deceit.

Vonnegut's handling of these three characters deserves close attention, for it resonates with his ambivalence and disgust over the implications of their mendacity, and that of all artists, comic or otherwise. The device that brings these three together is an arts festival in the imaginary Midland City, Ohio. It is an occasion that allows Vonnegut to explore the dangers of creative charm—its manipulation, mystification, and downright vileness—through the impact it has on both its practitioners and its victims. Vonnegut's warning is clear: "I can have oodles of charm when I want to." He echoes what Melville implies in both *Israel Potter* and *The Confidence-Man*, that the more charming an artist is, the more dangerous: "Charm was a scheme for making strangers like and trust a person immediately, no matter what the charmer had in mind" (20). Although Kilgore Trout may have no personal charm, his comic stories do—enough to secure his invitation to the arts festival, and to work *too* well upon the mind of at least one reader credulous enough to take him seriously. Dwayne Hoover, on the brink of madness, craves comedy, wanting "to laugh at his troubles, to go on living, and to keep out of the North Wing of the Midland County General Hospital, which [is] for lunatics." He is ripe for exploitation by any artistic trickster, "so open to new suggestions about the meaning of life that he [is] easily hypnotized" (195–96). The comic premise of one of Trout's stories—the ironic suggestion that the reader is the only organism of value in the universe—sends the unstable Dwayne into a violent rampage that leaves a score of injured in his wake. Given his realization that there is "no immunity to cuckoo ideas on Earth" (27), Trout is forced to accept his own guilt as the source of the "mind poison" that triggers the carnage. It does not matter that, like all comedians, he is only kidding: "Trout did not expect to be believed. . . . It shook up Trout to realize that even *he* could bring evil into the world—in the form of bad ideas" (15). In this, Trout stands as the comedian condemned.

Moreover, as a purveyor of "evil nonsense," Trout is obliged to admit his kinship with any number of playful deceivers, whose "nonsense was evil, since it concealed great crimes" (10). One of these, it is clear, is the second artistic confidence man to bear Vonnegut's scorn in *Breakfast of Champions*, the minimalist painter, Rabo Karabekian. Having sold his painting, "The Temptation of Saint Anthony," to the arts festival, Karabekian is forced to defend himself against irate citizens who are astounded to have been tricked into paying him "fifty thousand dollars for sticking a piece of yellow tape to a green piece of canvas" (214). He defends his work, and the price, with a spiel of rhetoric that, however eloquent, is invalid and a swindle. He gives his "'word of honor'" that this painting—already described as "meaningless"—depicts "'everything about life which truly matters, with nothing left out. It is a picture of the awareness of every animal'" (221). But how reliable is the "word of honor" of a man who admits to having "'no use for truth'"? As he says, "'You know what truth is?. . . It's some crazy thing my neighbor believes. If I want to make friends with him, I ask him what he believes. He tells me, and I say, "Yeah, yeah—ain't it the truth?"'" (209). Given his characterization as a shyster who "with his meaningless pictures had entered into a conspiracy with millionaires to make poor people feel stupid," it is clear that Karabekian's artistic "nonsense" is no less evil than Trout's (209). His painting is a joke, as is his pompous defense, neither of which earns Vonnegut's respect. With no little sarcasm, Vonnegut calls Karabekian's mumbo jumbo "the spiritual climax of this book, for it is at this point that I, the author, am suddenly transformed by what I have done so far" (218). He goes on to ridicule Karabekian's self-eulogy with more mock suggestions of his having been transformed by the avowed meaning of a "meaningless" painting. He assigns Karabekian's "unwavering band of light"—the vertical strip which is supposed to depict awareness—to the cores of so many characters that it becomes ridiculous. Of Kilgore Trout: "His situation, insofar as he was a machine, was complex, tragic, and laughable. But the sacred part of him, his awareness, remained an unwavering band of light." Of himself: "And this book is being written by a meat machine in cooperation with a machine made of metal and plastic. . . . And at the core of the writing meat machine is something sacred, which is an unwavering band of light." Of the reader: "At the core of each person who reads this book is a band of unwavering light" (225). Even Einstein's Theory of Relativity, $E=MC^2$, needs the revelations of the indispensable Karabekian to complete it: "It was a flawed equation, as far as I was concerned. There should have been an 'A' in there somewhere for *Awareness*" (241). He stops the action to carry the point home: "My doorbell has just rung in my New York apartment. And I know what I will find when I open my front door: an unwavering band of light." He concludes with a heavy dose of mock praise: "God bless Rabo Karabekian!" (225).

Given the narrator's own duplicitous voice and character, a perceptive reader like Leonard Mustazza may well take such praise at face value and conclude that this painting—this practical joke—could actually "rescue [the narrator] from doubt and give him the serenity he has long sought." But in accepting Karabekian's explanation that "the only ennobling feature of life is awareness, sacred consciousness, the unwavering band of light that animates the dead machinery of the body," Mustazza may also have been taken in—especially given the importance Vonnegut has always placed on *activity* as the means of social improvement, beyond mere "awareness."[36] Certainly, the citizens themselves are duped: prepared, only moments before, to lynch Karabekian for his swindle, they congratulate him for his explanation, saying, " 'If artists would explain more, people would like art more' " (235–36). In obliging them with a mystifying explanation, Karabekian doubly swindles them. They are still fifty-thousand dollars poorer, however mollified, and however more "aware" they may be about what the painting is supposed to represent. And in accepting at face value the narrator's assertion that "it is Rabo Karabekian who made me the serene Earthling which I am this day," the reader, too, is swindled (220).

The narrator is, after all, neither serene nor trustworthy, the third of the book's comedians to draw Vonnegut's rebuke. The narrator is both wounded and wounding, as he sits mouthing the word *schizophrenia*, "fascinated" by its appearance, its sound, and the slapstick image it conjures up of "a human being sneezing in a blizzard of soapflakes" (193). He admits his unsureness as to whether or not he has "that disease," and in one precarious moment appears to abdicate from all critical observation, worn down by the consequences: "I was making myself hideously uncomfortable by not narrowing my attention to details of life which were immediately important, and by refusing to believe what my neighbors believed" (194). It is, of course, incredible that Vonnegut could advocate the setting aside of the critical perspective in exchange for the willful adoption of blinders, in order to fit in with one's neighbors. Thus, as in *Slaughterhouse-Five*, his affectation of serenity here is not wholly convincing, especially given the scornful manner in which he depicts *himself* as a devious confidence man. The "I" of the book is a tyrannical user, inscrutable in his mirrored sunglasses, appearing in Midland City to gloat over his creative powers and to affirm his Godlike status: "I was on a par with the Creator of the Universe there in the dark in the cocktail lounge. I shrunk the Universe to a ball exactly one light-year in diameter. I had it explode. I had it disperse itself again." But he is really a petty trickster, a cheap vaudeville magician with cheap tricks, taking advantage of powerless characters and a credulous, willing audience: "Ask me a question, any question. How old is the Universe? It is one half-second old, but that half-second has lasted one quintillion years so far" (201). He reserves his greatest duplicity for poor old Kilgore Trout, the one character to whom he reveals himself at the end of the book, vilely playing with him like a cat with a mouse. Confronting the embittered, broken comedian as his omnipotent Creator, "Vonnegut" boasts: " 'I don't need a gun to control you, Mr. Trout. All I have to do is write something down about you, and that's it." And, as the Superior Manipulator, he proves it: "I transported him to the Taj Mahal and then to Venice and then to Dar es Salaam and then to the surface of the Sun, where the flames could not consume him" (292). As the old man crashes to his knees and cowers before him, the Creator teases him with the promise of comfort and release from literary servitude: "'Mr. Trout, I love you. . . . I have broken your mind to pieces. I want you to feel a wholeness and inner harmony such as I have never allowed you to feel before.'" But he is setting up Trout for a mean trick, casting him in the same vulnerable position as any dupe seeking the comforting delusions of comedy and art. He makes Trout think he is offering a mouth-watering, perfect apple, describing it with the saccharine eloquence of a veritable Karabekian: "'I hold in my hand a symbol of wholeness and harmony and nourishment.'" However, it is all a con; having made Trout see this tempting symbol, the narrator complacently admits to sheer sleight-of-hand in a smug aside to the reader: "'I had nothing in my hand, but such was my power over Trout that he would see in it whatever I wished him to see'" (292–93). As an artist and a jokester, this "Vonnegut" is as oily, devious, and sinister as any Confidence-Man—and cruelly playful as well. Tiring of his practical joke at Trout's expense, the narrator disappears, leaving his character an abandoned old man, crying after him into the void, "'*Make me young, make me young, make me young!*'" (295). If this is a depiction of a "serene" narrator, it must be the serenity of a man without a conscience—and this cannot be the case, given the book's final page: a self-portrait of a weeping Kurt Vonnegut.

With his depictions of these three comedians, Vonnegut condemns in *Breakfast of Champions* not only those who allow their attention to be diverted by comedic or artistic seduction, but also himself and all artists who, through their creativity and misplaced self-importance, are embarked on a truly monstrous deception. By calling attention to his own confidence game as an artist and comedian, he warns that escapism into art and comedy may well assist in the process of adaptation, but that it may also amount to self-blinding with dangerous consequences. By the end of the book, Vonnegut has pitted the comedian against himself in an apparent effort to somehow accept or adapt to the notion of, on the one hand, the comedian's questionable social usefulness, and on the other, his wickedly seductive power. As a confrontation with the comic self, *Breakfast of Champions* appears to have been an exorcism of profound bitterness and contempt for the requirements of playful deceit; and in reviewing Vonnegut's oeuvre, one can indeed see that there was no way he could go but up. But in his ascent, as it appears, the comedian was also and ever on the way out.

Laughing Like Hell

I would like to admit, after Lawrence Broer, that the period following *Breakfast of Champions* has been one of "resolution," at least in the sense that none of Vonnegut's succeeding comedians evince the same depth of bitterness that Kilgore Trout and the "I" of that novel do. But I would not go so far as to say that the paradox of the critic at warning and the comedian at play is ever comfortably resolved in Vonnegut's later writings. If anything, there is only a resigned preparedness to be recurrently foiled by the paradox rather than utterly destroyed by it; either that or there is the decision to dispense with the masquerade altogether, as Wilbur and Eliza Swain do in *Slapstick*. What comes after *Breakfast of Champions*— or, arguably, not until the demons of *Slapstick* are exorcised—is, I would admit, "Vonnegut's softer focus" as described by Michael Wood.[37] But this period, ushered in by *Jailbird* (1979), is not free of Vonnegut's rebellion against the constraints of the comic straitjacket, signaled in other places besides the avowed renunciations in *Slapstick*, *Hocus Pocus*, and *Fates Worse than Death* mentioned earlier. Such rebellion is flagged in the various failures or inabilities of all Vonnegut's narrators—from the recidivist jailbird Walter Starbuck on—to convince themselves of either the efficacy or the righteousness of their play. Perhaps the only exception to this rule would be Leon Trotsky Trout, the ghostly narrator of *Galapagos* (1985), who can offer Vonnegut's most joyful narrative only after his father Kilgore's misanthropic solution to the problem of deceitful mankind has come to pass. Kilgore Trout, it will be recalled, suggests the biblical Flood as the ideal conservation measure in *Breakfast of Champions*. Thus, his son can be an unbridled optimist only in the context of "A Second Noah's Ark"—that is, after humans and their oversized brains have been wiped out en masse through the combination of their economic and military madness and a natural virus, leaving only a handful to evolve into the harmless, furry pranksters and fisherfolk of Santa Rosalia, the fictive Galapagos island.[38] While I readily agree with Leonard Mustazza that, in *Galapagos*, Vonnegut is not "advocating a return to the Stone Age" and that "he likes and admires people too much to wish that they would turn into laughing animals," it is significant that he must go to such lengths to depict a genuine optimist.[39]

In the year 1,001,986, with no capacity for dangerous opinions, suggestions, or evil tool-making, humans—with their puny brains and flipperlike hands—are like the trained sea lions and seals that Leon Trout recalls in his childhood circuses of over a million years before. They are pranksters who can "balance balls on their noses and blow horns and clap their flippers on cue" but who can "never have loaded and cocked a machine gun, or pulled the pin on a hand grenade and thrown it any distance with any accuracy" (123). Thus, there are only innocent, harmless things to inspire comedy: "And people still laugh about as much as they ever did, despite their shrunken brains. If a bunch of them are lying around on a beach, and one of them farts, everybody else laughs and laughs, just as people would have done a million years ago" (165). Most important, the association between play and mendacity is finally broken, although the memory of the "distracting and irrelevant and destructive . . . great big brains of a million years ago" still enrages Trout: "If they had told the truth, then I could see some point in everybody's having one. But these things lied all the time!" (141). There are still the dangers of complacent distractions on Galapagos, but they have nothing to do with laughter; only full bellies in the company of sharks. There can be no belly full of lies, comic or otherwise, as in the tenth previous millennium, since lies no longer exist. Thus, in this ideal setting, where there is "still hope for mankind," the consolations of art are needless, given that there is no longer anything to inspire them: "Nobody, surely, is going to write Beethoven's Ninth Symphony—or tell a lie, or start a Third World War" (208). The loss of music and comedy is a small price to pay for a world that can be genuinely optimistic.

But back in the twentieth century, Vonnegut's latter narrators can only attempt to affect optimism in the lackluster efforts of sad and wounded old men who are only too aware of the agonies they wish to ameliorate with their comic self-deceptions. Thus, the narrators of *Jailbird* and *Deadeye Dick* (1982) both betray their lack of faith in the artistic or otherwise imaginative games to which they resort. In both novels, comedy is signaled as an unsuccessful evasion. In *Jailbird*, Starbuck, the aged namesake (ironically) of the truth teller in *Moby-Dick*, actually attempts to adopt the "free and easy sort of genial, desperado philosophy" that sustains Ishmael through the nightmare voyage under Ahab. This second Starbuck tries, like Ishmael, to see the vicissitudes of his life as a "vast practical joke," or, as he variously describes it, as "this dream," "theater," or "musical comedy."[40] Other than in his references to the diversions of comedy as "narcotic," Starbuck is a failed comedian only implicitly, if importantly. He resorts to comic songs like "Sally in the Garden" for the purposes of "mental vacancy"—to clear his mind of his mistakes, his bereavements, his son's contempt, his betrayals of friends to the inquisitors of the HUAC, and his terror of the future on the outside after his Watergate imprisonment (8). He indulges in comic escapism through the benefits of mental time travel and the unlikely dream of modest bartending with his "Doctor of Mixology" degree, enjoying fragile illusions of his own self-respect with the repeated comic punchline, "At least I don't smoke anymore." But his escapist time travel forces him to confront bitter memories as well as the imminent future of an old derelict; and his dreams become nightmares of self-betrayal and the betrayals of others. Ultimately, Starbuck's songs, fantasies, and jokes keep him from neither the padded cell nor the prison, and his comic illusions are the half-hearted graspings at fragile straws by a man who has lost faith in the saving power of his own lies. More than anything else, what presides over *Jailbird* is Starbuck's outright shame in his indelible buffoonery, from the opening of his narrative—"Life goes on, yes—and a fool and his self-respect are soon parted, perhaps never to be reunited even on Judgement Day" (1)—to his closing complaints about the culture of levity. "'You know what is finally going to kill this planet?'" he asks. "'A total lack of seriousness,'" he answers—and proceeds, in his failure, to give up "on saying anything serious," tells one last joke, and sits down (238–39).

In the context of this discussion, greater attention is owed to Rudy Waltz, the narrator of *Deadeye Dick*, given that, unlike in *Jailbird*, the association with comedy as a deliberate practice is much more explicit. Like Starbuck, Rudy is forced to admit the failure of a comic outlook in shielding him from criminal recollections, but in his case the admission is that of a self-acknowledged comedian. Moreover, in allegorical terms, the associations between crime, quackery, art, and comedy are as strong as in *Mother Night*; comedy and art are in fact complicit with crime. In this respect, *Deadeye Dick* refers not only backwards but forwards as well, to the artistic confidence games of Rabo Karabekian in *Bluebeard* (with its explicit renunciation of comedy) and beyond, to the deliberate comic vacuum of *Hocus Pocus*. The criminal associations in *Deadeye Dick* begin with the childhood game that sets the action in motion, recollected—significantly enough, after *Breakfast of Champions*—by a depressed fifty-year-old narrator. Rudy reconstructs through "a leaky old memory" a history of unsuccessful evasion of the consequences of an imaginative, though deadly, game.[41] Through his criminal play—which, in the preface, Vonnegut calls a symbol of "all the bad things I have done"—Rudy causes the shotgun death of a pregnant mother of two (9). It happens, Rudy recalls, through the seductive power of playful creativity, and the potency of symbolism. On Mother's Day in 1944, with his brother gone to war, Rudy is a twelve-year-old playing with a rifle in his father's gun room, in a childish daydream: "I wanted to sit up there for a while, and look out over the roofs of the town, supposing that my brother might be going to his death, and hearing and feeling the tanks in the street below. Ah, sweet mystery of life" (55). As an artist at creative play, he elects to use a real bullet on justifiable artistic grounds: "The bullet was a symbol, and nobody was ever hurt by a symbol. It was a farewell to my childhood and a confirmation of my manhood. Why didn't I use a blank cartridge? What kind of symbol would that have been?" (56). Now as an artist with blood on his hands, he joins company with other creative reprobates: his father, a Nazi sympathizer with no talent and an easel like a "guillotine"; Adolf Hitler, the budding young painter whom his father saves from starvation; Rabo Karabekian, about to sell his "Temptation of Saint Anthony" to the Midland City Arts Center for an unbelievable sum; and, as the preface asserts, Vonnegut as the guilty "I." Rudy looks back to his estrangement from innocent fellowship, imagining a bell hung around his neck as in the Dark Ages, himself a "leper" who, through play, has "shaken hands with Death" (83). He documents his attempts to utilize other creative palliatives as a means of escaping what his play has done: "I wanted to get into bed and pull the covers over my head. That was my plan. That is still pretty much my plan" (70).

Comedy, as we shall see, is both implicitly and explicitly a tool of Rudy's attempted evasion; and given Vonnegut's consistent references to comedy as a sugar-coated pill, a "narcotic," and other such pharmaceutical deceivers, it is significant that Rudy, like his failed artist of a father, is a pharmacist—a role that Vonnegut also uses as a symbol for himself in the preface. The connection between comic deceit, evasion, and harmful drugs is quite clear: Rudy's family fortune is based on the legacy of "a quack medicine known as 'Saint Elmo's Remedy'" (13). Even in trying to escape this legacy through an attempt at writing comic plays, Rudy is thrown into the role of a drug salesman, repeating the association of writing with drug-selling established by Philip Castle in *Cat's Cradle*. Rudy recalls, "The night I told Father I wanted to be a writer . . . he ordered me to become a pharmacist instead, which I did." His father had ordered him, "Be a pharmacist! Go with the grain of your heritage!"—a heritage, of course, based on pharmaceutical quackery (96). There is a more sinister presence than "Saint Elmo's Remedy," however, in what Rudy calls the "era of pharmaceutical buffoonery." The Waltz Brothers' Drugstore trades on "barbiturates and amphetamines and methaqualones and so on" (39); Celia Hoover's suicide is attributed to "psychosis, often indistinguishable from schizophrenia" brought on by her amphetamine abuse; and Rudy's brother ends up "bombed on Darvon and Ritalin and methaqualone and Valium, and God knows what else" (151). The contempt Rudy feels for the local doctor who sells his soul even as he sells his painkillers, cannot be disassociated from Vonnegut's references to the drugs of comic evasion. If a buffoon can be a pharmacist or a prescribing doctor, then a comedian, too, can build up "a big practice on the principle that nobody in modern times should ever be the least uncomfortable or dissatisfied, since there were now pills for everything" (131). When Rudy finally *does* write a play, and the New York critics pan it, they find it "hilarious" that the playwright should hold a pharmacy degree: but it is not so odd given that comedy is, as Vonnegut says, a drug.

As a budding playwright, Rudy's first inspiration is a comedian: "James Thurber, who had grown up right there in Columbus, and then gone on to New York City to write comically about the same sorts of people I had known in Midland City" (97). Even as he earns his pharmacy degree, Rudy studies play writing, hoping to follow in Thurber's footsteps. This merely continues an association with comedy into which he has already been cast through his crime of homicide. He has already starred in what he calls "The Rudy Waltz Show," produced by the policemen who fingerprint him and roll his face in ink until he looks like a blackface minstrel, caged and put on display behind bars: "I was a geek. I was a wild man from Borneo. . . . I was regional theater." Moreover, this demeaning exhibition is not distinct from the writing career he is to adopt later, thanks to the mention of Alexander Woollcott: "He coined that wonderful epithet for writers, 'ink-stained wretches.' He should have seen me in my cage" (67).

The comic plays that Rudy creates in his adulthood are failures, and acknowledged as such. As he says, "The consequences of my having shot a pregnant woman were bound to be complicated beyond belief"; and so he attempts comic renderings of such consequences anytime he is brought face to face with the guilt and agony of them: "I have this trick for dealing with all my worst memories. I insist that they are plays. The characters are actors.

Their speeches and movements are stylized, arch. I am in the presence of art" (71). Art has got him into this and art—notably comic art—will get him out, or so he thinks. He imagines a number of comic "playlets" designed to ameliorate the pain of a "confrontation scene" with Dwayne Hoover (159); or the deterioration of his beautiful muse, Celia, into an addled drug abuser—his "crazy-old-lady play" (144); or "Duplex, A New Comedy by Rudy Waltz," through which he attempts to cope with his family's contempt for him and his own self-contempt. As the character description reads: *"On the balcony sits* RUDY WALTZ. . . . *He considers himself a big mistake. He considers life a big mistake. It probably shouldn't be going on. It is all he can do to give life the benefit of the doubt"* (110). Finally, there is his flop, *Katmandu*, about Shangri-La, where nobody—including a pregnant mother of two—ever dies, "where no one ever tried to hurt anybody else, and where everybody was happy and nobody grew old" (93). As if to confirm the failure of these comic visions to mask the unbearable—and even the criminality of the *attempt* to mask it—Rudy's ironic code name for the rubble of Midland City, neutron-bombed by a duplicitous American government, is "Shangri-La" (94).

There is one other significant indication of Vonnegut's censure of the comic practice in *Deadeye Dick*, again a reference to *Breakfast of Champions*. At Celia Hoover's funeral, Rudy writes a veritable Kilgore Trout story in his head: "There was no reason to take us seriously as individuals. Celia in her casket there, all shot through with Drāno and amphetamine, might have been a dead cell sloughed off by a pancreas the size of the Milky Way." Rudy finds himself "smiling at a funeral," in spite of himself: "How comical that I, a single cell, should take my life so seriously." But the would-be comedian is upbraided smartly: "I stopped smiling. I glanced around to see if anyone had noticed. One person had. He was at the other end of our pew, and he did not look away when I caught him gazing at me. . . . He was wearing large sunglasses with mirrored lenses" (156–57). Thus, with his Creator having come from the pages of *Breakfast of Champions* to give him the evil eye, Rudy concludes in his epilogue, "It may be a bad thing that so many people try to make good stories out of their lives. A story, after all, is as artificial as a mechanical bucking bronco in a drinking establishment" (165). It can also be as comical and, as a ludic device, just as inappropriate to its surrounding circumstances—or so *Deadeye Dick* implies.

Like *Jailbird* before it, *Deadeye Dick* is hardly resolute in its scourging of comic deceit, however more explicit it may be. But it still must represent a significant stage in the evolution of Vonnegut's long debate with himself over the value and morality of the comic practice. From the nadir of *Breakfast of Champions* and, I would suggest, *Slapstick*, through the resignation of *Jailbird* over the ineffectual chimeras of comic self-deception, Vonnegut brings to *Deadeye Dick* a noticeably more direct evaluation of comedy as an art form, given the narrator's avowed attempt at becoming a professional comedian, and his application of professional "tricks" to his private view of life. But even through the writing of *Deadeye Dick*, there was an exorcism that Vonnegut had yet to make. He began it in *Breakfast of Champions*, with the flaying of the painter and confidence man, Rabo Karabekian. He ignored it through *Slapstick* and *Jailbird*, and returned to it in *Deadeye Dick*, in which Rudy's mother begins "'raising hell'" about "'a painting by somebody named Rabo Karabekian.'" As Rudy notes, "'It's green. It's about the size of a barn door. It has one vertical orange stripe, and it's called "The Temptation of Saint Anthony."'" According to his mother, it is "'an insult . . . to the memory of every serious artist who ever lived'" (149). Vonnegut ignored the implications of Karabekian's painting long enough to kill off all deceitful tricksters in *Galapagos;* but the painting and its creator remained to taunt him until the final exorcism of *Bluebeard*. In this book, Vonnegut explicitly says goodbye to art as a joke and to jokery as any kind of useful art. If, in *Hocus Pocus*, the narrator refuses to see himself as a comedian, it may be because comedy had already been banished in the previous novel.

Bluebeard is, among other things, about the repentance of a guilty "false player" for a life of joking. In this book it is not all artists who are condemned; only comic ones (although the preface does lament the tendency "to endow certain sorts of human playfulness with inappropriate and hence distressing seriousness" through "the grotesque prices paid for works of art" and "children's games" such as sports, dance, and music making).[42] In *Bluebeard*, Rabo Karabekian is finally made to own up to "having disgraced [himself] in the visual arts" by demeaning them with his outrageous trickery (21). As a "serious artist" he has been, by his own admission, a "Floparroo" (208) and ostracized by his peers for good reason: "Painters shun me, since the ridicule my own paintings attracted and deserved encouraged Philistines to argue that *most* painters were charlatans or fools" (20). He looks back and concludes: "I have done no useful work for decades" (18). Instead, he has been an abstract expressionist painter.

It is difficult not to conclude that in *Bluebeard* abstract expressionism is a metaphor for comedy, just as drugs were in *Deadeye Dick*. The associations are manifold and plain, not only in the repeated contrasts between abstract expressionism and "serious art." As Karabekian recalls, the whole premise for the school was "a kind of a joke" played by the founding members—Jackson Pollock, Terry Kitchen, and Karabekian himself. Even at the outset, Karabekian is told, "'I can't get over how passionate you guys are, and yet so absolutely *unserious.*'" He replies, "'Everything about life is a joke. . . . Don't you know that?'" (213). But it is a dangerous joke that plays itself out for the players: trapped in their defining roles, Pollock and Kitchen escape through suicide, leaving Karabekian to marvel at "how things got so gruesomely serious" (212). He ruefully concludes that their dalliance with this comic art form was like playing with a dangerous drug, "a master seducer against whose blandishments we were defenseless" (134). Rabo admits to having "discovered something as powerful and irresponsible as shooting up with heroin: if I started laying on just one color of paint to a huge canvas, I could make the whole world drop away" (128–29). This admission is especially guilt-ridden, given that before succumbing to the playful charms of abstract expressionism he had worked so painstakingly to satisfy the injunction of his mentor, the illustrator Dan Gregory: "'Draw everything the way it really is'" (124).

In his hysterical condemnations of abstract expressionism, Gregory, too, reinforces its association with a comic form to be vilified. He demands that the young Rabo loyally despise the school as "'the work of swindlers and lunatics and degenerates'" who cannot be taken seriously (123). When Rabo disobeys him by patronizing the Museum of Modern Art, Gregory's greatest outrage is reserved for the obvious comic pleasure that Rabo betrays when he is caught leaving the exhibition: "'It's how *happy* you were when you were coming out! What could that happiness be but a mockery of me and of every person who ever tried to keep control of a paintbrush?'" (147). Although, as an illustrator, Gregory is himself a formidable counterfeiter, it is the degrading *playfulness* of abstract expressionism that he hates and its open admission of itself *as* play rather than as the attempted reflection of "what really is." It is not surprising, then, that of all the people Gregory alienates in his "humorlessness and rage," the most noteworthy two should be *co-*

medians: "When I said to Gregory that first night that I had heard the famous voice of W. C. Fields from the top of the spiral staircase, he replied that Fields would never be welcome in his house again, and neither would Al Jolson" (126).

For Rabo, the joke takes its revenge in a particularly cruel way, not only on him but also on those he has made a career of swindling. His abstract paintings—the vertical stripes of "awareness" on the solid fields of color—become "notorious for falling apart everywhere" (320) because of chemical reactions in a paint supposed to "outlive the smile on the 'Mona Lisa.'" Thus, the last laugh is not only on whoever pays tens of thousands of dollars for an overpriced bad joke but on Rabo himself, a bested comedian: "The name of the paint was Sateen Dura-Luxe. Mona Lisa is still smiling. And your local paint dealer, if he has been in the business any length of time, will laugh in your face if you ask for Sateen Dura-Luxe" (29). Rabo's work has been poisoned by buffoonery, so much so that he offers the world a new dictionary definition, "karabekian": "Fiasco in which a person causes total destruction of own work and reputation through stupidity, carelessness or both" (231). Rabo attempts to undo the consequences of his misapplied comedy, resolving to paint a serious illustration over what had been an admitted joke: in effect, he sets out to take back the joke in "an exorcism of an unhappy past, a symbolic repairing of all the damage I had done to myself and the others during my brief career as a painter" (236). Again, for "painter" we can read "jokester," given Rabo's declaration: "'I have had all I can stand of not taking myself seriously'" (139).

Rabo is aided in his conversion to a "serious artist" by the writer, Circe Berman, who soon after moving in with him throws down the gauntlet: "'Maybe you can't stand truly serious art. Maybe you'd better use the back door from now on'" (117). It is Circe who pushes Rabo back into stark illustration and away from artistic camouflage, taunting him: "'I need information the way I need vitamins and minerals. . . . Judging from your pictures, you hate facts like poison'" (31). Circe wants to be informed, not deceived into valuing paintings that are "'about absolutely nothing'" except themselves and the humor in which they are conceived (42). By the end of the book, she has succeeded in convincing Rabo to paint a canvas "so realistic that it might have been a photograph" (240). To Circe it is as real, if as humorless, as "'a display in a museum of natural history'" (243). For Rabo, the transition from cynical comedian to serious artist marks his "Renaissance" (237), as he judges his new creation: "This is no shaggy dog story. . . . And there is no lame joke in there" (45). On the contrary, his giant painting is an intricate illustration of particular people in a particular place and time, "'when the sun came up the day the Second World War ended in Europe'" (240). Containing representations of so much horror and brutality that lay in the war's wake, the painting is a confrontation and reckoning with reality, rather than a comic evasion of it. Moreover, it is both an elegy for, and exorcism of, a comic spirit signaled by the rendering of various comedians as slaves and criminals, as Rabo points out to Circe: "'These two Estonians in German uniforms are Laurel and Hardy. This French collaborator here is Charlie Chaplin. These two Polish slave laborers . . . are Jackson Pollock and Terry Kitchen'" (250).

Given what Rabo calls the "melancholy roll-call of real-life suicides among the Abstract Expressionists," this final, realistic illustration suggests that his ultimate withdrawal from jokery is, for Rabo, very much a happy escape (251). The sheer relief with which he closes his narrative following this momentous conversion; the renunciation of the legacy of the awful confidence game introduced and scorned in *Breakfast of Champions* and *Deadeye Dick*; and his sense of being a "Lazarus" brought back to life by Circe, the writer who teaches him to confront the unbearable and illustrate with sincerity—all of these point to *Bluebeard* as a significant critique of the comic practice. No longer imprisoned in the comedian's role, Rabo can exult in closure, "Oh, happy Rabo Karabekian," with a career of deceit and degradation behind him, and a reprieve in the offing (256).

From here it is only a small step to what is at the time of writing Vonnegut's latest novel, and the outright declaration by its narrator that he is no comedian. Eugene Debs Hartke is sick of lying, given that he had been such a consummate performer as a public information officer during the Vietnam War. The war is characterized as a "dirty joke" (9), a "loony" enterprise (39), a "big hallucination," "nonsense" (67), and an unbelievable fable that, like a sophomoric joke to which it is compared, demands the credulity of the public who had been "watched to see how long they went on believing it, just as they had been watched when they were little, no doubt, to see how long they would go on believing in the Tooth Fairy, the Easter Bunny, and Santa Claus" (51). As an unwilling comedian who had been under orders to perpetuate the joke "that we were clearly winning, and that the folks back home should be proud and happy about all the good things we were doing there"

(22), Hartke recalls with shame, "I was a genius of lethal hocus pocus!" (126). It is as if he is signaling Melville's fears about the potential of evil witchery from the mouth of an accomplished, smiling liar; for Hartke sees himself as a confidence man wearing on his hands the blood of "all those, many of them Americans, who died as an indirect result of all my hocus pocus, all by blah blah blah" (127). Resolved afterwards to live up to the precept that "honesty is the best policy" (33), Hartke, like the reformed Karabekian before him, sets out to tell the truth henceforth, becoming a teacher whose aim is to "overthrow . . . ignorance and self-serving fantasies" (74). For Hartke, it is "a teacher's duty to speak frankly" to his students (120); and he has only contempt for diversionary uses of knowledge, comic or otherwise: "The lesson I myself learned over and over again when teaching at the college and then the prison was the uselessness of information to most people, except as entertainment. If facts weren't funny or scary, or couldn't make you rich, the heck with them" (55). Ultimately, in spite of a wistful predilection for jokery, he becomes a martyr to the truth when he effectively takes back all the dirty jokes he had told in Vietnam, and is fired for "having wobbled the students' faith in the intelligence and decency of their country's leadership by telling them the truth about the Vietnam War" (203).

Hartke's opinions of three other comedian figures also point to the high price that must be paid by any would-be truth teller who chooses instead to don the comic mask, either as a means of deceiving others or in order to protect himself. First there is Damon Stern, the aforementioned history professor who, to Hartke's astonishment, keeps his job in spite of the witch hunt: again, as Hartke reasons, "My guess is that he was a comedian, and I was not." As far as Hartke is concerned, through his comedic evasions Stern had taken the coward's way out: "Stern never told the awful truth about supposedly noble human actions in recent times. Everything he debunked had to have transpired before 1950, say" (106). In contrast, Hartke and another condemned teacher had "talked about the last half of the 20th Century, in which we had both been seriously wounded physically and psychologically, which was nothing anybody but a sociopath could laugh about" (95). It is in fact a sociopath who is the second comedian figure upon whom Hartke pronounces his damning judgment: Alton Darwin is a mass murderer with a deadpan comic's viewpoint and delivery, who speaks "of trivial and serious matters in the same tone of voice, with the same gestures and facial expressions" (61). In this he is likened explicitly to the third of the comedian figures, Jack Patton, Hartke's dead brother-in-law who, even when alive, is "a dead man" by virtue of his pathetic attempt to counterfeit a comic vision: "Everything, and I mean everything, was a joke to him, or so he said. His favorite expression right up to the end was, 'I had to laugh like hell.'" Patton threatens to so laugh at a number of propositions: the torturing of animals; marriage; the atomic destruction of New York; the body count in Saigon; his own death. And, in the end, Patton's failure even to crack a smile is perhaps the most eloquent testimony to a comedian who promises, tries, and fails to deliver: "Patton would tell about some supposedly serious or beautiful or dangerous or holy event during which he had had to laugh like hell, but he hadn't really laughed. He kept a straight face, too, when he told about it afterward. In all his life, I don't think anybody ever heard him do what he said he had to do all the time, which was laugh like hell" (38–39).

For Vonnegut to have arrived at this stable of characters thirty years after beginning, in *Mother Night*, his exploration of what it means and what it takes to be a critically-minded comedian, indeed suggests a grim trajectory. But as Vonnegut has stated, it is not a particularly unique one, being rather indicative of a pattern. As we have seen, Vonnegut shares this trajectory with a host of other American satirists. This includes his avowed mentor, Mark Twain, to whom we now—finally—turn.

Chapter 6

Mark Twain: "My hated nom de plume"

One night in 1962, Dick Gregory and Grover Sales sat in a smoky cabaret, watching Lenny Bruce for the first time. Gregory leaned across the table and whispered to Sales, "'You have to go back to Mark Twain to find anything like him, and if they don't kill him or throw him in jail, he's liable to shake up this whole fuckin' country.'"[1] Kurt Vonnegut's wishful associations with Twain are by now a matter of record. Sinclair Lewis eulogizes Twain briefly in *Main Street*; and Garrison Keillor sings somewhere that he "rode with a man named Twain," sharing with him the "cash crop" of humor. *Huckleberry Finn* was one of the last books Bill Hicks reread before he died. And who would wish to count the number of publishers' blurbs naming this or that comedian as "the funniest since Mark Twain"? He is the black hole of American comedy, the locus around and toward which so many comparisons whirl in a vortex. American comedians either recall him or anticipate him. But sometimes a kinship with Twain is a sign not of comic genius but of comic frustration. Lenny Bruce despaired of his mask and took to preaching: he shared that with Twain. Vonnegut signals the impotence of comedy as a force for social betterment and loses his sense of humor at the age of sixty-three: Twain signaled the same toward the end of his career. Keillor grows "old and irritable," wishing to exchange humor for irritation. Growing old, he says, is "a terrible mistake, and that's no joke."[2] Twain not only said this but demonstrated it. Whatever mastery or ineptitude a comedian shows in the negotiation of a comic masquerade, somewhere or sometime Twain shows the same. The tension between the false player and the spoil-sport animates Twain in a career marked by the heights of confidence and the depths of faithlessness.

Historically, the illusion known as Mark Twain appeared on February 3, 1863, when Samuel Clemens first signed the pseudonym beneath a travel letter in the *Virginia City Territorial Enterprise*. (It was a great improvement on his earlier *nom de plume*, W. Epaminondas Adrastus Perkins.) Taken from the parlance of the Mississippi riverboat pilots, to "mark twain" meant to measure the waters at a depth of two fathoms; but as Clemens used it, Mark Twain became the alter ego of an increasingly embittered artist compelled to lead a precarious—and, at times, galling—double existence. With Mark Twain, Clemens established the identity of a professional comedian subject to the limitations of expression which, according to the conventions of every age, give comedy its license. As James Cox has noted, the disguise of Mark Twain allowed Clemens to invade "the very citadel of seriousness, transforming it into humor with each encroachment."[3] But Clemens throughout his life rebelled against his necessary disguise. It demeaned him, it threatened to take him over, it embarrassed him, and yet—most outrageously—it was indispensable. With "each encroachment," only a fabrication—Mark Twain—could camouflage the critical, misanthropic, and often anarchic intentions of his creator, becoming at once his mouthpiece, his shield, and his bane.

In 1966, James Cox laid down the lines for much of the subsequent discussion about Twain as a comic persona, in *Mark Twain: The Fate of Humor*. As he described it, the object of "the art of impersonation" mastered by Samuel Clemens was to enable him to "seem *serious* without necessarily being so" (my italics). His great problem, according to Cox, lay in satisfying those "serious minded and culturally ambitious readers who formed such a sizeable and influential segment of his audience."[4] I think it is true to say that Clemens did face this problem of impersonating seriousness *at times*, whether in the rendering of a particular character—such as Huck Finn throughout the first half of his adventures—or when negotiating the competing claims of his own ironic identity, such as in his repeated reactions against the sense that the buffoon was overpowering the serious critic in him. Cox declared that Clemens was "fated" to humor; but with all respect to the importance of his study, I don't think that Clemens's comedic status was necessarily so assured or ordained. As I hope to demonstrate, impersonating *seriousness* often appeared the least of Clemens's problems; on the contrary, he seems to have been more troubled the other way, with his greatest and ultimate difficulties lying in the convincing impersonation of *play*. As Aristotle, Huizinga, Eastman, and Eco (among others) have stated, and as the fates of numerous comedians from Rabelais onwards have shown, it is more vital for the jester to seem in jest without necessarily being so than the reverse. It is one thing to be frivolous, with derision as the worst response—and of course Clemens feared this greatly. But it is another thing to bear the reputation and suffer the consequences of being an iconoclast, or to repeat Huizinga once more, any one of the variety of spoil-sports: "apostates, heretics, innovators, prophets, conscientious objectors, etc." Clemens did indeed set out to demolish through "the art of impersonation," but I believe that his greatest task lay in disguising his violence and rage rather than his frivolity. With all his contempt for what he called "the damned human race," living as he did in a country and a century that had earned as much of his hatred as his admiration, his disguise nevertheless must win the indulgence of an easily unforgiving audience, themselves as often as not the objects of his scorn. As his later works especially reveal, Clemens's commitment to the deceptions of comic placation through the persona of the genial, befuddled Mark Twain was often grudging enough to betray the bitterness it was designed to conceal. But his resistance to the rules of the game showed itself long before he set to work on *Letters from the Earth*, *What Is Man?*, or *The Mysterious Stranger*, notorious in their misanthropic savagery. Hence his troubled execution of Huck's benign tolerance in the latter half of *Huckleberry Finn*, and the final, forced burlesques of play. Hence the cool ghostliness of *Pudd'nhead Wilson*, culminating in the explicit abdication of the ironist in deference to the serious practitioner of the law. These two works are especially noteworthy in that they not only reveal their creator's awareness and despair of confidence games in society at large but also demonstrate the varying unease with which Clemens participated in such machinations as a comedian. For this reason, I wish to approach both texts in detail, in the light of their being particular indications of an uneasy comic masquerade spanning forty-seven years.

"My hated *nom de plume*"

By the time he first signed the pen name "Mark Twain" as a twenty-eight-year-old journalist, Clemens had already abandoned a number of occupations—shop clerk, journeyman printer, apprentice riverboat pilot, Confederate soldier, secretary, prospector in silver and gold, quartz miner. Each of these failed attempts inspired the material that would eventually find its way into the written works of Mark Twain: the medieval newspaperman in *A Connecticut Yankee*; the riverboat characters in *Life on the Mississippi*, *Tom Sawyer*, and *Huckleberry Finn*; the guilt-ridden Confederate in "The Private History of a Campaign That Failed"; the hapless clerks, secretaries, and miners in "To the California Pioneers" and *Roughing It*. All had developed out of the true-to-life failures of Samuel Clemens and were comedically exploited by him as the artistic illusion, Mark Twain.

While Clemens had indeed discovered a potent comic device through which he could capitalize upon and transform his failures and disillusionments, he would also rebel repeatedly against the very persona he had created, and which to his dismay threatened so often to overpower or—even worse—define him. Possibly he invented the reckless businessman, Mr. Clemens, in order to compete with Twain; yet he also had to realize that the comedian's was the hand that fed him, even in business. Mark Twain's name was ultimately more profitable, and it was Mark Twain on the world lecture circuit who rescued Sam Clemens, the failed businessman, from financial ruin. Occasionally, Clemens's resentment toward his comedic double led him to challenge Mark Twain—pitifully—upon his own territory, the written page. The results, although Clemens would often refer to them as his "nobler" works, were in fact such ponderous, flat creations as *Joan of Arc* and *What Is Man?*, both published under the conspicuous authorship of Samuel Clemens instead of Mark Twain, and loaded with the manifest teaching and preaching that Clemens himself said was the death of humor. It was more than a case of a clown hankering to play Hamlet: the relationship between Clemens and Mark Twain at times resembled an outright wrestling match. And although it was Mark Twain who would become a citizen of the world, the disarming charm of his comedy was in the end a poor match for the corrosive misanthropy of his creator.

As in the cases of the comedians we have encountered so far, it is not necessary to look solely toward the end of Twain's dual career for compelling evidence of the struggle. The tension between the "noble," serious-minded writer and the comedian he grew sometimes to despise reveals itself as early as in the conflicting descriptions of his first tale, "The Celebrated Jumping Frog of Calaveras County," which introduced him to the publishing circles of New York. On the heels of its publication, in 1868, Clemens was calling it "'a villainous backwoods sketch'" and "'an infamous volume.'" But a year later, he would write to his wife, "'Between you and I, privately Livy dear, it is the best humorous sketch America has produced yet, and I must read it in public some day.'"[5] This is the first in a long line of contradictions: for nearly every utterance of praise for Mark Twain from the lips or pen of his creator, there is an epithet of exasperation and denial from the same source.

Consider his earliest explicit admission of a calling "'to literature of a low order—i.e. humorous,'" as he wrote to his brother from the Far West. He had tried everything else, he said; he had nothing to lose as a comedian. "'I would long ago have ceased to meddle with things for which I was by nature unfitted, and turned my attention to seriously scribbling to excite the *laughter* of God's creatures. Poor, pitiful business.'"[6] As early as this, with Mark Twain in the mere embryonic stage, Clemens maintains two paradoxical stances: his denigration of humor is, of course, an ironic implication of the opposite opinion; but at the same time it *is* his opinion, as he would repeat it throughout his life. James Cox is right to quote this letter as early evidence of the artistic conflict between Clemens and Twain, notably with the oxymoronic "seriously scribbling." As Cox suggests, Clemens's dependence on the comic persona of Mark Twain, coupled with his admitted need to assert himself seriously and critically, enabled him in his best creations to reach into formerly sanctified territory and truly keep his comedy from the "low order" in which he feared it lay. The tragedy, however, is that Clemens was never fully confident in the mastery of his deceptions and so suffered through a life of alternating opinions of himself and his alter ego. When he failed as a businessman and artist, he would assert himself as Mark Twain; and when Twain was attacked for irreverence, amateurism, or buffoonery, a wounded, noble, *serious* Clemens would attempt a rescue.

This conflict shows itself, in one aspect or another, in all of Mark Twain's writings—not only as a source of debilitation, of course, but of creative energy as well. It allowed Clemens the dual vision through which he became famous, beginning with his first book, *The Innocents Abroad*, wherein the experiences of the traveling reporter, Clemens, were comedically exaggerated and mocked by the wide-eyed newcomer, Mark Twain. The nominal Innocent intruding into the exalted territory of the Holy Land and the shrines of Europe is the unsophisticated and remarkably naive Mr. Twain, immune from retaliation as he reports with unintentional irreverence the blemishes identified by his cynical creator, seemingly unaware of the barbs issuing from his mouth. In mastering this deception, Clemens found the approach he would most successfully employ in *Huckleberry Finn*. Yet even as early as *The Innocents Abroad*, the anarchic Clemens was at war with the demands of convention, relying as he would do throughout his career on the editorial judgment of friends and his own Victorian, Calvinist conscience to excise what he and they considered the coarseness of his comic delivery.

Early on, too, the conflict between the raw iconoclast and the deceptive trickster extended beyond the confines of the written page and into the personal relations between Clemens and his closest acquaintances, determining as much as any other factor the development of the imaginary Mark Twain. Clemens's courtship and marriage to Olivia Langdon is a case in point, directly indicative of the opposing emotions he felt as a serious writer and a comedian. The early weeks of his courtship were among the most shameful that Clemens ever experienced, owing to an insulting character investigation launched by Olivia's mother. It was quickly apparent that after a young manhood of roughing it on the Mississippi and the Pacific Slope, Clemens would need a character change like Saul's on the road to Damascus to satisfy Mrs. Langdon. In the end, he was forced to resort to a deception worthy of the Duke and the King: as a demonstration of his Christian inspiration he wrote for Mrs. Langdon an overblown essay on the Nativity, describing as a sanctified idyll the very Bethlehem that with his own eyes he had seen as a stinking pit of poverty, leprosy, and corruption. Mrs. Langdon was impressed, and the courtship was allowed to continue; but after Clemens had demonstrated with utmost gravity his capacity for the noble word, the demon in him went to work, disguising his iconoclasm through the quizzical naïveté of Mark Twain. When *The Innocents Abroad* soon appeared, the Bethlehem he described was the awful one he had seen. Of course, he got away with it: there is no record of Mrs. Langdon taking offense.

Clemens appears to have learned much about the persuasive powers of his comic voice during his courtship and its crucial role in tempering his critical impulses. But he also repeatedly demonstrated his unease in the adoption of that voice, mostly because of his concerns about the social status of a comedian. As he wrote to Mary Fairbanks about his fiancée, "Poor girl, anybody who could convince her that I was not a humorist would secure her eternal gratitude! She thinks a humorist is something pretty awful."[7] The good opinions of the likes of Mary Fairbanks and the Langdon family must have been instrumental in the anxieties Clemens felt about the new double identity he was developing. Mrs. Fairbanks herself—in a sense his first unofficial editor, having coaxed him into softening some of the more critical passages of *The Innocents Abroad*—was apparently aware of his destructive tendencies. Yet if she accepted that he needed the mask of humor, she was unhappy with its coarseness as it had so far been developed. "I want the public, who know him now only as 'the wild humorist of the Pacific Slope,' to know something of his deeper, larger nature," she said. "I remember being quite incensed by a lady's asking, 'Is there anything of Mr. Clemens except his humor?'"[8] It was largely owing to the efforts of Mary Fairbanks that Clemens wrote and published the dishonest, flatulent passage on the Nativity that so filled him with self-disgust afterwards.

The outright necessity of Clemens's comic mask more than once clashed with his fear of the designation "buffoon." After many contributions to the *Atlantic Monthly*, he told the editor, William Dean Howells, that he most liked the magazine's readership because it didn't "require a 'humorist' to paint himself stripéd and stand on his head every fifteen minutes."[9] Later identically presented in the tacky Royal Nonesuch performance of *Huckleberry Finn*, this derisory image is precisely the one Clemens feared would define him when he most resented bearing the identity of Mark Twain. "'I am demeaning myself,'" he once complained aloud to George Washington Cable during a lecture tour. "'I am allowing myself to be a mere buffoon. It's ghastly. I can't endure it any longer.'"[10] One thing that rescued him from the fate of buffoonery, he declared, was his wife's constant vigilance against his sacrificing of morals or points of instruction for the sake of a laugh; and it was this opposition between, on the one hand, moralizing and instruction, and the assurance of play on the other, that he was to have such difficulty in negotiating, especially in his later works, and in spite of his autobiography's explicit warning about manifest preaching. Yet as an old man, Clemens would have reason to consider himself justified in his periodic resistance to the encroachments of the clown, Mark Twain, if he took at face value the sentiments of a congratulatory letter from George Bernard Shaw on the occasion of his receiving an honorary Oxford doctorate: "'My dear Mark Twain—not to say Dr. Clemens (although I have always regarded Clemens as mere raw material—might have been your brother or your uncle) . . . '"[11] Clemens frequently enough despaired of just such an impression; yet he was forced to recognize, as Shaw did, that Mark Twain's dominance was necessary for the protection of his creator. To repeat Shaw's reference to Clemens: "'He is in very much the same position as myself. He has to put things in such a way as to make people who would otherwise hang him believe he is joking.'"[12]

The strain of attempting to create and maintain such a belief shows itself in, among other things, Clemens's decision to resort to retrospection and the juvenile viewpoint first employed in *Tom Sawyer*. He had come to an important realization in the early 1870s, having identified and, in collaboration with Charles Dudley Warner, savagely attacked the political corruptions and bloodsucking mania of speculation in the postwar period they together named the Gilded Age. When the book of that title was finished, Clemens saw that he was in danger of treating what he called "the wash of today" with a sarcastic bitterness too caustic to be contained by Mark Twain's voice; he confessed to his difficulties in adopting a medium flexible enough to accommodate his outrage while still remaining comedically adept. As he wrote to Howells, "a man can't write successful satire unless he be in a calm judicial good humor. . . . I don't ever seem to be in a good enough humor with ANYthing to *satirize* it; no, I want to stand up before it and *curse* it, and foam at the mouth—or take a club and pound it to rags and pulp."[13] It was partly the experience of writing *The Gilded Age* that steered Clemens toward the comedic devices of *Tom Sawyer*, set, as *Huckleberry Finn* and *Pudd'nhead Wilson* would be, in the antebellum South, the society in which Clemens had matured and that he ultimately rejected. Tom Sawyer's world is one of bloodlust, slavery, and dread; yet it is also charmed, for with the device that would become one of his most protective defenses—the viewpoint of a child—Clemens could coax the reader's indulgence and forestall censure, disguising contemporary adult machinations of power, greed, violence, and sex as the juvenile play of the past. Although he told Howells that he had kept Tom Sawyer as a child simply to prevent him from becoming "like all the one-horse men in literature," he must have also realized the defensive potential of the child's viewpoint.[14] It is reasonable to assume that this was instrumental in his decision to begin his next book in the form of a semiliterate backwoods boy's autobiography.

Immediately upon the publication of *Tom Sawyer* in 1879, Clemens began work on *Huckleberry Finn*, coming to a dead stop at chapter 16, wherein a depressed Huck battles with his conscience— as though it were a separate entity—and sees his idyllic raft destroyed. If, as Henry Nash Smith suggested, Huck's depression and hatred for his conscience were a reflection of a crisis buried deep in the psyche of a divided Clemens, such an opinion is supported by a short story written just before the completion of *Tom Sawyer*, "The Facts Concerning the Recent Carnival of Crime in Connecticut." In this bitter tale, the narrator, Mark Twain, destroys a deformed twin dwarf, his conscience, who had been tormenting him all his life. The consequent euphoria of a man without a conscience, immune to remorse, drives the narrator into murdering, pillaging, and swindling his way across the state. The tale is, if nothing else, an indication of Clemens's capacity to see himself—and even depict himself —as engaged in the violent negotiation of two conflicting halves of an identity, just as he was to envisage and depict Huck Finn.

The immediate period following the first of many creative blocks preventing the progression of *Huckleberry Finn* is also instructive. The first silencing of Huck's comic voice coincided with the critical reception in some genteel corners of *Tom Sawyer*, swiftly judged by the self-proclaimed guardians of youthful morality as a bad influence and frivolous. Injured and ashamed, Clemens began as a reaction against unfavorable criticism a pattern of withdrawal from the comic responsibility to which his pen name had committed him. In this instance he commenced work on the relatively tame, sometimes pompous *The Prince and the Pauper*. With a colossal chip on his shoulder, Clemens vowed to publish it anonymously, " 'such grave and stately work being considered by the world to be above my proper level.' "[15] An indication of the reactions that may have caused Clemens to pit his gravity against Mark Twain's comedy lies in a passage from his daughter Susy's juvenile biography of him, written when she was fourteen, after the publications of both *The Prince and the Pauper* and *Huckleberry Finn*. She recoiled from the praise flowing in for the latter book. *The Prince and the Pauper*, she said, was " 'unquestionably the best book he has ever written.' " The more letters congratulated her father on his return to his " 'own style' " with *Huckleberry Finn*, the less Susy liked it: " 'That enoyed me that enoyed me greatly, because it trobles me to have so few people know papa, I mean really know him, they think of Mark

Twain as a humorist joking at everything.'"[16] Before she died, she uttered the wish that she had never heard of her father's alter ego and despaired of being known only as Mark Twain's daughter—feelings that he could not have ignored.

Other friends frequently rallied to bolster Clemens's reputation as a serious author, as though to protect him from his degrading association with Mark Twain. Howells welcomed *The Prince and the Pauper* in a review for the *New York Tribune* in which he praised, to Clemens's immense gratification, the "'fascination of the narrative and the strength of the implied moral'" which could only "'surprise those who have found nothing but drollery in Mark Twain's books, and have not perceived the artistic sense and the strain of deep earnestness underlying his humor.'"[17] This is almost verbatim in sentiment to a review of Mark Twain's *Sketches, New and Old* that Howells had written a few years earlier, applauding "a growing seriousness and meaning in the apparently unmoralized drolling" of a "*subtle* humorist."[18] Clemens had replied with ecstatic thanks, not only on his own behalf but on his wife's as well: "You see, the thing that gravels her is that I am so persistently glorified as a mere buffoon, as if that entirely covered my case—which she denies with venom."[19] There is, of course, no telling precisely to what degree Howells, Olivia, Susy, Mary Fairbanks, or anyone else influenced Clemens in the development of his comic voice; but as James Cox points out, although Clemens was not obliged to write comedy, Mark Twain was. I wish to place more emphasis on the word *obliged* than perhaps Cox does; for the extent to which Clemens actively courted such acknowledgments of his own seriousness is not necessarily an indication that he was fated to humor but rather that he resisted the obligation to humor that was implicit in Mark Twain's identity. For this reason, although *The Prince and the Pauper* was initially published under the authorship of Mark Twain, a growing number of companies took to publishing later editions crediting Clemens, as though they accepted that the comedian had somehow withdrawn. Clemens's indecision over whether or not to publish it anonymously had ended with the glowing delight of Howells's review; yet the indecision, both in itself and as it was manifest in the strained comedy of the book, clearly reveals the unease between Clemens and his fabricated alter ego.

In 1877, as the manuscript of *Huckleberry Finn* lay resting in a pigeonhole and *The Prince and the Pauper* was being hailed as the finest production of a noble career, it is clear that as a comedian Clemens felt more insecure than ever. When asked by Howells to take a public part in the presidential campaign of Rutherford B. Hayes, he declined: "When a humorist ventures upon the grave concerns of life, he must do his job better than another man or he works harm to his cause."[20] His comedic insecurity was magnified that same year by the most severe blow he would ever receive as a comedian, the universal public outrage over a joke that had painfully proved itself an insufficient shield. It was especially demoralizing as the offense occurred in the immediacy of a live performance rather than through the relatively protective distance offered by the printed page. At a banquet in Boston on the occasion of Whittier's seventieth birthday, Clemens managed to convey his class-bound resentment through a story in which three disreputable tramps gain entry to Mark Twain's mining shack by passing themselves off as Emerson, Holmes, and Longfellow, misquoting from their works over a poker game. For an audience he had the humorless cream of Boston Brahmin society, including the three dignitaries themselves. Howells, who was also present, remembered that they responded, not with laughter, but with a silence "'weighing many tons to the square inch.'"[21] Embarrassed for his friend, Howells kept his eyes glued to his plate, looking up only once to find Clemens visibly dying on his feet, trapped between a scandalized audience and a fatally inept joke. Clemens spent the next months in extreme shame and remorse, begging forgiveness both publicly and privately in letters and speeches. He wrote to Howells afterwards, "My sense of disgrace does not abate. It grows. I see that it is going to add itself to my list of permanencies."[22] And he fled to Europe.

It was fortunate that upon his return the next year, he had the opportunity to regain his confidence in another public appearance before an equally illustrious audience, where he was convinced as never before or, arguably, afterwards of the disarming power of Mark Twain's comedy: at a banquet for former president Grant, he gave a speech that reduced the immobile Iron General himself to hysterics. That the authority and austerity of the former Union commander could be so undermined by the drawling, shuffling, defiant teasing of a former Confederate private established Mark Twain with impunity as the comic antihero victorious over the hero, with laughter as the vanquishing weapon and shield. Ostensibly a toast in honor of America's babies, with all their potential as the coming generation, the speech that sent Grant and the veterans of the Army of the Tennessee into howling agonies was a double-edged tribute depicting Grant as the scourge of the battlefield but bumbling and helpless with an infant in his arms. "You could face the death storm at Donelson and Vicksburg and give back blow for blow," Twain taunted, "but when he clawed your whiskers, and pulled your hair, and twisted your nose, you had to take it." Easily as provocative and irreverent as the Whittier fiasco, the speech drew a response that completely erased the shame and embarrassment of the former event. Depicting Grant as once a baby himself, preoccupied with the Herculean task of getting "his own big toe into his mouth," Clemens hovered on the brink of disaster, with, as he later recalled, "a sort of shuddering silence" abruptly descending as it had done in Boston—until he rescued himself with the redeeming punch line: "And if the child is but the prophecy of the man, there are mighty few who will doubt that he *succeeded*."²³ The roar that reclaimed the hall rang in Clemens's ears for hours afterwards, as he shook hands and accepted praise well into the morning. His joyous letters written the next day glow with his recognition of the extent to which Mark Twain's comic shield could protect even a lowly Confederate private in an assault against the vanquisher of Robert E. Lee. To Olivia, he wrote, "I fetched him! I broke him up utterly! The audience *saw* that for once in his life he had been knocked out of his iron serenity." He told Howells, "I knew I could lick him. I shook him up like dynamite. . . . My truths had wracked all the bones of his body apart." And to his brother: "He laughed until his bones ached."²⁴

The resounding success of this return to the comic stage revived for a shining moment all of Clemens's faith in the ability of Mark Twain to shield him from the repercussions of his critical intent. Not only could he now face the Mississippi of an embarrassed youth to collect the material for *Life on the Mississippi* but he experienced a surge of energy that smashed through his creative block and drove him to complete *Huckleberry Finn*. In 1883, he wrote to his mother, "I haven't had such booming working days for many years. This summer it is no more trouble to me to write than it is to lie."²⁵ Yet as the comedic inconsistencies of that very book demonstrate, lying was more difficult than Clemens would here admit. In this tale of a mendacious boy whose heart is filled with contempt for the hypocrisies that surround him; who sees himself as a divided persona, his "sound" half at war with his "deformed" half; who embarks on a series of confidence games in order to confound the vilest of confidence men; whose childish voice so struggles to contain the vitriol of its creator's derision that it almost dies away, only to be revived as the voice of a hollow phantom in a grotesque burlesque—in this tale Clemens signals his unease over the poten-

tial of comedy as a valid means of social criticism and his own diminishing faith in his masquerade.

Huckleberry Finn: "Low-down humbugs and frauds"

Mark Twain began *Huckleberry Finn* in America's cente-
nary year, 1876, in the heart of the corrupt era that he himself had
named "the Gilded Age." At its inception, he intended it to be nothing more than a sequel to the boys' adventure book *Tom Sawyer*,
published the same year. A letter to Howells shows how casually
he appeared to view his new creation in its early stages, with four
hundred pages already written. "Began another boy's book," he
writes, "more to be at work than anything else." He declares only a
tolerable liking for it thus far, and either playfully or otherwise
threatens to "pigeonhole or burn the MS when it is done."[26] Although he fortunately never chose the latter course, he did indeed
pigeonhole the manuscript before it was done—repeatedly. His first
creative block lasted for two years as he consciously and unconsciously wrestled with the technical and moral difficulties in deciding whether the book would be merely "another boy's book" or the
provocative social critique it was to become. He overcame this first
impasse in 1879 or 1880, only to pigeonhole the manuscript again
until 1884, when it was completed in a final burst—eight years and
seven books after its conception.

In deciding to present the book as Huck Finn's autobiography, Mark Twain placed himself in the position of creating the
first full-length book in an American vernacular. But more important, in comedic terms, he provided himself with a calculated voice
of ignorance, innocence, and reverence that was to transmit to the
world the irreverent rage of the sophisticated, embittered Samuel
Clemens. The voice and the vernacular were even more than the
means of describing the serious issues that Clemens saw between
1876 and 1884: they were his protective charm and the deceptive instruments of his attack. The decision to use Huck as the narrative
persona not only resolved some difficulties with literary style and
viewpoint that had plagued Twain's earlier creations, it also enabled him to add an overwhelming degree of humanity and conflict
to a character who might otherwise have been a mere voice or
transparent persona. But with this decision, Twain was faced with a
difficulty that caused him to pigeonhole his manuscript time and

again, for what began as a comic adventure story developed increasingly serious implications that countered and threatened to destroy the initial premise and spirit of the book. This was revealed in chapter 16, when Huck and Jim bypass Cairo, Illinois, the last free-soil outpost, with their raft destroyed in a fog. Here, after an irksome four years of indecision, Twain chose to commit himself to a critical process through which his disarming comic shield, Huck Finn, would have to confront such issues as child abuse, murder, sadism, racism, greed, guilt, religious hypocrisy, and social corruption at large. With this commitment Twain faced the necessity of imbuing Huck with varying degrees of innocence, ignorance, deference, reverence, and, notably, contempt. One of his greatest problems, comedically, lay in calculating just how much of these various attributes Huck must and could display in order to serve as an effective insulator and mouthpiece for the increasingly misanthropic Clemens.

Along with Twain's difficulties in presenting Huck as a mitigating shield came the opportunity to establish a conflict between a decadent, dominant culture and alternative, subversive values. As Tony Tanner noted, this conflict belies the impression of Huck's narrative as merely "a good, healthy vernacular protest blowing in from the West to disperse the stagnant rhetorical mists hovering over Brahmin New England," the reigning court of literary excellence into which Clemens had insinuated himself.[27] Much more than this, the character of Huck Finn personified in a single consciousness the corrupt moral codes of the society that bore him and the anarchic spontaneity and vision that could potentially undermine them. Through the act of creation that produced Huck Finn, Mark Twain came to discover for himself the issues he seemingly had no initial intentions of confronting. As the most popular comedian of the Gilded Age it was of course only through implication that he could at once damn his society and gain its indulgence. In choosing a backwoods American vernacular to carry his implications, Twain not only employed the familiar comic device that had already endeared a generation of Southwestern humorists to the English-speaking world. He also turned notions of propriety and respectability on their heads; for in spite of its grammatical imperfections, Huck's vernacular is understood to be in a precarious state of purity in relation to the corrupt, though linguistically correct, expressions of society. Indeed, the purity of his vernacular is constantly threatened and sometimes contaminated, especially when he is most obviously seen as a product of his decadent social environment; but when he distances himself from society, the implied purity of his vernacular becomes not only the accepted form of expression but the defining, threatened character of Huck himself.

Twain employs one other device that not only strengthens the defensive efficacy of Huck's character but sustains the poignancy and, ultimately, the tragedy of the book: this is Huck's conviction that he is evil and beyond redemption. What the reader sees as his most admirable attributes Huck sees as his worst—the more he chastises himself for doing the "bad" things that will land him in hell the more the reader applauds him for precisely those actions. If Huck's ironic state of ignorance should ever be rectified, his immunity, as well as the humor of the book, would be threatened. When he looks within himself and is confused by the conflict between what Twain called his sound heart and deformed conscience, his confusion arouses laughter that is at once critical and indulgent. In order to control this response, Twain had to negotiate with three areas of perception and voice: Huck Finn's, the knowing reader's, and his own, conscious of both Huck's ignorance and the reader's sophistication. By maintaining and regulating Huck's misconceptions about his moral status in relation to that of the community, Twain created in Huck a mouthpiece that—in its most effective moments—allowed the bitterest of criticism to stand while convincing the reader that from the mouth of a humorous ignorant will come words of deep insight, morality, and compassion.

Thus, one important aspect of the mask that is Huck Finn's narration is his continual self-denunciation, as he berates himself to the opposite effect in the reader's eyes. His natural compassion gives him a misplaced resignation to impending doom in hell, since that compassion so often opposes the values that the St. Petersburg folk deem proper. He has pitted his innate goodness against his conscience so often that anytime he feels compassion for one of society's victims, it is accompanied by a strong dosage of self-criticism. This is shown early in the raft voyage, when he tries to prevent some bandits from drowning aboard a sinking steamboat: "I begun to think how dreadful it was, even for murderers, to be in such a fix. I says to myself, there ain't no telling but I might come to be a murderer myself, yet, and then how would I like it?"[28] He avers this with a straight face, and by projecting into the boy's future sense the abhorrent qualities of a murderer, Twain not only reinforces the contrast between the morality of Huck Finn and that of the thieves over whose predicament he suffers, he also implants the sinister warning that Huck's humanity is seriously in danger. Huck has, after all, been forced to point a gun at his own father, whose physical abuse he has constantly suffered. Thus his unsure prophecy highlights the fragility of his juvenile compassion, grimly suggesting that he may yet become his father's son.

When his heart aches over the plight of another pair of "rapscallions," the Duke and the King, Huck believes that his pain is just punishment. Having been tormented enough by an innate morality at odds with a socially conditioned one, he develops a scorn for his own conscience. As the Duke and King are tarred, feathered, and ridden out of town on a rail, Huck makes the obvious though crucial observation that "human beings *can* be awful cruel to one another." Yet in spite of this awareness, which produces one of his few explicit social judgments, he still misplaces the blame for the pair's misfortune on himself: "I warn't feeling so brash as I was before, but kind of ornery, and humble, and to blame somehow—though *I* hadn't done nothing." Rather than direct his contempt outward at the confidence men who deserve it, Huck directs it inward: "It don't make no difference whether you do right or wrong, a person's conscience ain't got no sense, and just goes for him *anyway*. If I had a yaller dog that didn't know more than a person's conscience does, I would pison him" (302). Just as intense as the hatred of Clemens for his own conscience, as witnessed in his biography and "The Carnival of Crime in Connecticut," among other writings, Huck's self-hatred is based on the irony of the mistaken conviction of his own moral depravity. Being at odds with his conscience causes him to cast himself as no better than a murderer or arch villain and traitor, as he reflects upon Mary Jane Wilks's determination to pray even for *him*: "She had the grit to pray for Judas if she took the notion" (258).

By here juxtaposing such assertions of Mary Jane's legitimate faith with passages describing the clerical burlesques of the Duke and the King, Twain provides the same contrast as in the internal monologues of Huck Finn, who tries to distinguish religious faith from pretension and show. Nowhere are his pathetically erroneous impressions so plainly exemplified as in his arguments over his own lack of faith. In his literal-mindedness, he cannot accept the irrelevancies of religious convention; yet he believes it is because he cannot be touched by that grace that distinguishes the "good" from the "wicked." The reader senses that Huck merely cannot be swayed by church-bound finery and hollow pretense, while Huck himself believes that he can *never* be touched by divine goodness, inspiration, or grace. This conflict embodied in him over the separation of spiritual wheat from chaff—faith from hypocrisy—is of the same sort experienced by his creator, a Calvinist who would come to write exceptionally vitriolic attacks against organized religion and the concept of a merciful, meaningful God. By presenting Huck as an ignorant, albeit moral, boy who agonizes over the illogic of religious convention, Twain attempted to secure his own impunity and shield his audience from the rancor with which he plainly treated religion later in *What Is Man?* and *The Mysterious Stranger.* Here, in *Huckleberry Finn*, he does not so much question the concept of God per se but rather the irrelevancies or hypocrisies that surround worship to the point of taking precedence over Christian behavior on the part of professed Christians. This is dangerous territory for a popular author and comedian of the nineteenth century; so his skepticism is disguised as the Socratic musing of an ignorant child. He wonders whether he has been misinformed about the efficacy of prayer: "I says to myself, if a body can get anything they pray for, why don't Deacon Wynn get back the money he lost on pork?" He questions the disparity between the forgiving deity of the liberal Christian sects and the vindictive God of John Calvin: "I judged I could see that there was two providences, and a poor chap would stand considerable show with the widow's Providence, but if Miss Watson's got him there warn't no help for him any more." He concludes that he would turn to the former deity if given the chance; but he doubts the possibility, given that his conscience has convinced him of his being "so ignorant and so kind of low-down and ornery" (60–61). His self-denunciation, however pathetic, is in keeping with the comedian's ancient tactic of attacking himself before others have the chance, while still allowing Twain to propose ironically the near-blasphemy that there must be more than one God to satisfy the moral claims of all the self-righteous.

After praying for the "courage" to betray Jim, Huck declares with a guilty heart, "You can't pray a lie—I found that out" (282). On one hand, and fortunately for the nineteenth century's reception of Mark Twain, this may be taken as an admission of Huck's faith in "the widow's Providence" as pitted against the drawing-room piety of Miss Watson. But more subversively, it could be taken to mean that *all* prayer is a lie, and therefore Huck cannot earnestly pray. This is revealed in the pointedly contrasting example of the Duke, who gloats while running his hands through the gold coins of the pilfered Wilks inheritance, "'Thish-yer comes of trust'n to Providence'" (230). If Huck cannot pray for the courage to do an evil thing, it is only because in *his* eyes he is a coward afraid to do the "right" thing. Hence the contrast between his evident courage in boldly lying to a pair of bounty hunters looking for Jim and the ignorant conviction of his own cowardice. In taking the daring step of convincing these two violent men that Jim is white, Huck feels that he isn't "man enough" to betray him, that he hasn't "the spunk of a rabbit." The reader stands assured of Huck's innate morality in thus risking his life, however much Huck concludes that he will never learn "to do right, when it's troublesome to do right and ain't no trouble to do wrong, and the wages is the same" (149). His conclusion, while an indication of his inner torment over the conflict between a "sound heart" and "deformed conscience," reinforces his capacity as a disarming comic shield. Twain depends upon this conflict, especially when Huck is at his most critical. In fact, the conflict is never resolved: it caused two of Twain's creative blocks, only to be sidestepped by the burlesque end sequence on the Phelps plantation, and left dangling with Huck's determination to "light out for the territory."

The history of these creative blocks—the points at which they interrupted the narrative's progression—are indicative of Twain's difficulty in maintaining the comic deception to which he had committed himself with the adoption of Huck's divided persona. The raft's approach to Cairo—where Melville's Confidence-Man acquired his most hellish overtones—is where Twain experienced the first impasse in the unconscious debate between the comic adventure writer and the misanthropic critic; for it is here that Huck first, and most explicitly, reveals that his socialized conscience is indeed at battle with his innate sense of justice or compassion. Up to now he has been willing to maintain Jim's secrecy without hesitation, but here—the point at which Jim can escape up the Ohio River to freedom—Huck declares: "I begun to get it through my head that he *was* most free—and who was to blame for it? Why, *me*. I couldn't get that out of my conscience, no how nor no way." The surprise that Huck actually now feels guilty is sprung in a reversal of the reader's expectations. Compounding the impact is the ironic inversion of two interpretations of the word "free": Huck's interpretation, connoting criminality, and the reader's, connoting natural justice. This is the book's first real indication that the main issue is not the mechanics of Jim's escape, as it would have been in an adventure story; nor is it an indictment of slavery itself, since the book was begun thirteen years after emancipation. At this point Twain is about to attack the very society corrupt enough to have produced and maintained the institution of slavery in the first place—the Southern society that bore him and the Northern society that had largely acquiesced in the practice until secession had forced the issue—the American society that was still his audience.

But as Twain found, as the narrative progressed it was not easy to maintain the comic inversion upon which his shield would depend; and the difficulty shows itself when Huck's voice is at its most brutal and critical of others rather than himself. On the one hand, Huck presents the sheer illogic of the slaveholding rationale when he reflects: "Here was this nigger which I had as good as helped to run away, coming right out flat-footed and saying he would steal his children—children that belonged to a man I didn't even know" (146). But his reduction of his friend Jim to the status of a bigoted, impersonal epithet is out of keeping with his former regard for him, and the defiant promise he had made earlier: " 'People would call me a low-down Ablitionist and despise me for keeping mum—but that don't make no difference' " (96). Huck's change of mind may have been necessary in order to establish and foreshadow the recurring conflict upon which Twain depended; but it demonstrates in its vicious language how close Huck comes to losing his immunity from corruption. This problem shows itself elsewhere, as when Huck reflects, "Just see what a difference it made in him the minute he judged he was about free. It was according to the old saying, 'give a nigger an inch and he'll take an ell' " (146). The contrast between the ignorant cruelty of this maxim in the mouth of a fourteen-year-old boy and the spontaneous affection for Jim that Huck otherwise speaks from the heart is evidence of two things: the conflict between Huck's generous impulse and conditioned belief, and Twain's precarious balancing act in maintaining a blameless voice. One might question whether Huck is even aware of the maxim's literal meaning. At moments when his social brainwashing is most apparent, his conscience addresses him in the language of his society, either corrupt and debased, as above, or in a caricature of an elevated style that Henry Nash Smith noted as the verbal equivalent of the gaudy ornaments in the Grangerford parlor. A twisted, exalted language is especially prevalent in the words of the Duke, the King, and Pap Finn; it is also the language of Tom Sawyer when he is at the height of his romantic pretensions. In Huck's own narration, it is at its strongest during his final debate on whether to betray Jim, at which time his conscience torments him in the language of a backwoods Jonathan Edwards in a Klansman's hood: "Something inside of me kept saying, 'There was the

Sunday school, you could a gone to it; and if you'd a done it they'd a learnt you, there, that people that acts as I'd been acting about that nigger goes to everlasting fire'" (282). Here Jim is again viciously reduced to "that nigger," while the only thing protecting Huck from censure is that such language comes in the context of his self-denunciation.

That Huck's goodness *is* innate, and that it would entail his *complete* socialization to remove it, is apparent in the comparison of his own honest vernacular with the debased or ornamental language of his conscience. In spite of the inverted viewpoint, the language is powerfully direct and spontaneous, pure in spite of its grammatical imperfections. Whereas at moments of farce the comedy is produced by the contrast between a corrupt vernacular and a "pure" one, the comedy of Huck's heartfelt soliloquy over whether or not to betray Jim with an informing note depends on the ignorance with which he asserts his own irredeemable depravity: "And I about made up my mind to pray; and see if I couldn't try and quit being the kind of boy I was, and be better. So I kneeled down. But the words wouldn't come." It is clear that here, as elsewhere, Huck honestly believes he is evil, whatever opinion the reader might hold of him. Hence his failure at prayer, testifying his inability to accept what is immoral; and hence his ironic assurance of his own damnation to hell when he finally decides to rescue Jim from the Phelps plantation. The fragility of this assurance as a comic device is all the more remarkable when one considers that, by the time he concludes he is hell-bound for his compassion, Huck has already been fed to the teeth with evidence of *real* social decadence: the evil confidence games of the Duke and the King, the shooting of Boggs and the townsfolk's relish over it, the murder of Buck Grangerford and the brutal feud, and, of course, the anguish of Jim and a race in chains. Surely more aware of shore life and its corruptions, Huck is by now *still* unable to draw the proper conclusions about his own morality in relation to that of his society. Until those conclusions are drawn, he is devoid of proper knowledge, sheltered from the truth, and thus fertile for comic exploitation.

As long as he can maintain Huck in such a state of ignorance, Twain has at hand an effective comic shield. But his troubles in maintaining Huck's ignorance, and the unconsciously precocious, critical voice that reflects it, are part of the history of the book and Twain's own shifting comic stance. An entry from 1891 in his notebook gives a hint of what might have followed were Huck Finn ever to have resolved his conflict, losing his innocence in the final disillusionment of an old man who has learned that there is neither a heaven nor a hell to go to: "Huck comes back, 60 years old, from nobody knows where—& crazy. Thinks he is a boy again, & scans always every face for Tom & Becky & c." The comedy of Twain's projected sequel would obviously not be light: "Tom comes, at last, 60 from wandering the world, and tends Huck, & together they talk the old times; both are desolate, life has been a failure, all that was loveable, all that was beautiful is under the mould. They die together."[29] With such a plot, one course *might* lie in exploiting the pseudo-innocence of Huck's craziness, but that would probably be too pathetic and sentimental to sustain the comedic screen through which Clemens could vent his pessimism on his audience. In such a work, Huck necessarily must have come to face an unthinkable truth: "life has been a failure." If the only relief from this truth were craziness or death, as opposed to the sustained ignorance given Huck in the complete text, another comedic approach could lie in an absurdist gallows humor—too much so for Clemens's popular audience, unprepared as they surely would be were he to anticipate Kafka. So, in *Huckleberry Finn*, rather than killing the reader's hope, Mark Twain kills Huck's, consigning him to the permanent, torturous conviction that whatever causes his conscience to torment him is the deserved result of his *own* faulty internal wiring. Twain is merciful enough, though, to give Huck that self-preserving instinct that compels him to "light out for the territory" where his remaining soundness of heart may survive until society's next encroachment. But the lighting-out itself may be an admission of defeat, the silencing of a voice that had threatened too many times to betray the God-hating, man-hating condemnations of its creator.

This threat of betrayal is especially apparent in the latter half of the book, that is, between Huck's arrival at the Grangerford house and his part in the almost inexplicable burlesque at the Phelps plantation—inexplicable because his passivity then seems so out of place with his reactions to the downriver experience, especially the horror of the feud. The rise and fall of Huck's awareness is exceptionally steep between his meeting of the Grangerfords and his game playing on the plantation at Jim's expense. The comic voice through which his awareness is transmitted between these two sites conversely follows a drastic alternation between the grimmest gallows humor, total silencing, and the tragically burlesque— all exemplifying Twain's difficulty in maintaining the blameless voice of the comedian without slipping into the bleakest satire, mere clownishness, or giving up on the deception completely. At times he falls into all three situations: the thievery of the Duke and the King, the murder of Boggs, and the brutality of the feud are more than a match for Huck's good-natured innocence, while the burlesques on the Phelps plantation undermine the directness of the social critique that precedes them, with Huck consigned to a supporting role, and only a hint of his late critical awareness remaining. In between, as in the instances of Buck's death and Sherburn's diatribe on cowardice, the comic voice is stilled altogether.

Given the subject matter Twain found himself treating during Huck's downriver experience, it is not surprising that he diminished Huck's role as an object of humor, choosing instead to highlight the bleak incongruities within society rather than those within Huck concerning his own morality and conscience. In order to recognize how Twain could treat human barbarity *as* a comedian, one must focus on his attention to incongruity, by which he simultaneously depicts such contrasts as those between piety and murder, gentility and animalism, pretension and action. Such contrasts are embodied especially in the persons of the Grangerfords and the Duke and the King. The varying intensity of Huck's comedy depends upon these incongruities and the decreasing degree of innocence with which he reveals them. Through the build-up to the first blow to that innocence—the death of Buck Grangerford—and beyond it to the Duke and King episodes, Huck's narration develops from mere precocious observation to undisguised disillusionment and disgust. This decrease of his innocence coincides with the swift shedding of the fake gentility of the feudists and confidence men, who eventually are portrayed purely as animals.

It is significant that at Buck's death Huck utters his first unmasked betrayal of disgust: "It made me so sick I most fell out of the tree" (175). From here onwards, until the appearance of Tom Sawyer, Huck's critical revelations are never as unconsciously uttered as they have been previously, suggesting a diminished capacity in the comic device that sustains the blameless voice. Huck betrays a contemptuous misanthropy as he pronounces on the Duke and the King: "It was enough to make a body ashamed of the human race" (226), and "I never see anything so disgusting" (228). In one sense it is only natural that Huck should be moved and changed by the corruption he witnesses on shore; but as he witnesses it and grows increasingly direct in his criticism, it is apparent that Twain cannot deal with these issues without revealing more of his own cynicism and disgust than previously. Huck himself no longer remains the focus of the humor or the reader's primary concern. He becomes a reporter directing the reader's attention to the horrors he sees, with those horrors themselves becoming the objects of Mark Twain's fury.

Plotting the rise of Huck's conscious awareness, and the concomitant hardening of his critical voice, is instructive. When he arrives at the Grangerford house, he appears relatively free of opinion. He reports, rather than editorializes, on being interrogated at gunpoint by a "gentleman" and his sons and on the shuffling entrance of Buck, rubbing his sleepy eyes and dragging a shotgun twice his size. He does not judge the oddity of Colonel Grangerford's fatherly reassurance that Buck, too, will have *his* chance to kill some Shepherdsons. If the passages give rise to laughter, it is more sardonic than benign; there is an awareness and foreboding on the part of the reader from which Huck is yet spared. Short, pointed references to shooting and murder are nearly swamped by Huck's childish banter with Buck about dogs and rabbits and skipping school. Huck is unaware of the implications as he comments on the gaudiness of the house and its furnishings; he merely reports what he sees and hears: "There was a little old piano, too, that had tin pans in it, I reckon, and nothing was ever so lovely as to hear the young ladies sing 'The Last Link Is Broken' and play 'The Battle of Prague' on it" (163). The total extent of Huck's present inability to pronounce judgment is made apparent as he admires and mistakes for art the obsessively warped elegiac creations of Emmeline Grangerford. The morbidity of her drawings affects him adversely, but Twain does not permit him to place the reason: "These was all nice pictures, I reckon, but I didn't seem somehow to take to them, because if ever I was down a little, they always give me the fan-tods." He *appears*, as he must, baffled and awed by what he thinks is Emmeline's artistic perseverance and command of poetic technique: "She would slap down a line, and if she couldn't find anything to rhyme with it, she would just scratch it out and slap down another one, and go ahead." Two voices are activated here: the cynical voice of Mark Twain, aware of the reader's sophistication, and the awed, ignorant voice of Huck Finn, who delivers unawares Twain's sarcasm with no hint of his dual role as admirer and critic. He opens himself to both appreciation and ridicule with his envious, though unconsciously double-edged declaration: "Every time a man died, or a woman died, or a child died, she would be on hand with her 'tribute' before he was cold" (162).

These initial passages present Huck as cushioned in a padding of deceptive familial warmth whose seaminess informs only the reader that all is not harmonious in the Grangerford household. Huck's awful awakening will be all the more powerful when the cushion is torn apart at the seams. The disparity between his innocent appreciation and Emmeline's morbid, mechanical sentimentality is apparent at the outset, but the passages do more than merely display the Grangerford superficiality. More important, they provide a contrasting foreshadow of the simple and honest force of Huck's own elegy on the loss of his friend: "I cried a little when I was covering up Buck's face, for he was mighty good to me" (175). This, the sole mention in the book of Huck Finn shedding an honest tear, while he otherwise "lets on" to cry to save himself or Jim in a scrape, is a telling indication of the damaging blow to his psyche as well as to the resilience of his comic voice.

Another factor making the loss of Huck's innocence all the more crippling is the initial admiration he feels for Colonel Grangerford, the chief adherent to that brand of barbarism called chivalry. The colonel is the closest thing to a father that Huck might wish to have, after the neglect and mistreatment at the hands of Pap Finn. In his admiration for a father figure, Huck is unaware of the thick, deceptive coat of gentility worn by the colonel—"He was a gentleman all over; and so was his family"—yet, more than comically suggesting that the Grangerford women, too, are "gentlemen," Huck unconsciously reveals another side to the colonel: "He was well born, as the saying is, and that's worth as much in a man as it is in a horse" (164). Huck does not realize that he here implies the opinion of a critical observer— one that he himself will soon have cause to believe—that in spite of his genteel trappings, Grangerford is at bottom a brute. Huck is awed and respectful of the Grangerford manners that shroud the savage animal psyche and of the power with which the colonel commands these manners at church, at the table, and in the parlor. Thinking that he is reporting on Grangerford's command of etiquette, Huck unwittingly reveals the man's hidden brutality as he repeats his admonition following Buck's close brush with a Shepherdson: " 'I don't like that shooting from behind a bush. Why didn't you step into the road, my boy?' " (166). Huck himself is coming closer to a more conscious knowledge of such brutality, a knowledge that crystallizes in the boughs of a tree as Buck is killed; and as he approaches this point, his comic voice undergoes a progressive strangulation.

Buck's close encounter with Harney Shepherdson signals the rise of Huck's own consciousness, while Buck, still with a child's characteristic naïveté, explains the workings of the feud: " 'A man has a quarrel with another man, and kills him; then that other man's brother kills *him*; then the other brothers, on both sides, goes for one another; and then the *cousins* chip in—and by-and-by everybody's killed off, and there ain't no more feud'" (167). Buck is of course revealing unconsciously the process of his own family's extinction, with the comedy, however bleak, depending on the distance between Buck and his subject. The feud is described as an abstract process, a schoolboy's elementary subtraction problem mastered with smug pride. But when Buck shortens the distance—in this case the primary comedic device—by describing the cornering of his fourteen-year-old cousin by old Baldy Shepherdson, the only comic element remaining is a pitiful irony: "'So at last Bud seen it warn't any use, so he stopped and faced around so as to have the bullet holes in front, you know, and the old man he rode up and shot him down'" (168). The voice is the same in each description, as is the incongruity between the deadpan narration and the subject matter—not to mention the incongruity *within* the subject matter itself, namely, the emphasis on the niceties of procedure and show in a hopelessly terminal process. What changes the quality of humor is the shortened distance between the narrator and the subject matter: although Buck maintains an almost ghostly mask of innocence, the reader perceives the extent to which the boy is scarred and doomed by the grotesqueness of his family.

These two paragraphs demonstrate the same manner in which Huck's humor will darken over the next four pages, as he approaches the apocalyptic death of Buck. Huck likewise is drawn into immediate contact with the subject matter: the death of his friend, almost his twin in name and age, brings it from the general to the particular; and he will become emotionally and verbally altered. The extent to which Huck henceforth reveals his bitterness and disgust for what he sees outside of himself shows how Twain could not maintain the disarmingly unaware mouthpiece of the earlier chapters. With Huck's decreased innocence comes an inevitable decrease in comic intensity. The final, undeniable *increase* created during the Phelps burlesques depends on the regression of Huck Finn to a prefeud distance and somnambulistic innocence, in which he seems almost hypnotized into forgetting all he has seen, merely to accommodate the romantic fantasies of Tom Sawyer. It appears an almost desperate strategy to regain Huck's lost comic voice, first silenced with the death of Buck Grangerford, and only fitfully apparent in the succeeding episodes.

When Huck sees Buck pursued and shot to pieces by a band of grown men, his voice—the sole instrument of Mark Twain's comedy—is temporarily arrested. To have made him anything other than speechless might have made his reporting as incredibly detached as Buck's own, or as insincere and obsessively gushy as Emmeline's. He is not even given the benefit of the precocious backwoods allegory that his limited vocabulary had previously allowed him. Instead he can only answer with an impotent silence: "I ain't agoing to tell all that happened—it would make me sick again if I was to do that" (175). It is here that Huck's innocence and juvenile precocity—which up to now had characterized his comic voice—receive their death-blow. Scarred by this shattering revelation of the alliance between outward honor and inward brutality, he henceforth delivers a comedy that remains bitter as long as his consciousness is his own, that is, before he is anesthetized into the final burlesques. As he says of the bloody events that had sickened him, "I wished I hadn't ever come ashore that night, to see such things. I ain't ever going to get shut of them—lots of times I dream about them" (175). Thus irreversibly crippled, Huck from now on stingily guards his spirit of acceptance, and he is noticeably less ready to forgive, or even to *appear* forgiving. By allowing Huck to show outwardly his bitterness for actions and objects outside of himself, Mark Twain to a large extent reduces his capacity for comic implication. Again, for him to have done otherwise would have threatened to keep Huck so detached as to seem unnatural and incredible; but this is precisely what happens in the final passages. To be sure, Twain would indeed resort to such eerie detachment in his later works, notably *Pudd'nhead Wilson* and *The Mysterious Stranger*, but by then he would have already given up any intentions of presenting a model alternative through comedy, as he still tries to do in *Huckleberry Finn*.

A further indication of Twain's need to juggle with the comic device to which he was committed from the book's outset is Huck's recurring pattern of attempting a return to the solace of play or juvenility following Buck's death. This in fact is one way of explaining the end sequence, wherein Huck becomes totally absorbed in Tom Sawyer's game playing: since he *is* after all a child, it seems a natural enough course of action. But the fact remains that without exception these returns to innocence are only temporary, always thwarted or compromised by corruption in the surrounding adult world. Immediately after covering up Buck's face, Huck runs back to the fatherly or big-brotherly comfort of Jim, the maternal warmth of the Mississippi, and the protection of the raft: "We said there warn't no home like a raft, after all. Other places do seem so cramped up and smothery, but a raft don't. You feel mighty free and easy and comfortable on a raft" (176). The pattern of escapism thus begins, but Huck finds his rejuvenation by the raft and the river to be short-lived. He is immediately saddled with the Duke and the King, and his unnaturally heightened sense of perception, whose revelations have just caused his flight, forces him to continue making such accurate and critical social judgments from which most children are spared. Immediately sizing up the Duke and the King as "low-down humbugs and frauds," Huck remains silent only in the interests of keeping peace aboard the raft and preserving Jim's safety (185). But when they land ashore in a hellish Arkansas village, he willingly and consciously represents the townsfolk as the sadists they are, with a capacity for judgment denied him at the Grangerford household: "There couldn't anything wake them up all over, and make them happy all over, like a dog fight—unless it might be putting turpentine on a stray dog and setting fire to him or tying a pan to his tail and see him run himself to death" (202–3). The comedy here, if a sick and helpless chuckle can be counted as such, is based on the incongruity between the townspeople's delight and their means of obtaining it. The deadpan of Huck's narration caused by his limited vocabulary cannot hide the evident disgust in his voice, whether in describing the shooting of Boggs, the townspeople's jostling for choice viewing spots to watch him die, or their gross parodies of it afterwards. If any laughter arises from these passages, it is not owing to a boy's disarmingly precocious commentary on grown-up affairs but rather to the ignorance of the adults themselves of the hell they create. If the reader laughs at all, it is out of that sour, sardonic despair that characterizes black comedy: we can do nothing but laugh.

The presence of Boggs's assassin, Colonel Sherburn, creates the one instance in the book wherein Huck, as narrator, is so out of character that he can repeat verbatim Sherburn's lengthy and verbally sophisticated monologue on cowardice, with no trace of his own stunted dialect. Henry Nash Smith gives as a reason for this Twain's impatience with being a passive observer through the persona of Huck Finn, suggesting his need for "an alternative persona who was protected against suffering by being devoid of pity or guilt"—again, an indication of the comedian's inability to proceed with the comic premise originally initiated.[30] Sherburn in fact does more to erase Huck's character than does Tom Sawyer in the final sequence. It is as though Huck is speaking strange tongues while demonically possessed, for this occasion is the only one in the book wherein his narration sustains a vocabulary and diction he cannot possibly have mastered, showing that Twain felt it necessary to erase totally the comic voice in order to deal with a subject he could not present comedically.

In order to reintroduce Huck with the character of the child he is, while still commenting on the adult capacity for sadism, Twain causes him to express his disgust in a more appropriate and credible manner: he runs away, this being the only protest in his power. As he had done after Buck's death, he again attempts a retreat into innocence as a reaction against his disgust, taking refuge in a circus audience. He enjoys the circus in a brief moment of play, but *his* enjoyment comes from the relief of seeing who he thinks is a drunk escaping death on a runaway horse. The passage is a brief reaffirmation of Huck's innate compassion, sincerity, and noteworthy lack of a sense of humor, which allow him to make unwittingly pointed statements about social behavior. While Huck hopes for the rider's safety, the townspeople lust after his injury as he bounces like a rag doll on the horse's back. Thus Huck's attempted escape into the relief of juvenile play ultimately provides yet another example of adult sadism, for the crowd are as unaware as he that the drunk is actually an expert circus horseman in disguise. Amidst their laughter, Huck alone is "all of a tremble to see his danger" (212). Had Huck seen the show before witnessing the feud, his character suggests, his reaction might have been the same; he might have been just as relieved to find the rider out of peril. The circus, however, and the relief it provides, would seem less of a stop-gap for his intensified disillusionment than it does now. As the downriver experience continues, the broadest comedy is to come from the fitful bursts of slapstick and burlesque at Huck's expense in the fleeting moments of innocence that vie with his increasingly weary cynicism, as he approaches the almost complete erasure of character on the Phelps plantation. After seeing the Duke and the King con a town with the Royal Nonesuch and its parodies of Shakespeare, Huck is quick and merciless in passing critical judgment on them, figuring them for "rapscallions." As they swindle the Wilks girls out of their father's bequest with their farcical impersonations of his deaf and dumb brothers, Huck can only respond with previously uncharacteristic rage and epithets of contempt for the human race.

Then, as quickly as he has learned to judge, he seems to forget. Immediately upon vowing to set Jim free after escaping from the Duke and the King, he is at the Phelps plantation. If he indeed plans on going to hell, he takes a good time in going, unheroically diminishing into a shadow behind Tom Sawyer's antics. The only critical remarks he makes on the plantation are about Silas Phelps, who "never charged nothing for his preaching, and it was worth it, too" (297), and about Tom's contemptible romances: "'He had a dream . . . and it shot him'" (351). Such remarks as these seem more unwitting than pointed, as though Twain were attempting to reinvest Huck with his former unconscious precocity rather than his later, bitterly earned critical awareness. While there is indeed more comedy to be found in the book, it is pure burlesque; and one must look to Tom Sawyer and Jim for it. As for Huck, his days as both social observer and comic mouthpiece are over. However broad is the comedy of the final ten chapters, it carries with it an undercurrent of impotence and defeat. That the conflict between Huck's "sound heart" and "deformed conscience" is left unresolved suggests—by virtue of Twain's having separated comedy from Huck's late critical awareness—Clemens's dawning conclusion that comedy, as artistic deception, might not stand as a weapon against the social realities he deplored. In this sense, Huck's sustained *lack* of social judgment in the closing chapters may in fact be the final judgment of Mark Twain: if the audience demands comedy and belly laughs, he would provide them—at the price of everything else. Referring to the "'inharmonious burlesque'" of the final sequence, Bernard De Voto wrote, "In the whole history of the English novel there is no more abrupt or more chilling descent."[31]

The implications of Twain's having abandoned Huck's resolve for the sake of a hearty last laugh are even more drastic than those suggested by Henry Nash Smith, who believed that the final sequence amounted to nothing more than the means by which Twain beat his way back from incipient tragedy to comic resolution. Likewise there is more to the ending than its being the "final joke" at the complacent reader's expense, as James Cox suggested— "the moment when, in outrageous burlesque, it attacks the sentiment which its style has at once evoked and exploited."[32] However likely these conclusions are in themselves, from the comedic standpoint there is another implication revealed in the final burst of creative energy that produced the end sequence. Cox notes that by the time Clemens was engaged in the final phase of *Huckleberry Finn*, he was also swamped in a plethora of speculative business, having overextended his investments in such ventures as vineyards, history games, a steam pulley, a watch company, an insurance house, a steam generator, a new process of marine telegraphy, and a kaolo-type engraver. This was not all: Clemens was about to become the senior partner and chief investor in the Webster Publishing Company, the disaster-ridden firm whose first project would be *The Adventures of Huckleberry Finn*. Most of these ventures were doomed to failure, recurrently dragging Clemens to the brink of bankruptcy and despondency. If his disillusionments with the corruptions of the Gilded Age, compounded by his own business disasters, caused him to lose confidence in the power of his comedy as a potent force for betterment—his society's or his own—it is conceivable, then, that the end of the book is an indictment of comedy itself as a critical weapon, represented in the final impotence of Huck Finn against the gimmicks and posturing of Tom Sawyer.

The implications of the ending were also carried into Twain's plans for a sequel entitled "Huckleberry Finn and Tom Sawyer Among the Indians." In this story, Huck still plans to "light out for the territory"—but not to escape pointedly the corruptions of society. He merely wishes to "cut for the Injun country and go for adventures" along with Tom and Jim, the latter of whom evidently decides that his wife and children are not worth finding. Even this plan is postponed as Huck accommodates himself to the society from which he had planned to escape. As he says, he and Jim "kind of hung fire. Plenty to eat and nothing to do. We was very well satisfied."[33] Such feebleness may well have been the price of comedy in Mark Twain's eyes—in spite of his later protestations to the contrary.

But if *Huckleberry Finn*, especially its ending, indicates the degree to which Twain not only noted the illusions maintained by society and himself but despaired of both their perniciousness and necessity, then it also indicates that same fitfulness in which he would repeatedly abandon the deceptions of the comedian throughout his career. The worldly realities from which he could not fully divert his attention, and which frequently caused him to lose confidence in his own game of confidence, were not merely those business ventures that preoccupied him during the completion of *Huckleberry Finn*; nor were they the particular social corruptions of America in the Gilded Age. As the previous section showed, among the actualities that could not be displaced or transformed by the illusions of comedy were the internal conflicts and questions in Samuel Clemens over his own ironic identity—because it was precisely these illusions that determined the makeup of his alter ego and contributed to the conflicts. *Huckleberry Finn*, itself both a condemnation of pretense and a product of it, exemplifies the paradox inherent in the duality of Clemens, the cynical critic, and Twain, the winsome comedian. Just as the book's ending indicates a denunciation of comedic deception on the part of Clemens, it is a manifestation of a trend that had plagued him since the inception of Mark Twain, and which would continue to do so. As his biography shows, the comic illusions of Mark Twain came nowhere near to assuaging the conflicts in his creator; they appear only to have exacerbated them. Thus can the inconsistencies and ending of *Huckleberry Finn* be seen as products of the crisis that influenced the overall development of the fabrication, Mark Twain, pointing the way to a final resignation.

Pudd'nhead Wilson: "'pears to be a fool"

The period between the release of *Huckleberry Finn* and the writing of *Pudd'nhead Wilson* reveals a protracted battle between Clemens and Mark Twain that, while not signaling the final blow to the comic impulse, certainly foreshadows it. In a sense, *Pudd'nhead Wilson* is Clemens's full-scale, implicit rejection of comedy, signifying the defeat of the comedian figure and betraying—as in *The Confidence-Man*—an outright suspicion of a visible world constructed, as the aging Twain implies, through layers of untrustworthy illusion. The contest between the confidence man and the earnest revelator that gains its fullest expression in *Pudd'nhead Wilson* is a continuation of the conflict only barely lulled by the completion of *Huckleberry Finn*. It is a contest that manifests itself in a variety of circumstances.

Even as *Huckleberry Finn* neared its release date, the businessman in Clemens stepped up his activities with a fervency to suggest that he was less fulfilled as a comedian than he might otherwise have been. Perhaps the seemingly newfound confidence with which he had viewed his creative powers ("It is no more trouble to write than it is to lie") was transferred to those business preoccupations that were such a bane to him, and would so remain. In any event, the ink of *Huckleberry Finn* was hardly dry when Clemens launched his publishing firm, invented his history game, poured his earnings into vineyards and insurance and manufacturing companies, and devoted himself to the other affairs that would combine to ruin him. His subsequent writings, private and public, show that the retreat of his confidence in the manipulations of both business and artistry, combined with the darkening of his outlook on the entire course of human progress in his own century, led in a direct path to the cynical depression and bitterness that variously characterized the remainder of his works, against which no pretense of gaiety could stand. It was a retreat of confidence that also led in a direct path to *Pudd'nhead Wilson*.

Just as Melville had utilized the Franklin of *Israel Potter* in preparation for a greater rendering in *The Confidence-Man*, so too did Twain—unconsciously or otherwise—prepare for the explorations of *Pudd'nhead Wilson* with an earlier critique. As he sank into the mire of failure and bankruptcy with his doomed Paige typesetting machine, Clemens began to toy with an idea that had started out as a hurried notebook entry: "Dream of being a knight errant in armor in the middle ages. Have the notions & habits of thought of present day mixed with the necessities of that." The potential for innocent slapstick was considerable: "No pockets in armor. No way to manage certain requirements of nature. Can't scratch. . . . Make disagreeable clatter when I enter church. Can't dress or undress myself. Always getting struck by lightning. Fall down, can't get up."[34] This was, of course, the germination of Hank Morgan, the doomed Connecticut Yankee in King Arthur's Court. Twain's treatment of Morgan reveals much about the inspiration behind *Pudd'nhead Wilson* and about the latter book's place in the struggle between Clemens and Mark Twain.

Critics have twinned Clemens's obsession with the ill-fated Paige typesetter and the technological nightmare of Hank Morgan's Camelot, claiming that the personal and financial failures of Clemens, the Gilded Age businessman, determined the fate of Morgan, the Middle Age confidence man. This may be so; but even a year before becoming embroiled with the disasters of the typesetter, Clemens was already toying with the doom scenario that would make *A Connecticut Yankee* one of his grimmest tales: "He mourns his lost land—has come to England & revisited it, but it is all changed & become old, so old!—& it was so fresh & new, so virgin before. . . . Has lost all interest in life—is found dead next morning —suicide."[35] The timing of this notebook entry makes it clear that despair was seeping into Mark Twain's projected burlesque before his business failures began to mount up. They certainly must have affected the development of the book, but it was not merely disillusionment with business, or technology, or America in the Gilded Age that doomed the book to its ultimate holocaust. It was something much deeper that motivated Hank Morgan to betray the most cynical, godless, misanthropic thought yet published by Mark Twain: "All that is original in us, and therefore fairly creditable or discreditable to us, can be covered up and hidden by the point of a cambric needle." As for the rest of the human makeup, body and spirit—in 1886, with the reviled Darwin only six years dead—it is merely "atoms contributed by, and inherited from, a procession of ancestors that stretches back a billion years to the Adam-clam or grasshopper or monkey from whom our race has been so tediously and ostentatiously and unprofitably developed."[36]

The protagonist who utters this—the book's comic persona and supposedly the author's comic shield—is also the condemned object of Mark Twain's satire, the confidence man who lives by American know-how, destroys by it, and is himself eventually destroyed by it. Hank Morgan is Twain's projection of Franklin, though without the wit, good humor, social conscience, or philosophical depth ascribed to him by Melville. He is, as he proudly proclaims, "a Yankee of Yankees" and "nearly barren of sentiment"; in Clemens's estimation, he is "an ass."[37] With a half-baked, populist idealism as the justification for boosting himself and his shallow gimmicks—or, as he calls them, "effects"—he dupes the unavoidably credulous subjects of Camelot with his seemingly miraculous mastery of such nineteenth-century commonplaces as plumbing, explosives, solar calculation, and shooting people with pistols. Through his easy deceptions he earns the status of a magical demigod, "the Boss"—until he is put to sleep for thirteen centuries by an exasperated Merlin. But before he can be thus disarmed, he and his Gatling guns succeed in massacring twenty-five thousand knights in ten minutes, all in the name of progress. This was Mark Twain's *comedy*, a runaway nightmare spawned from an innocent burlesque. *A Connecticut Yankee* provides the starkest example of a comic voice in unequal contest with its subject matter. Far from being imbued with the comic pretense of innocence or reverence that in his best moments had made Huck Finn such a canny mouthpiece for the embittered Clemens, Hank Morgan has little more than a con man's patter and slickness as his defining qualities. Such a transparent voice could not contain enough unwitting wit, intelligence, or compassion to accommodate and disguise the cynical rage that drove the story to its bloody conclusion. Hank Morgan is a crank, a failed confidence man in terms of the comedy as well as the plot, only capable of betraying the misanthropy that Huck Finn, at his most disarming, could disguise.

There may of course be more to Hank Morgan's failure than mere shallowness of voice. In 1885, the year of the notebook entry predicting Morgan's unfunny suicide, *Huckleberry Finn* had come out to reviews of its "blood-curdling humor" and its "course and dreary fun." Mark Twain, it was charged, had "no reliable sense of propriety"; and newspapers from the Atlantic to the Mississippi echoed the lofty sentiments of Louisa May Alcott: "If Mr. Clemens cannot think of something better to tell our pure-minded lads and lasses, he had best stop writing for them."[38] He had in fact already done so, even with *Huckleberry Finn*, though nearly all of the negative reviews were based on the erroneous assumption that Twain was still a children's writer. The Concord, Massachusetts, library committee voted to expel the book from its shelves as "trash suitable only for the slums." Clemens put on a defiant face in public, proclaiming in a newspaper, "That will sell 25,000 copies for us sure."[39] But his private letters reveal his sense of injury and persecution; so if, once again attacked as a coarse buffoon, he lost confidence in the power of his comedy, it is possible that he was driven to make his next book, *A Connecticut Yankee*, serious to the point of tragedy. And, just as he had turned to a fangless project like *The Prince and the Pauper* after the hostile reception of *Tom Sawyer*, he fell back upon a number of risk-free sequels that would prove safe and reliable—but not before he proceeded to ruin himself in business.

By 1891, still not convinced of the hopelessness of the Paige typesetter, Clemens was investing in it to the tune of three thousand dollars a month. His resources nearly dissipated, he began to borrow from friends and relations; and in an effort to economize his meager holdings, sailed with his family for the relatively cheaper economy of Europe. He continued to manage the typesetter affairs along with a handful of other ventures, making eight Atlantic crossings over the next three years and finally returning to Europe a bankrupt. In 1894, after a loss of thirteen years and $190,000, Clemens wailed to his partners in New York, "Get me out of business! and I will be yours forever gratefully." He would henceforth, he said, "wallow in ink."[40] With little more to lose, he began writing a story that, like *A Connecticut Yankee*, began as a simple burlesque —this time exploiting the comic possibilities of identical twinship, as in innumerable farces before it. At its inception it was primarily an effort to stave off his creditors, a serialization for *Century Magazine* that indeed succeeded in keeping them at bay. Like *Huckleberry Finn*, it ran away from its initial premise, invading territories its author had had no apparent intention of crossing and emerging as the most enigmatic of all Mark Twain's comedies. As it turned out, it was also—in spite of its comic mastery—his final rejection of the comic mask itself.

Pudd'nhead Wilson was Twain's last look at particularly *American* impostures, written in 1894 from the distant vantage point of Italy, nearly sixty-five years after the time of its setting. The distance factor is important, not only in geographical and temporal terms but comedically as well, for it allowed Twain to explore—after Melville and from the depths of his own depression—the frightening degree to which human relations depend on the manipulations and interpretations of outward appearance. His debate over the slavery of men and women to their own uncertain identities, as well as to the world's posturing, is to a great extent a manifestation of Clemens's own obsession with the ironic identity he shared with Mark Twain. Although the final implications of *Pudd'nhead Wilson* are easily as grim—if not more so—than those of *A Connecticut Yankee*, it is nevertheless the greater comedy. For rather than employing as ineffectual a mouthpiece as the blustering, shallow confidence man, Hank Morgan, Twain utilized the deadpan voice of a detached observer, embodied in both the omniscient narrator and the character of the outcast comedian, Pudd'nhead Wilson himself. These two personae combine into a mastery of controlled, ironic distance that allowed Twain to present one of his bleakest fables as the effective comedy not attained in his next and last novel, *The Mysterious Stranger*. As the outcome of *Pudd'nhead Wilson* suggests, however, the book is, in spite of its own comic success, Clemens's ultimate denial of comedy as an instrument of social criticism or change and, as such, his ultimate denial of Mark Twain.

Clemens's sense of imprisonment by his twin, the "freak" Mark Twain, and his resistance to it are by now well known. Hence his repeated treatment of twins as freaks, either with the joined Chang and Eng in "The Personal Habits of the Siamese Twins" or the joined Capello brothers in "Those Extraordinary Twins," out of which grew his rendering of the separated Capellos in *Pudd'nhead Wilson*. Through all of these he as much confronts his own personal enslavement to what he saw as the comic expectations of the buffoon, as the broader question of general human enslavement to fictions of identity. When, in *Pudd'nhead Wilson*, the twin Capello brothers arrive in Dawson's Landing, Angelo reveals the degradation of a man forced, out of monetary necessity, to exploit his own seeming oddity in order to get a laugh. The result for the brothers had been two years of "'slavery'" among "'the attractions of a cheap museum in Berlin.'"[41] As he began writing *Pudd'nhead Wilson*, Clemens himself was about to begin a worldwide lecture tour to regain his lost finances, after having frequently rebelled against the necessity of stepping onto the lecture platform, each time vowing never to do so again for any price. Notable in his complaints was his repugnance over the possessiveness of his audiences, so that his impression of his own enslavement to the identity of Mark Twain was exacerbated by the unmerciful grasp of public adulation. In *Pudd'nhead Wilson*, the twins' first appearance at the home of the widow Cooper and her daughter, Rowena, culminates with all the neighborhood rushing in to see the new, fine, foreign birds, who are obliged to set about "winning approval, compelling admiration and achieving favor from all." The widow Cooper follows "the conquering march with a proud eye," while Rowena says to herself, "'And to think they are ours—all ours'" (93).

The narrator is ironically distant enough to prevent the same resentment that Clemens often felt toward his audience from appearing in its brutal immediacy on the page, a resentment that had once prompted fellow lecturer Oliver Wendell Holmes to write to him in commiseration, "These negative faces with their vacuous eyes and stony lineaments pump and suck the warm soul. They are what kill the lecturer."[42] Although Clemens readily concurred with this damning opinion, in *Pudd'nhead Wilson* the ironic narrator transforms his contempt into playful condescension for the widow and Rowena as they bask in the cheap thrills of hosting "their" celebrities. Each of the women "recognized that she knew now for the first time the real meaning of that great word Glory, and perceived the stupendous value of it, and understood why men in all ages had been willing to throw away meaner happinesses, treasure, life itself, to get a taste of its sublime and supreme joy" (94)—sarcastic, yes; but nevertheless in this instance transformed and softened just enough to suggest the narrator's fictional indulgence (94). Similarly, when Judge Driscoll, wishing to be the first to display the twins in public, takes them on a whirlwind showing-off of the town's most stultifying landmarks, the sentiment expressed is an ironically softened echo of many vitriolic descriptions in Clemens's letters written during his exhausting lecture tours. The bitter resignation with which he had to ingratiate himself to well-meaning, thoughtless hosts—when at times all he wanted was a good night's sleep after a grueling performance—is comedically transformed into the twins' responses to the judge's attention. Spoken, they "admired his admiration, and paid him back the best they could"; unspoken, "they could have done better if some fifteen or sixteen hundred thousand previous experiences of this sort in various countries had not already rubbed off a considerable part of the novelty of it" (96–97).

That Clemens did feel an actual slave to his comedic alter ego, and a sort of freak as well, is particularly evident in letters written in the fatigue of his globe-spanning lecture tours, or at other times when "being funny" seemed a monstrously inhuman expectation. As early as 1871, when his financial troubles were nowhere near their magnitude as during the writing of *Pudd'nhead Wilson*, Clemens had despaired to his brother about the necessity of "seeing my hated nom de plume (for I do loathe the very sight of it) in print *again* every month."[43] His other sufferings had also piled on, irrespective of the public demands upon the genial comedian. When they became too heavy, he resigned as a regular contributor to the *Galaxy Magazine* with the public admission that after eight months of deathbed vigils and sickbed watches, with two of his family taken and two others nearly so, he was still "under contract to furnish 'humorous' matter once a month"—some of which "could have been injected into a funeral sermon without disturbing the solemnity of the occasion."[44] One of those funereal pieces had been "Mark Twain's (Burlesque) Autobiography," in which Clemens assigned his "hated nom de plume" to a direct ancestry of history's most infamous criminals and outcasts, from Guy Fawkes to Nebuchadnezzar to Baalam's Ass. The hostility and contempt for Mark Twain that so pervades this sketch must have informed Pudd'nhead Wilson's speculation—in one of his later aphorisms—that "the secret source of Humor itself is not joy but sorrow. There is no humor in heaven."[45]

As he began *Pudd'nhead Wilson* with the conscious intent of staving off bankruptcy, Clemens faced the realization that he must again exploit *his* sorrows in the name of an alter ego whose identity forever threatened to eclipse his own. Were the question of his *own* identity the sole inspiration for the book, he might not have been able to extend the dilemma so far into the metaphysical, social, political, economic, and moral spheres; but this he did do upon recognizing—as Melville had done—that his own internal struggle might be embodied in the impostures of all human relations. Clemens's internal debate about the nature of his own identity was embodied on a universal scale during the 1890s in the questions of heredity and environment, where religious—and thus moral—certainties were swiftly losing ground. In America at least, along with the increasing moral and spiritual ambivalence after Darwin came a seemingly heightened susceptibility and sensitivity to manipulations by grinning confidence men, politicians, robber barons, carpetbaggers, and land speculators—all of whom flourished to a large extent through the exploitation of a prevailing moral insecurity, as Twain and Warner had shown in *The Gilded Age* and Melville before them in *The Confidence-Man*. Clemens's abiding suspicions over whether morality itself was not just another socially acquired pretense caused *Pudd'nhead Wilson* to remain as unresolved as Clemens himself during his deathbed ravings about dual identity and "the laws of mentality."[46] As a comedic deception that sets out to damn imposture, *Pudd'nhead Wilson* is at once an apology for and critique of manipulations of appearance, morality, and belief. The grim conclusion, however, is that such manipulations are inescapable, motivated as they are by the general slavery to both heredity and environment.

Thus could Pudd'nhead Wilson offer two equally caustic aphorisms in his calendar, demonstrating in combination such slavery. One aphorism presents the fickleness of the environment: "Training is everything. The peach was once a bitter almond; cauliflower is nothing but cabbage with a college education" (84). The second laments an incurable *inheritance* of human corruption: "Adam was but human—this explains it all. He did not want the apple for the apple's sake; he wanted it only because it was forbidden" (61). Twain depicts this combination in the character of Tom Driscoll, whose depravity is owing as much to his "native viciousness" as to the unavoidable circumstances in which he has been placed. Thus the underlying irony of the book places a hopeless, "native" determinism in a paradoxical alliance with that "training [that] is everything." The unmaking of Tom Driscoll hinges on the one piece of evidence that all his pretenses—themselves beyond his control—could not disguise: his fingerprints.

Mark Twain's conviction that "the skin of every human being contains a slave" motivates a plot as tortured as the conclusion that is drawn from it.[47] Tom Driscoll is, on the one hand, a slave by virtue of his *inherited* portion of African blood, while on the other hand he is designated a slave because his society had been *trained* into accepting the righteousness of slavery. Thus is he cast by an inescapable inherited condition into a bondage that is arbitrarily imposed. The paradox is further represented by the fact that the only given depiction of Tom as a culpable being is as an unwilling impostor, since everything the reader knows about his character comes after his mother has exchanged him in the cradle. Underlying all this is the reader's knowledge that he is not in fact the "white" Tom Driscoll but the "black" Valet de Chambre. Then, in a *further* compounding of the paradox, the reader is reminded that the standard designating the babies as "black" or "white" by virtue of the proportion of blood in their veins, rather than their outward appearance, is but "a fiction of law and custom" (64).

The inability to conclude the source of human impressions, resulting in a plot depending on the preordained and the arbitrarily imposed, establishes the one inescapable certainty in the book, as damning as in *The Confidence-Man*: judgments based on outward appearance are both unavoidable and unreliable. Hence the appearances of gentility in the Virginian aristocrats in contrast with the barbarism that inspires them, or the impressions of David Wilson as a "pudd'nhead" in contrast with the cleverness he reveals at the end, or the appearances of Roxy and Tom as white in contrast with the "fiction of law and custom" designating them as black slaves. But if Twain's intention is to attack the gullibility in which people depend on appearances, he offers no alternative lying between sheer credulity and cynical mistrust—a bleak prospect, validating the comedy's seemingly ironic designation as *The Tragedy of Pudd'nhead Wilson*. Just as the Confidence-Man's victims could only argue to exhaustion the question as to whether the trickster is a "genius," "fool," or "knave," Angelo and Luigi are doomed to puzzle over Tom's trustworthiness. To Angelo, he has "a good eye"; to Luigi there is "something veiled and sly about it." To Angelo, his manner of speech is "pleasant" and "free and easy"; to Luigi it is "more so than . . . agreeable." Angelo thinks he is "a sufficiently nice young man"; Luigi isn't so sure (123–24). Tom in fact displays all these multifarious qualities in the course of the novel, some of which are calculated, some of which show themselves in *spite* of his attempts to camouflage them. The trouble for the twins comes in determining not the existence of such incongruous attributes but rather which are genuine and which are not. While the reader is often privy to the omniscient narrator's guidance in making a judgment (if, indeed, the *narrator* can be trusted), the implication remains that in life we are without such guidance.

In Twain's treatment of the town's aristocrats, he repeats the caution of *Huckleberry Finn* against trusting the impressions of a smooth gentility, which can hide an inner savagery. Sometimes he does this solely through ironies inherent in the dialogue, as when

York Driscoll, *himself* a respected judge, vents his rage on Tom for settling an assault case off the dueling ground: "'You cur! You scum! You vermin! Do you mean to tell me that the blood of my race has suffered a blow and crawled to a court of law about it?'" (141). At other times Twain handles the gentility of Dawson's Landing with a blatant sarcasm that, unlike in his treatment of the widow Cooper and Rowena, suggests even here a difficulty in comedically distancing himself from the objects of his scorn, opening him to the accusation of employing the lowest form of irony. Yet it is upon just such an irony that a valid interpretation of the book frequently rests, however much it threatens to betray the narrator. Hence the description of Percy Driscoll, who resolves to sell three slaves down the river for an unsolved petty theft. First described as "a fairly humane man towards slaves and other animals" and "an exceedingly humane man toward the erring of his own race," Driscoll relents at the last moment when all three, in understandable terror, confess. He withdraws in private to reflect upon his magnanimity and the "noble and gracious thing" he had just done; "and that night he set the incident down in his diary, so that his son might read it in after years, and be thereby moved to deeds of gentleness and humanity himself" (68). Here Twain is open to two accusations: either he is employing a facile sarcasm, or—as F. R. Leavis thought—he "unmistakenly admires" these petty aristocrats.[48] In any case, the narrator here comes uncharacteristically closer to the object of his criticism and indicates Twain's impatience with the requirements of distance.

But to a degree such confusion is understandable, for another problem in grasping Twain's comedic treatment of a class he despises—and one with unhappy implications—is that he offers no opposing faction or model of good for the reader's approbation. Although ridiculing the corrupt elite and their preposterous codes of honor, these are no worse than the populist bigotry of the townspeople themselves. It is an indictment of the entire community when the local newspaper not only reports the unwitnessed murder of Judge Driscoll but tries and executes the wrongfully suspected assassin (Luigi) in its pages. The whole community likewise stands condemned in their barbaric support of the eventual duel between Luigi and Judge Driscoll: their farcical democracy is no alternative to the remnants of the aristocracy's feudal code. Not only are the participants deified by the community on the morning after the duel but so are their seconds, "wherefore Pudd'nhead Wilson was suddenly become a man of consequence" (163). But it is no compliment to Pudd'nhead Wilson that the townspeople choose him as mayoral candidate, for it is not owing to his merits but rather to his foolhardy participation in a barbarous ritual. Thus even *he* is not an alternative worthy of praise. However much he may be the most rational and good-natured character in the book, Pudd'nhead Wilson nonetheless takes no pains to dismiss either the absurd democracy or the feudal code; his best friend is in fact Judge Driscoll.

Neither is Roxy offered as a model alternative. Her outrageous confidence game—the switching of the babies in the cradle—is at least understood, given that she is "the heir of two centuries of unatoned insult and outrage" (109). Yet for all her potential of acting as an opposing force to a decadent society, Twain attaches to her the same mindless conditioning as to the community itself, thus again compounding the slavery of blood with that of the environment. In the search for justification in committing the deception on behalf of her son, she repeatedly emulates her aristocratic masters. It begins the moment she debates her decision to make the switch in the cradle, as she recalls an old fable about such a trick by the queen of England: "'Dah, now—de preacher said it his own self, en it ain't no sin, 'ca'se white folks done it . . . en not on'y jis' common white folks nuthur, but de biggest quality dey is in de whole bilin!'" (73). Roxy's inhumanity is at least equal to that of Judge Driscoll and Colonel Grangerford when she berates her only son for refusing to risk his life in the duel with Luigi, given his illegitimate paternity in Colonel Cecil Burleigh Essex and his questionable descendancy from John Smith, Pocahontas, and an African king—"'en yit here you is a-slinkin' outen a duel en disgracin' our whole line like a ornery low-down hound! Yes, it's de nigger in you!'" (158). Her ridiculous pretensions and pride at being one of "de Smith-Pocahontases" reduce her from being a potentially powerful adversary and representative of justice to the demeaned status of a darky minstrel. Her emulation of the corrupt white aristocracy gives validity to the words of Driscoll's real heir, exchanged for Tom's sake into slavery, and who responds to Roxy's angry taunt of being an "imitation nigger": "'If I's imitation, what is you? Bofe of us is imitation *white* . . . we don't amount to noth'n as imitation *niggers*'" (103).

Thus with no one in the world represented by Dawson's Landing to act as the sort of model alternative precariously embodied in Huck Finn, it is apparent that Mark Twain could offer no contest against the irreconcilable and—to his mind—unchangeable forces of human nature that manifest themselves in a greedy survival of the fittest. Even Roxy's apparently unselfish motives in sacrificing all for her son attract a critical eye when one considers her obsession, at the risk of that very son's life, with keeping alive her dubious aristocratic heritage. Each major character carries out his or her plans with no sense of internal division or conflict, with no little space of undeformed morality, as Huck Finn had, in which an alternative might germinate. Twain's apparent lack of faith in the hopes of altering this inescapable state gives a caustic ring to the blanket pronouncement in Pudd'nhead Wilson's Calendar over *all* displays of faith, echoing the implications of *The Confidence-Man* in *its* all-embracing April Fool setting: "April 1.—This is the day upon which we are reminded of what we are on the other three hundred and sixty-four" (211). The fact is that Twain, like Melville, offers no other choice.

Twain's faithlessness is cast in another way, besides in such maxims worthy of an embittered Poor Richard; he actually demonstrates it in the collective fate of the two changelings. Having usurped his master's identity so as *not* to be sold down the river, the false Tom is convicted of Judge Driscoll's murder and exposed as a slave. Because of his economic value as a slave, he is pardoned—in order to be sold down the river. This final, ironic reversal of Tom's fortune might not at first seem so unjust, since all along he had been acting in the "native viciousness" ascribed to him: the implications for the brainwashed society that transmuted his sentence could conceivably be camouflaged by the conviction that Tom got his just desserts (uncharitably assuming that native *anything* is a just grounds for punishment). Yet in presenting the fate of the *real* Tom, consigned since infancy to the identity of Valet de Chambre, Twain depicts the same ironic bondage of those who have done nothing in particular to deserve it. It is not an expression of judgment or justice, but merely the presentation of a cruelly indifferent reality, when the attempt is made to restore the innocent man's identity after decades of conditioning: "The poor fellow could not endure the terrors of the white man's parlor, and felt at home and at peace nowhere but in the kitchen. The family pew was a misery to him, yet he could nevermore enter into the solacing refuge of the 'nigger gallery'—that was closed to him for good and all" (225).

Thus even the real, blameless Tom is still a slave. As the one most tragically duped by Roxy's confidence game and the inescapable determinist paradox of heredity and environment, *The Tragedy of Pudd'nhead Wilson* pertains more to him than to anybody, for his fate expresses the knowledge that the same absurdity will bind the undeserving as well as the deserving. The question remains as to how the irredeemably cynical Mark Twain could depict such a hopeless conclusion in a comic success. He needlessly goes to the extent of including isolated comic effects as if to remind the reader that this is a comedy in spite of its title. Various bits of slapstick and diversion, the burlesque appendix of "Those Extraordinary Twins," and Twain's own admission therein of being "a jackleg novelist" almost beg the reader to take it all as a joke. But the novel succeeds as comedy in spite of these efforts, depending for the most part—with the admitted exceptions mentioned above—on a calculated narrative distance and the refusal to pronounce judgment. In choosing the perspective of an unruffled, impartial observer, the narrator is in the elevated position of viewing as a whole the ironic relationships between humanity, predeterminism, and chance. He can see humans as both agents and victims of their confidence games, and describes the situation with an indispensable deadpan.

What is troubling for the comedian, however, is Twain's implicit suggestion that the comedy depends more on the ironic relationships within the world than on one's own efforts as a comedian; for in *Pudd'nhead Wilson* the comedian suffers a grave defeat. The townspeople brand David Wilson a "pudd'nhead" and an outcast because of his jokes, which they cannot understand: "Irony was not for those people; their mental vision was not focused for it. They read those playful trifles of his in solid earnest, and decided without hesitancy that if there had been any doubt that Dave Wilson was a pudd'nhead—which there hadn't—this revelation removed that doubt for good and all" (86). At the end of the book, the only way for Wilson to gain respect from the community is to prove himself a master of the most expressively serious of professions, the law. Pudd'nhead's value thus lies in his capacity to reveal *earnestly* the slavery of humanity to predetermination (in the form of a fingerprint) and to environment (in the form of Tom's legal status as a slave). His courtroom revelations expose both the untrustworthiness of appearance and the inescapable dependence upon it; and in their seriousness, their earnestness, they indicate the necessity—as George Toles notes—for Wilson to "take back his jokes" and through the law renounce his status as a comedian—foreshadowing Lenny Bruce by nearly a century.[49] Pudd'nhead drops the comic mask, succumbs to the will of Dawson's Landing and as a lawyer actually executes it, making no effort to criticize or undermine it. His comic utterances are reduced to the *private*, cynical grumblings of Pudd'nhead Wilson's Calendar, with which Twain forecasts his own abdication from the comic stage.

Spoil-sport

Near the end of his life, Mark Twain was to direct his attention to one last pair of twins—not identical, to be sure, but conceived in the same moment, though with disguised paternity. These were his last major literary projects, the nonfictional *What Is Man?* and the ostensible comedy, *The Mysterious Stranger*. Twain worked on them concurrently at times, and with the same "pen warmed up in hell." The former was published anonymously and privately, and the latter posthumously, after heavy editorial bowdlerization. Clemens called *What Is Man?* his "Bible." In a letter to Howells in 1899 from Austria—the setting of *The Mysterious Stranger*—he betrayed the conviction that had fueled both works: "I suspect to you there is still dignity in human life, & that Man is not a joke—a poor joke—the poorest that was ever contrived—an April fool joke, played by a malicious Creator with nothing better to waste his time upon." Clemens maintained that he was through with playing the mirthful fool, since he was fed up with such "poor jokes" as these: "Man is not to me the respect-worthy person he was before; & so I have lost my pride in him & can't write gaily nor praisefully about him any more. And I don't intend to try."[50] Eight years later, when *What Is Man?* furtively appeared, Clemens explained in the preface why he had waited so long to publish this God-hating, man-hating sermon: "Every thought in [it] has been thought (and accepted as unassailable truth) by millions of men—and concealed, kept private. Why did they not speak out? Because they dreaded (*and could not bear*) the disapproval of the people around them." He himself was no different: "Why have I not published? The same reason has restrained me, I think. I can find no other."[51] His offering was hardly comic but rather a barely contrived Socratic dialogue in which an Old Man harangues a Young Man with scornful teachings on determinism and general human corruption. As Jesse Bier notes, it was basically an atheistic Calvinist's "orthodox invective against sinful humanity. . . . All Sunday churchgoers, even in optimistic and sentimental America, expected as much as he gave them and in the manner he gave it, traditionally."[52] Yet even with his outright declaration of contempt for the polite conventions he had inherited —and the public deceit into which he had been coerced all his creative life—Clemens could not cut himself off from Mark Twain. Even when he loathed him, he could not let him go.

Out of this realization came the halfhearted fantasy of the other twin, *The Mysterious Stranger*, the final scrawl of the sickened Mark Twain who could no longer compete with the faithlessness—"the dark anarchy of consciousness," in Lewis Simpson's words—of his creator.[53] The victorious Stranger of the title is Little Satan, the heartless practical joker whose closing words of scorn for all that God created could have come straight from the pages of Clemens's "Bible." God is a wicked urchin "'who could make good children as easily as bad, yet preferred to make bad ones; who could have made every one of them happy, yet never made a single happy one; who made them prize their bitter life, yet stingily cut it short; . . . who mouths justice and invented hell—mouths mercy and invented hell—mouths Golden Rules, and forgiveness multiplied by seventy times seven, and invented hell.'" Clemens's final comic mouthpiece slips in vituperative confusion between his damnations of God and his atheistic nihilism: "'It is true, that which I have revealed to you; there is no God, no universe, no human race, no earthly life, no heaven, no hell. It is all a dream—a grotesque and foolish dream.'" In the now tattered disguise that had once belonged to Vonnegut's winsome teddy bear, Clemens pushes his Satan forward to spit in the face of the young Everyman unfortunate enough to receive the demonic word: "'Nothing exists but you. And you are but a *thought*—a vagrant thought, a useless thought, a homeless thought, wandering forlorn among the empty eternities.'"[54] It could not be put plainer than this. More than anything else, *The Mysterious Stranger*, although written under Mark Twain's name, is the epitaph for the comedian who had already been buried with *Pudd'nhead Wilson*, along with all the trappings of the comic masquerade upon which he had been compelled to depend.

At one point in the novel, Satan tells the narrator that his despised, forsaken race has only "'one really effective weapon'" to commend it. "'Power, Money, Persuasion, Supplication, Persecution—these can lift at a colossal humbug,—push it a little, century by century: but only Laughter can blow it to rags and atoms at a blast. Against the assault of Laughter nothing can stand.'"[55] Of course, it would be foolish for any comedian to admit outright such a subversive intent: this alone might suggest that Twain was through with his confidence game. But it is really the final lie in the career of Mark Twain, for his creator had already come to think otherwise, and had in fact demonstrated it with Pudd'nhead Wilson's abandonment of jokes for the law.

CHAPTER 7

Conclusion: A Bad Case of Irony Fatigue

Why, Kurt Vonnegut asks, is there such a startling ten-dency for comedians to turn into "intolerably unfunny pessimists" the longer they attempt "to laugh rather than weep about demoral-izing information"? As this study has shown even in its admitted selectivity, there are indeed exceptions that can prove his rule—most notably, in this case, Benjamin Franklin. At the end of his life, Franklin could look with pity upon the earnest, agitated youth around him, and declare: " 'Since growing older, since my passions have dimmed, I feel a peace of mind and heart that I never felt be-fore, that these young people cannot know.' " His soul, he said, could look " 'out upon the noisy passers-by without becoming in-volved in their quarrels.' "[1] Oh, happy Benjamin Franklin.

Still, if I were to cast about for a picture of the most geni-al, serene comedian I have yet encountered, I would not look to American history for it, nor to American literature (pace Melville). I would have to go to the protagonist of Thomas Mann's last novel, *The Confessions of Felix Krull, Confidence Man*. No one shall persuade me that Felix Krull could ever fall victim to Vonnegut's Law. He is an actor, thief, liar, pimp, forger, flatterer, jailbird, seducer, smiling hypocrite, and impostor. His mentor is Hermes the Thief. He is an artist, "a natural costume boy"—a supreme ironist who declares: "To live like a soldier but not as a soldier, figuratively but not liter-ally, to be allowed in short to live symbolically, spells true free-dom."[2] He avers with a straight face: "He who really loves the world shapes himself to please it" (57)—and he actually "shiver[s] with joy at the thought of the equality of seeming and being" (226). Not for him any sense of imprisonment in an ironic identity by which his real self might be canceled out, as he becomes by day a lowly waiter in a Parisian hotel and by night a pilfering, moneyed aristocrat—"a kind of dual existence, whose charm lay in the ambiguity as to which figure was the real I and which the masquerade" (204). If anything, the erasure of his self is the source of his exhilaration: "The undisguised reality behind the two appearances, the real I, could not be identified because it actually did not exist" (205). As a self-styled "entertainer and illusionist" divesting all who come before him of their wealth, their self-possession, and their apprehension of "reality," he is—like Melville's Franklin—at his most scrupulous with the tricks of his trade: "'Frivolity is not my style, especially in the matter of jokes'" (221). He has no scruples, however, for the objects of his divestments, the victims of illusion. They are, to him, like "the giant swarms of poor moths and gnats, rushing silently and madly into the enticing flame! What unanimity in agreeing to let oneself be deceived!" (28). And for anyone ever to rupture the confidence game—"'to destroy belief in beauty and form, image and dream'"—is to become "'a spoil-sport, and to spoil the game of life is not only sinful, it is simply and entirely devilish'" (322). Felix Krull is Huizinga's "false player" to the end.

Back to the question that Vonnegut poses—and why Ben Franklin, like Felix Krull, should prove such a noteworthy exception to his pessimistic rule. An answer may also lie, along with Krull, beyond the pale of American history and literature; beyond the pale of pure comic theory. It may lie in the area where comic theory and political theory meet—politics being the daily activity of worldly affairs, in John Seery's words, "the art, or the rough-and-tumble, of diverse persons trying to live together."[3] It may lie, in fact, in a debate initiated in 1918 by Krull's creator. That year, Thomas Mann published *Reflections of a Nonpolitical Man*, his inquiry into what he regarded as the antithetical relationship between art (or, as he sometimes calls it, "estheticism") and political activity. It is also one of the twentieth century's first major critiques of irony and—as Seery points out—one of its trickiest examples. Determined to locate irony as a positive force for political activism and social change, Seery has looked to Mann's *Reflections* in the effort to rescue irony from the stigma of parasitism and evasion that political theorists since Plato have assigned to it. Seery argues that Mann's elaborations on the evasiveness of irony are in themselves ironic and in fact undercut any suggestion of irony's incompatibility with social or political activity. Indeed, Mann's *Reflections* are highly ironic in terms of their voice, as he signals in his introduction a "trace of the actor, the lawyer, of play, artistry, detachment, of lack of conviction and of . . . poetic sophistry" informing the book— "and still, what I said was at every moment truly my intellectual conviction, my heartfelt emotion." Effectively, Mann throws down the gauntlet, at once inviting a reader to believe and disbelieve his protestations of honesty: "It is not for me to solve the paradox of this mixture of dialectics and genuine, honestly striving will to truth. In the end, the very existence of this book vouches for my seriousness."[4] The problem with Mann's irony lies in making the choice between believing and disbelieving. To some degree, Seery and his colleague, Daniel Conway, choose to disbelieve Mann's apparent "skepticism" about the political efficacy of irony—which Mann calls "the self-betrayal of the intellect." Mann may *appear* to accept "the either/or dilemma posed to the Athenian judges [by Socrates]: Irony or Politics"; but to Conway and Seery, the opposite is possible: "What if Mann's 'nonpolitical' separation of irony and politics were *itself* ironic? . . . Mann's exercise in self-referential irony introduces the idea that irony can betray even its own antipolitical character, thus enabling an unexpected and unlikely turn toward politics." It is a hopeful conclusion they offer: "Under certain unique conditions, [Mann] seems to suggest, the self-betrayal of the intellect itself becomes political and yields a fleeting, fragile moment of affirmation and empowerment."[5] Perhaps this is so.

But even if it is so, is it not possible that such moments are *too* fleeting, and *too* fragile for the ironist who would be politically and socially engaged? Seery and others have argued persuasively for the commitment and engagement that irony might actually allow; but the fact remains that the *perception* of irony as escape, negation, and retreat not only exists generally but is perhaps overwhelming. Moreover, the connotations of deceit and parasitism also appear indelible—even to Mann himself, and in spite of the self-referential, ironic voice of his *Reflections*. Whatever irony's secret capacity to "woo" and to "win," he says, "it is still weak in will and fatalistic, and it is at any rate very far from placing itself seriously and actively in the service of desirability and of ideals. Above all, however, it is a completely *personal* ethos, not a social one . . . not a means of improvement in the intellectual-political sense" (13). It is highly ironic, of course, that such a shameless con-

fession should come from one of Western literature's master ironists; but it is one that he makes on behalf of all artists.

For to Mann, art (or "estheticism") is by definition ironic
and—one can hear the howls of protest—deeply uncommitted to
anything other than an abstract intellectual freedom. It is thus by
nature an evasive form of play: "Someone who is used to creating
art, never takes spiritual and intellectual things *completely seriously,*
for his job has always been rather to treat them as material and as
playthings, to represent points of view, to deal in dialectics, always
letting the one who is speaking at the time be right" (165). In contrast to "art" or "estheticism," there is "politics": "The true definition of the concept, 'politics,' is only possible with the help of its
opposite concept; it says: 'Politics is the opposite of estheticism.' Or:
'Politics is salvation from estheticism.' Or, stated quite strictly: 'To
be a politician is the only possible way of not being an esthete'"
(160).

Again: Thomas Mann is perhaps neither right nor honest
here—Conway and Seery would certainly hope so. But Mann is at
least *voicing* a pervasive impression, one that may also work upon
any practicing ironist who wishes to go beyond the bounds of his
irony. Of all the subjects of this study, only Benjamin Franklin was
able to dispense with the ironic stance of the hoaxer and the comedian and to step completely and indivisibly into the realm of political activity. He was free to drop irony, comedy, art—altogether—
and to pick them up again as and when he chose. The same cannot
be said even for Sinclair Lewis and Herman Melville, who, although not explicitly avowing themselves as comedians, bound
themselves to the ironic chimeras of art—even Melville, who in his
embittered old age looked to poetry as his only salvation from the
mundanities of the customs dock. Benjamin Franklin could indeed
ask rhetorically: Where is the irony—conscious, at any rate—in my
founding of the first American public library; in my delegation to
the Continental Congress; in my contributions to the Declaration of
Independence; in my negotiations for the Treaty of Paris; in my
presidency of the Pennsylvania Executive; in my presence at the
Constitutional Convention? By contrast, how potentially galling it
must be to be locked into the ironic identity and obliged to dismiss
your life's work with the falsehood, "Bob, they're just jokes"; or to
be condemned merely to *satirizing* a social or moral evil, when what
you want is "to stand up before it & *curse* it, & foam at the mouth—
or take a club & pound it to rags & pulp." Perhaps Franklin was a
serene ironist to the end only because he was a part-time ironist.

If this appears facile, look to Mann again—to Felix Krull. True, irony is the totality of his life and yet he is serene; but it is the serenity of a man without a conscience, a man without any social or political commitment, a reveler in his own parasitism. (If I do him a disservice in interpreting him thus, he has only the artistry of his irony to blame.) The same cannot be said for those in this study who are at once obligated to irony and committed to social change. Moreover, the rendering of Felix Krull, coming as it does at the end of Mann's life, must add weight to the author's reflections upon irony of nearly four decades previous—and upon the ironist with his "touch of seeming unscrupulousness, frivolity, dialectic, and pettifoggery" (166). It must add weight to Mann's damnation of irony's "artistic nature" as "something *one can retreat behind* when the objective world becomes a bit confused—behind which one is happily sheltered and still derives honor from the confusion" (403). Even the satirist does not escape the damnation: "We know the political moralist, the man of domestic policy and of national self-criticism, as a satirist. Satire, 'scourging' satire, is obviously the most important instrument of his political-social-critical pedagogy. But satire, since it is art, is always to a certain extent an end in itself: it gives pleasure, it pleases the one who exercises it as well as the one who receives it—regardless of its pedagogical value" (415). A satirist, like any comedian, "does not want to be thought of as a simple moralizer"—in fact, he must avoid such an impression at all costs: "Therefore he is intent on veiling and camouflaging the morality in an artistic-psychological way: he takes virtue a bit pathologically— oh, not too much so, just so far that one can still take its blarney seriously, but so that it also seems all right not to take it seriously" (403). Even worse is the observation that Lenny Bruce was to echo almost fifty years after Mann: "To a certain extent . . . the satirist *likes* the object of satire, the 'conditions,' for they are what make his effects possible" (415). Even the most politically direct satire is, in the end, only art—"estheticism; but a half-baked, cowardly one that retreats behind virtue. It is also virtuousness, but a half-baked and cowardly one that uses art as a breastplate" (404).

For a committed, radical social activist, Mann seems to say, irony (and, in its ironic nature, art) should be the last—the least thinkable—tool, given that it is inherently "conservative," an agent of stasis in which "being and effect contradict one another" (430). So back to Franklin: however conservative and stonily he now sits in statuary or on the American bank note, no one could credibly deny his radicalism *or* his bravery in becoming a traitor in the face of the hangman's noose. True, he is said to have faced the threat of that noose with a joke—"We must all hang together, or most assuredly we shall all hang separately"—but in no way was his jokery responsible for the threat.[6] His ironic hoaxes and bagatelles alone could not have earned him that honor, and even the most incendiary of them remained long undiscovered. It was not his artistry that earned him the name of "the grand Incendiary" or "the dangerous Engine" among Tories.[7] By contrast, imagine the cartoonist Herblock ruefully shaking his head as a giggling Haldeman or Erlichman walks away with the originals of his caricatures; or Vonnegut noting his satire as an effective agent of "lubrication" oiling along the reelection of Nixon—as though these satirists had earned a medal from *their* Tory adversaries instead of the threat of the noose.

When Thomas Mann asserts that "the artist-activist does not think of action at all" but rather "fame, money, love, applause, applause," perhaps he is being either too harsh or—as John Seery would hope—ironic (428). As Seery knows, Mann himself had elsewhere said, "Nothing would be more erroneous than to regard [art's] irony—the irony of all mediation—as a nihilistic escape from struggle and from human obligation."[8] It is such an apparently unguarded statement as this that allows Seery to build upon the hope that Mann does *not* mean what he says in his *Reflections* and that irony may indeed be an agent of social and political activism. "Like Mann," he writes, "I believe politics requires earnest commitment and thus may be at odds with irony's ambivalence; but this commitment may also rest upon a pretense of sorts, about which the serious politician may be able to learn a great deal from the enigmatic ironist."[9] For Seery, it is enough to say that "the pretense of irony reveals a certain kind of commitment, the value of exchange for its own sake, which is for the sake of a kind of remote contact with other human beings" (187). Looked at in this way, "irony is not, after all, a negative or destructive temperament and technique but instead gives way . . . to a substantive, world-affirming ethos" (139). By extension, Seery suggests, politics must be inherently ironic, as it "acquires its meaning and form and direction only by recognizing its essential if underlying irony: that all is part pretense, play, fiction, temporality, construct, indirection." What Seery in fact argues for, if not explicitly, is the absurdism of Camus—or, indeed, Kurt Vonnegut—as the informing political agent: "Politics is *ironic*, because it requires an acceptance of the pretense, the possible fiction, that living together matters in the face of death" (10). Politics, to Seery, relies "not upon positive or true criteria, but [upon] the acceptance of a possible falsehood, a noble lie, e.g., that all men and women are brothers and sisters, that all peoples are interrelated solely by virtue of their common humanity." This could have come straight from one of Vonnegut's early graduation speeches, were it slightly less theorized: "The advantages of using a falsehood as the basis for community are potentially enormous, for it relieves the theorist, as well as the practitioner, of having to find some substantive and verifiable One over the Many, some cosmopolitan standard that actually encompasses the entire globe" (327).

In a bold conclusion, Seery speaks the truth: "I have labored repeatedly against viewing irony as a merely deflationary, corrosive technique" (323). And he has done it convincingly; he makes it clear that irony can indeed be life-enhancing and affirmative. But the question remains: Is it enough? Is it enough for the ironic practitioner who—sooner or later—cannot accept the absurdism, the fragility, the fleetness of the affirmation? If, for instance, Gandhian nonviolent resistance was, as Seery suggests, an ironic stance against British colonial rule, would it have worked against a power structure like Nazism, which was impervious to *Swiftian* irony, let alone Gandhian? Seery's epitomizing image, in fact, is that of a solitary disabled woman comically floating a toy balloon in the midst of an antinuclear protest, in an affirmative act of "ironic *pretense.*" On the one hand, he argues, this slight figure "exhibits a pretense toward the balloon as a technique of opposition against the weapons lab, the state, and the police—the balloon cannot *literally* counteract these institutions." But on the other hand, "the balloon also suggests a broader pretense toward life—*as if* it matters." What is most pertinent, of course, is the exactitude with which her motivation matches that of the comedian as social critic: "The woman's pretense betrays on the one hand an underlying skepticism; the whimsy in her act is finally an appeal to the skeptical rather than to the credulous, and it is also designed to provoke a skepticism, a questioning attitude, in the otherwise unreflective observer." At the same time, "we must understand her actions, her deliberate affirmation of life (also symbolized in the balloon), *against* the background of her countervailing skepticism." Fair enough. Her balloon is, in fact, her joke: "Her pretense, while implicitly condoning disengagement from life, at the same time invites the skeptic to play along. She has revealed her conscious decision to affirm life in the nuclear age" (322).

But the question *still* remains: Is it enough—even if it is all she has? Seery himself faces this question squarely: "In the nuclear age, holding a balloon while holding up traffic is an act of absurdism, escapism, or sheer nihilism *unless* that act is backed by the chastening attitude of irony—and in our example, the handicapped woman's obvious deliberateness suggests that her actions are ironic in a most profoundly unsettling way." Her balloon—her little joke—"is a symbol of life—but what a pathetic, fragile symbol!" For Seery, however, it *is* enough: "Upon reflection, we realize that the woman is *truly* floating the balloon, that her act is not so innocent and naïvely childlike as it first appears, that it reveals more skepticism than sanguinity about our nuclear future" (321).

But in the end—"upon reflection"—what has happened? Seery has brought us back, full circle, to the *starting* point of satiric irony: skepticism. After the ironist has floated her balloon to signal the skepticism that had brought her there in the first place, where can she then go? Disturbingly—and Seery's idealism notwithstanding—the answer may be: Nowhere. So thinks the philosopher Richard Rorty, who, under Seery's protest, disarms the ironist as the slave of a self-acknowledged "contingency"—"the contingency of his or her own most central beliefs and desires" as well as the ironic language in which the world is to be described.[10] To Rorty, irony is "largely irrelevant to public life and political questions"; and the ironist who employs it can be neither "progressive" nor "dynamic," since all he or she can do is redescribe the world in a highly idiosyncratic, contingent manner. Thus, the woman who uses a joke balloon to redescribe for you the relation between yourself and, say, a nuclear reality "cannot claim that adopting her redescription of yourself or your situation makes you better able to conquer the forces which are marshaled against you. On her account, that ability is a matter of weapons and luck, not a matter of having truth on your side."[11] Rorty points to Sartre's description of ironists as "'meta-stable': never quite able to take themselves seriously because always aware that the terms in which they describe themselves are subject to change, always aware of the contingency of their final vocabularies, and thus of their selves."[12]

Contingency, meta-stability, truth without weapons—it is small wonder that an ironist may eventually succumb to a kind of irony fatigue. Famously, it happened to Sartre himself, for whom the ironic absurdity of existentialism ultimately proved no match for the stark image of a starving child. He escaped into Marxism, according to whose founder irony was fit for the subjectivity and individualism of art but hardly appropriate for collective politics, social activism, objective criticism, and the inspiration of "world-historical" movements.[13] Less famous, but more intriguing, is the recent example quoted by Linda Hutcheon of a group of literary critics who had concluded that they must quit being comedians and *just say it straight*—their intention being "to restore public confidence and sidestep further press attacks on the profession." Even in their ironically titled manifesto, "Regulations for Literary Criticism in the 1990s," their message is clear: Regulation VII reads, *"No irony."* The reason: "Employing irony, speaking tongue in cheek, talking wryly or self mockingly—these smartass intellectual practices give our whole profession a bad name." Unlike Thomas Mann's ironic attack on irony, there is no abundance of clever self-referentiality here: "We cannot mince words about irony. Knock it off, and knock it off now." The authors invoke a number of reasons for thus encouraging the spoil-sport in the critic: "In the first place, nobody understands your little ironies but you and your theory-mongering friends. In the second place, even if someone *does* understand your ironies, they still won't translate into newsprint and you'll wind up looking foolish anyway." But it is with their last reason that they nail shut the ironist's coffin: "In the third place, great literature demands of us a high seriousness of purpose—not disrespectful laughter and clowning around. So just wipe that smirk off your face."[14] Irony fatigue shows itself elsewhere in contemporary critical life, reflecting equally negatively on concepts of ironic play and elevating the critic as spoil-sport. Against the followers of Barthes, Bakhtin, and Derrida—postmodernists who, in Seery's words, accept "playfully and joyfully the breakdown of determinate meanings, the loss of certainty, the deconstruction of critical dichotomies and differences" (199)—there are the likes of Alex Callinicos, whose *Against Postmodernism* explicitly attacks the comic/ironic impulse in current social and textual criticism. His goal is "to challenge the strange mixture of cultural and political pessimism and light-minded playfulness with which—in a more than usually farcical reprise of the apocalyptic mood at the end of the last century—much of the contemporary Western intelligentsia apparently intends to greet our own *fin de siècle*."[15]

Of course, I may be opening myself to the charge that these last examples refer to indivisible social critics, while *comedians* are the subject of the present discussion. But this has been precisely my point throughout this study: certain comedians who have been divided between the urge toward serious criticism and the concomitant, requisite urge toward play may well be subject to irony fatigue, even though their peculiar identities commit them to an irony from which other critics are free to escape. And if the serious critic who is not bound to irony can *still* evince signs of such fatigue, how potentially enervating it must be for the comedian who *is* so bound—for whom irony is at once a necessary refuge and an agent of self-betrayal. "Irony's guns face in every direction," says D. J. Enright—including that of the comedian who is identified by it.[16] Linda Hutcheon notes the relentless "flipping from negative to positive" that characterizes "the evaluative rhetoric of discourses about irony"; it is no less present in the actual practice of irony, nor in the self-assessment of many ironists.[17] Hence Garrison Keillor's simultaneous revelry in the "cash crop" of humor and his urge to give it up for the straightforwardness of "irritation"—an urge tempered by the lessons of Carol Kenicott in *Main Street*. Hence Melville's "madness and anguish" over the impossibility of frankness, and his amazement and worry at Franklin's own ironic capacity. Hence Lenny Bruce's dismissal of comedy from the very stage on which he stood, and the uneasy accommodation of Bill Hicks to the requirement of the comedic lie through which the truth might be told. The schizophrenia of Vonnegut's comedians is yet another symptom of irony fatigue, while Mark Twain slipped, sickened, into the Great Dark in which reality and appearance—life and dream—were ultimately indistinguishable.

When the strain of negotiating the slippery meanings of (and behind) irony takes its toll on comedians who acquire an addiction to plain speaking—in Linda Hutcheon's words, comedians "whose political [and, I would add, social] commitments lead them to desire . . . an unambiguous discourse of engagement"—they are the most at risk *as* comedians.[18] They are then in danger of losing what Empson called that "generous skepticism which can believe at once that people are and are not guilty."[19] However sensitive they are to the connotations of irony as "corrosive" and, at best, "episodically political";[20] however much they may agree with Czeslaw Milosz that irony is "the glory of slaves"—that there is only one small step "from what is a desperate protest masked with a smile to nihilistic acquiescence";[21] and however much Artemus Ward may be speaking for them when he says, "The pen's more mightier than the sword, but which, I'm afraid, would stand rather a slim chance beside the needle gun"[22]—they have no options as comedians except to be faithful to their ironic identities, no matter how tired the marriage.

Possibly this study has led to a consideration that extends beyond the peculiarities of comedians alone, into those of artists in general. If there is indeed an urge to escape from an ironic identity, it may be that of any artist who loses faith in the efficacy of his or her art. But what D. C. Muecke says of all artists must go doubly for the comedian, for whom ironic play is the overt and acknowledged defining characteristic: "The artist is in an ironic position for several reasons: in order to write well he must be both creative and critical, subjective and objective, enthusiastic and realistic, emotional and rational, unconsciously inspired and a conscious artist." He must be content to offer to the world "work [that] purports to be about the world and yet is fiction." He must acknowledge his "obligation to give a true or complete account of reality but he knows this is impossible, reality being incomprehensibly vast, full of contradictions, and in a continual state of becoming, so that even a true account would be immediately falsified as soon as it was completed." Given such reckonings, "the only possibility open for a real artist is to stand apart from his work and at the same time incorporate this awareness of his ironic position into the work itself."[23] As if this were not challenging enough, if the artist is a comedian, one further obligation overrides all others: and no matter how sickening, degrading, or contemptible the injunction, Gary Cooper said it best.

Notes

Introduction

1. Kurt Vonnegut, *Breakfast of Champions* (London: Vintage, 1992), 86.
2. Quoted in Justin Kaplan, *Mr. Clemens and Mark Twain* (London: Jonathan Cape, 1967), 382.
3. Johan Huizinga, *Homo Ludens: A Study of the Play Element in Culture* (London: Routledge and Kegan Paul, 1949), 11.
4. Kurt Vonnegut, *Fates Worse than Death* (London: Jonathan Cape, 1991), 183.
5. Ibid.
6. Herman Melville, *Pierre, Israel Potter, The Confidence-Man, Tales, and Billy Budd*, Library of America edition (New York: Literary Classics of the United States, Inc., 1984), 935.
7. Kurt Vonnegut, *Palm Sunday* (London: Jonathan Cape, 1981), 166.
8. Kurt Vonnegut, "Opening Remarks," in *The Unabridged Mark Twain*, ed. Lawrence Teacher (Philadelphia: Running Press, 1976), 1:xv.

Chapter One

1. Justine Kershaw and David Helton, "Dressing for Dinner," *Hunters in the Wild*, BBC-TV (1993).
2. Owen Wister, *The Virginian* (New York: Penguin, 1988), 22, 23.
3. Umberto Eco, *Travels in Hyper Reality* (London: Picador, 1987), 275.
4. "Mark Twain's Burlesque Autobiography," in *The Unabridged Mark Twain*, ed. Lawrence Teacher (Philadelphia: Running Press, 1976), 2:xi.
5. Johan Huizinga, *Homo Ludens: A Study of the Play Element in Culture* (London: Routledge and Kegan Paul, 1949), 11.
6. Max Eastman, *Enjoyment of Laughter* (London: Johnson Reprint Co., 1970), 3.
7. Huizinga, *Homo Ludens*, 11.
8. Sinclair Lewis, *Main Street* (London: Penguin, 1991), 6. All further references are from this edition, with page numbers quoted in the text.
9. Garrison Keillor, on *Desert Island Discs*, BBC Radio 4, February 12, 1995.
10. Garrison Keillor, *We Are Still Married* (London: Faber, 1993), xvi.
11. Ibid., 138.

12. John E. Miller, "The Distance Between Gopher Prairie and Lake Wobegon: Sinclair Lewis and Garrison Keillor on the Small Town Experience," *Centennial Review* 31 (Fall 1987): 432–46.

13. *The Man from Main Street*, ed. Harry E. Maule and Melville H. Cane (London: Heinemann, 1954), 59, 203.

14. Ibid., 204.

15. Keillor, *We Are Still Married*, 141.

16. *The Autobiography of Mark Twain*, ed. Charles Neider (London: Chatto and Windus, 1960), 273.

17. Garrison Keillor, *A Prairie Home Companion*, National Public Radio broadcasts, 1980–81.

18. Keillor on *Desert Island Discs*, BBC Radio 4, op cit.

19. Huizinga, *Homo Ludens*, 11.

20. Judith Yaross Lee, *Garrison Keillor: A Voice of America* (Jackson: University Press of Mississippi, 1991), 2.

21. Miller, "Distance," 445.

22. Stephen Wilbers, "Lake Wobegon: Mythical Place and the American Imagination," *American Studies* 30 (Spring 1989): 8.

23. Lee, *Garrison Keillor*, 2.

24. Doug Hanson, "A Hometown Look at *Lake Wobegon Days*," *Minnesota Daily*, September 30, 1985, 28; quoted in Wilbers, "Lake Wobegon," 17.

25. Donald E. Morse, "Monkeys, Changelings, and Asses: Audience, Fantasy, and Belief," in *Aspects of Fantasy*, ed. William Coyle (Westport, Conn.: Greenwood Press, 1986), 198.

26. Jacques M. Laroche and Claude J. Fouillade, "A Socio-Cultural Reading of *Lake Wobegon Days*, or Can You Go Home Again to Mid-America?" *Revue Francaise d'Etudes Americaines* 14 (November 1989): 434.

27. Garrison Keillor, *Lake Wobegon Days* (London: Faber, 1989), xi. All further quotations are from this edition.

28. Quoted in Michael Kline, "Narrative Strategies in Garrison Keillor's 'Lake Wobegon' Stories," *Studies in American Humor* 6 (1988): 141.

29. Quoted in Lee, *Garrison Keillor*, 57.

30. Ibid., 4.

31. Ibid., 9–10.

32. Ibid., 36, 68–69, 76.

33. Ibid., ix, 49.

34. Peter Hans Schreffler, "Caught Between Two Worlds: The Spiritual Predicament and Rhetorical Ambivalence of Garrison Keillor" (Ph.D. diss., Bowling Green State University, 1990), 1, 9.

35. Laroche and Fouillade, "Socio-Cultural Reading," 434.

36. Lee, *Garrison Keillor*, 12, 46–51.

37. Ibid., 57–60.
38. Bruce Michelson, "Keillor and Rolvaag and the Art of Telling the Truth," *American Studies* 30 (Spring 1989): 33.
39. Keillor on *Desert Island Discs*, op cit.
40. Schreffler, "Caught Between Two Worlds," 67.
41. Laroche and Fouillade, "Socio-Cultural Reading," 436.
42. Keillor, *We Are Still Married*, xvi.
43. Wayne C. Booth, *The Rhetoric of Irony* (Chicago: University of Chicago Press, 1974), 176.
44. John E. Seery, *Political Returns: Irony in Politics and Theory from Plato to the Antinuclear Movement* (Boulder: Westview Press, 1990), 162; D. J. Enright, *The Alluring Problem: An Essay on Irony* (Oxford: Oxford University Press, 1986), 5; Linda Hutcheon, *Irony's Edge: The Theory and Politics of Irony* (London: Routledge, 1994), 3.
45. Mick Eaton, quoted in Susan Purdie, *Comedy: The Mastery of Discourse* (London: Harvester Wheatsheaf, 1993), 73.
46. Erich Heller, *The Ironic German: A Study of Thomas Mann* (Boston: Little, Brown and Co., 1958), 235.
47. G. G. Sedgewick, quoted in Seery, *Political Returns*, 165.
48. Enright, *Alluring Problem*, 1.
49. Booth, *Rhetoric of Irony*, 5.
50. Patrick W. Colfer, "The Spirit of Irony and the Problem of Negativity" (Ph.D. diss., University of Edinburgh, 1981), ii, 60–61.
51. Quoted in Seery, *Political Returns*, 179.
52. Purdie, *Comedy*, 117.
53. Booth, *Rhetoric of Irony*, 178.
54. R. Chambers, quoted in Hutcheon, *Irony's Edge*, 100.
55. Benjamin DeMott, "The New Irony: Sickniks and Others," *American Scholar* 31 (Winter 1961–62): 110.
56. Peter Conrad, quoted in Enright, *Alluring Problem*, 13.
57. Hutcheon, *Irony's Edge*, 120.
58. C. Jan Swearingen, *Rhetoric and Irony: Western Literacy and Western Lies* (New York: Oxford University Press, 1991), ix.
59. Daniel W. Conway and John E. Seery, *The Politics of Irony: Essays in Self-Betrayal* (New York: St. Martin's Press, 1992), 1.
60. Swearingen, *Rhetoric and Irony*, 130–31.
61. Malcolm Bradbury, quoted in Elaine B. Safer, *The Contemporary American Comic Epic* (Detroit: Wayne State University Press, 1989), 160.
62. Graham Greene, Herblock, and Kurt Vonnegut, quoted in William Keough, *Punchlines: The Violence of American Humor* (New York: Paragon House, 1990), 121.

Chapter Two

1. Benjamin Franklin, "Silence Dogood," nos. 1–4, in *The Papers of Benjamin Franklin*, ed. Leonard W. Labaree and Whitfield J. Bell (New Haven: Yale University Press, 1960), 1:12–18.
2. "A Witch Trial at Mount Holly," in *Papers of Benjamin Franklin*, 1:184.
3. "The Speech of Miss Polly Baker," in Franklin, *The Autobiography and Other Writings*, ed. Kenneth Silverman (London: Penguin, 1986), 209–12.
4. Max Hall, *Benjamin Franklin and Polly Baker: The History of a Literary Deception* (Pittsburgh: University of Pittsburgh Press, 1990), 3–4.
5. Jefferson's account of Reynal's meeting with Franklin, in *Ben Franklin Laughing*, ed. P. M. Zall (Berkeley: University of California Press, 1980), 383.
6. Franklin, "A Traveller," in *The Writings of Benjamin Franklin*, ed. Albert Henry Smyth (New York: Macmillan, 1906), 4:368–69.
7. Zall, *Ben Franklin Laughing*, 39–40.
8. Walter Blair and Hamlin Hill, *America's Humor: From Poor Richard to Doonesbury* (New York: Oxford University Press, 1978), 82–83.
9. *Writings of Benjamin Franklin*, 8:448.
10. Franklin, "To the Royal Academy of Brusselles," in *Franklin's Wit and Folly: The Bagatelles*, ed. Richard E. Amacher (New Brunswick: Rutgers University Press, 1953), 67–69.
11. Justine Kershaw and David Helton, "Dressing for Dinner," *Hunters in the Wild*, BBC-TV (1993).
12. Kurt Vonnegut, *Fates Worse than Death* (London: Jonathan Cape, 1991), 183.
13. Kenneth Silverman, introduction to Franklin, *Autobiography*, ix.
14. Ibid., xiii.
15. Gary Lindberg, *The Confidence Man in American Literature* (New York: Oxford University Press, 1982), 116.
16. Franklin, *Autobiography*, 73. All further quotations from are from this edition, with page references indicated in the text.
17. D. H. Lawrence, *Studies in Classic American Literature* (London: Penguin, 1971), 20, 22.
18. Ibid., 25.
19. D. H. Lawrence, *The Symbolic Meaning* (New York: Centaur, 1962), 43.
20. Silverman, in Franklin, *Autobiography*, xiii.
21. Lawrence, *Symbolic Meaning*, 36.
22. Ibid., 47.
23. Mark Twain, "The Late Benjamin Franklin," *The Complete Humorous Sketches and Tales of Mark Twain*, ed. Charles Neider (Garden City, N.Y.: Doubleday, 1961), 139.
24. Edgar Allan Poe, "Diddling Considered as One of the Exact Sciences," *Comedies and Sketches* (Harmondsworth: Penguin, 1988), 150–52.
25. Lindberg, *Confidence Man*, 6.

26. *The Letters of Herman Melville*, ed. Merrell R. Davis and William H. Gilman (New Haven: Yale University Press, 1960), 96.

27. Ibid., 79–80.

28. Herman Melville, "Hawthorne and His Mosses," in *Pierre, Israel Potter, The Confidence-Man, Tales, and Billy Budd*, Library of America edition (New York: Literary Classics of the United States, Inc., 1984), 1164.

29. Ibid., 1160.

30. Herman Melville, *Mardi* (Evanston: Northwestern University Press, 1970), xvii.

31. Ibid., 284.

32. Herman Melville, *Moby-Dick* (New York: W. W. Norton, 1967), 126, 195–96.

33. *Letters of Herman Melville*, 142.

34. Lawrence, *Symbolic Meaning*, 46.

35. Herman Melville, *Israel Potter*, in *Pierre, etc.*, 479. All further quotations from *Israel Potter* are taken from this edition, with page references cited in the text. The quotation from Silverman comes from his introduction to Franklin, *Autobiography*, xiii.

36. Herman Melville, *The Confidence-Man*, in *Pierre, etc.*, 842. All further quotations from *The Confidence-Man* are taken from this edition, with page references cited in the text.

37. Lindberg, *Confidence Man*, 19.

38. Ralph Ellison, *Shadow and Act* (London: Secker and Warburg, 1967), 49.

39. Ralph Ellison, *Invisible Man* (London: Penguin, 1965), 17.

Chapter Three

1. Mark Twain, "On the Decay of the Art of Lying," *The Unabridged Mark Twain*, ed. Lawrence Teacher (Philadelphia: Running Press, 1976), 1:742.

2. Norman Mailer, "The White Negro," *Advertisements for Myself* (London: Corgi, 1961), 283.

3. James Thurber, "The State of the Nation's Humor," *New York Times Magazine*, December 7, 1958, 26.

4. Malcolm Muggeridge, "America Needs a *Punch*," *Esquire*, April 1958, 60.

5. Hugh Dalziel Duncan, *Communication and Social Order* (New York: Oxford University Press, 1962), 377.

6. W. T. Lhamon, *Deliberate Speed: The Origins of a Cultural Style in the American 1950s* (Washington, D.C.: Smithsonian Institution Press, 1990).

7. Lenny Bruce, *What I Was Arrested For* (Douglas Records 2). Hereafter cited in the text as *WIAF*.

8. Caroline Bird, "Born 1930: The Unlost Generation," quoted in Mailer, "White Negro," 281.

9. Mailer, "White Negro," 283.

10. Kenneth Tynan, "Foreword," in Lenny Bruce, *How to Talk Dirty and Influence People* (St. Albans: Panther, 1981), 10.

11. Andrew Ross, *No Respect: Intellectuals and Popular Culture* (London: Routledge, 1989), 91.

12. Orrin Keepnews, "Without Apology: The Existential Jazz Aura of Lenny Bruce," *Downbeat*, November 3, 1966, 42.

13. Jonathan Miller, "The Sick White Negro," *Partisan Review* (Spring 1963): 150.

14. Bruce, *How to Talk Dirty and Influence People*, 46.

15. Jack Kerouac, *On the Road* (London: Penguin, 1991), 177.

16. Mailer, "White Negro," 292–93.

17. Ross, *No Respect*, 85.

18. Lenny Bruce, *Thank You, Masked Man* (Fantasy Records 7017).

19. Bruce, *How to Talk Dirty and Influence People*, 63.

20. Roy Carr, Brian Case, and Fred Dellar, *The Hip: Hipsters, Jazz and the Beat Generation* (London: Faber, 1986), 63.

21. Lenny Bruce, *The Midnight Concert* (United Artists Records 6794). Hereafter cited in the text as *MC*.

22. "Dick Gregory Is Back," *New York Times*, June 6, 1993, B1.

23. Albert Goldman, *Ladies and Gentlemen . . . Lenny Bruce!!* (New York: Random House, 1974), 192.

24. Lenny Bruce, *The Sick Humor of Lenny Bruce* (Fantasy Records 7003). Hereafter cited in the text as *SHLB*.

25. Lenny Bruce, *Lenny Bruce Is Out Again* (Phillies Records 4010). Hereafter cited in the text as *LBOA*.

26. Lenny Bruce, *The Essential Lenny Bruce: Politics* (Douglas Records 788). Hereafter cited as *ELBP*.

27. Lenny Bruce, "Commercials," *Lenny Bruce: American* (Fantasy Records 7011). Hereafter cited as *LBA*.

28. Gershon Legman, *No Laughing Matter: An Analysis of Sexual Humor*, 2 vols. (Bloomington: Indiana University Press, 1982).

29. Mary Douglas, *Implicit Meanings: Essays in Anthropology* (London: Routledge and Kegan Paul, 1978), 97.

30. Bruce, *How to Talk Dirty and Influence People*, 146–47.

31. Ross, *No Respect*, 91–92.

32. *The Essential Lenny Bruce*, ed. John Cohen (St. Albans: Panther, 1981), 208–9. All further references from this text will be cited by page numbers in parentheses.

33. Ioan Davies, "Lenny Bruce: Hyperrealism and the Death of Jewish Tragic Humor," *Social Text* 22 (Spring 1989): 93.

34. Sarah Blacher Cohen, "The Varieties of Jewish Humor," in *Jewish Wry: Essays on Jewish Humor*, ed. Sarah Blacher Cohen (Bloomington: Indiana University Press, 1987), 8.

35. Lenny Bruce, *The Berkeley Concert* (Bizarre/Reprise Records 6329). Hereafter cited as *BC*.
36. Bruce, *How to Talk Dirty and Influence People*, 22.
37. Sigmund Freud, *Jokes and Their Relation to the Unconscious* (New York: Norton, 1960), 112.
38. Cohen, "Varieties," 4.
39. Sanford Pinsker, "Lenny Bruce: *Spritzing* the *Goyim*/Shocking the Jews," in Cohen, *Jewish Wry*, 91.
40. Cohen, "Varieties," 4–5.
41. John Oldani, "*Is the Pope Catholic?* A Content Analysis of American Jokelore About the Catholic Clergy," in *Humour in Society: Resistance and Control*, ed. Chris Powell and George E. C. Paton (London: Macmillan, 1988), 69–70.
42. Frank Kofsky, *Lenny Bruce: The Comedian as Social Critic and Secular Moralist* (New York: Monad Press, 1974), 88.
43. Bruce, *How to Talk Dirty and Influence People*, 211–12.
44. Kurt Vonnegut, *Breakfast of Champions* (London: Vintage, 1992), 86.
45. Bruce, *How to Talk Dirty and Influence People*, 171.
46. Lenny Bruce, *I Am Not a Nut, Elect Me!* (Fantasy Records 7007). Hereafter cited as *IANN*.
47. Bruce, *How to Talk Dirty and Influence People*, 214–15.
48. Ibid., 33.
49. Pinsker, "Lenny Bruce," 89–90.
50. Bruce, *How To Talk Dirty and Influence People*, 176.
51. Grover Sales, "Dagos and Niggers and Kikes, Oh My," *Nation*, December 7, 1992, 2.
52. Bruce, *How to Talk Dirty and Influence People*, 145–46.
53. Duncan, *Communication and Social Order*, 407.
54. Mikhail Bakhtin, *Rabelais and His World* (Bloomington: Indiana University Press, 1984) and *The Dialogic Imagination* (Austin: University of Texas Press, 1981).
55. Kurt Vonnegut, *Palm Sunday* (London: Jonathan Cape, 1981), 225.
56. Umberto Eco, *Travels in Hyper Reality* (London: Picador, 1987), 275.
57. Kurt Vonnegut, *Hocus Pocus* (London: Vintage, 1991), 3.
58. Bruce, *How to Talk Dirty and Influence People*, 221.
59. Kofsky, *Lenny Bruce*, 119.
60. Bruce, *How To Talk Dirty and Influence People*, 63.
61. Miller, "Sick White Negro," 150.
62. Jacob Levine and Frederick Redlich, "Failure to Understand Humor," *Psychoanalytic Quarterly* 24 (1955): 560.
63. Stephanie Koziski, "The Standup Comedian as Anthropologist," *Journal of Popular Culture* 18 (1984): 60.
64. Ibid., 60–61
65. Pinsker, "Lenny Bruce," 97.
66. Albert Goldman, *Ladies and Gentlemen*, 375.

67. Ralph Gleason, "The Trials of Lenny Bruce," *Guardian*, April 27, 1965, 9.
68. Clive Barnes, "Lenny: The Fine Art of Obscenity," *Times* (London), June 5, 1971, 7.
69. Malcolm Muggeridge, "Books," *Esquire*, November 1965, 65.
70. Albert Goldman, "The Comedy of Lenny Bruce," *London Magazine* 3 (January 1964): 68–75; *Ladies and Gentlemen*; and *Freakshow* (New York: Atheneum, 1971).
71. Goldman, *Ladies and Gentlemen*, 290.
72. Bruce, *How to Talk Dirty and Influence People*, 265.
73. Ibid.
74. Pinsker, "Lenny Bruce," 99.
75. Eric Bogosian, introduction to Lenny Bruce, *How To Talk Dirty and Influence People* (New York: Fireside, 1992), vii–x.
76. Ross, *No Respect*, 91–92.
77. Ibid., 92.

Chapter Four

1. Bill Carter, *The Late Shift: Letterman, Leno, and the Network Battle for the Night* (New York: Hyperion, 1995).
2. John Lahr, "The Goat Boy Rises," *New Yorker*, November 1, 1993, 113.
3. "It's Just a Ride," produced by Rupert Edwards, in *Totally Bill Hicks* (Tiger Aspects/Channel 4 Video, 1994). Hereafter cited in the text as *IJR*.
4. Mike Sager, "The Gospel According to Hicks," *GQ*, September 1994, 290.
5. Letter from Katrina vanden Heuvel, editor of the *Nation*, to Hicks's co-manager, Colleen McGarr, October 31, 1993. Quoted courtesy of Katrina vanden Heuvel.
6. Bill Hicks, "Revelations," in *Totally Bill Hicks*. Hereafter cited in the text as *REV*.
7. H. D. Rankin, "A Modest Proposal About the *Republic*," *Apeiron* 2 (1968): 21.
8. D. C. Muecke, *Irony and the Ironic* (London: Methuen, 1982), 45.
9. D. J. Enright, *The Alluring Problem: An Essay on Irony* (Oxford: Oxford University Press, 1986), 75.
10. Bill Hicks, *Relentless* (Invasion Records, 1992). Hereafter cited as *RC*.
11. Rankin, "Modest Proposal," 21.
12. Quoted in Edwin M. Good, *Irony in the Old Testament* (Philadelphia: Westminster Press, 1965), 23.
13. Wayne C. Booth, *The Rhetoric of Irony* (Chicago: University of Chicago Press, 1974), 47.

14. James Wolcott, "The Dennis Menace," *New Yorker*, June 6, 1994, 89; Mark Edwards, "The Grin Reality," *Sunday Times* (London), May 21, 1995, 5.
15. Bill Carter, "Lots of Political Humor, and No Morton Kondracke," *New York Times*, February 27, 1994, Section 2, p. 33. This article appeared the day after Bill Hicks died.
16. Quoted in Lahr, "Goat Boy," 113.
17. Sager, "Gospel," 290.
18. Edith Sorenson, "In the Outlaw Area," *Houston Press*, June 3, 1993, 21.
19. Compare Bill Hicks, *Sane Man* (Sacred Cow video, 1989) and *Dangerous* (Invasion Records, 1990) with Denis Leary, *No Cure for Cancer* (video and album conceived in 1990; recorded 1992). See also Doug Stern, "Profile: Bill Hicks," *Austin Comic News*, February 1993, 7; and Anita Sarko, "Bill Hicks is the Missing Link American Comedy Has Been Looking For," *Ray Gun*, August 1993, 5.
20. Dennis Miller, on *The Dennis Miller Show* (syndicated), October 15, 1992.
21. Bill Hicks at Igby's Comedy Club, Los Angeles, November 17, 1993. Unreleased video footage provided by the Strauss-McGarr Entertainment Agency. Further quotations from this source will be denoted by *I*.
22. Carter, *Late Shift*, 280–81.
23. *Letters of Herman Melville*, ed. Merrell K. Davis and William M. Gilman (New Haven: Yale University Press, 1960), 142.
24. Ken Auletta, "Late-Night Gamble," *New Yorker*, February 1, 1993, 39.
25. Quoted in Carey Goldberg, "Welcome to New York, Capital of Profanities," *New York Times*, June 19, 1995, B3.
26. Quoted in Jack Boulware, "Bill Hicks: High Plains Jester," *Nose*, March 1993, 29.
27. Hicks on the *Howard Stern Show*, WXRK Radio (New York), October 7, 1993.
28. "Comedy Mission," *48 Hours*, CBS-TV, October 4, 1991.
29. Quoted in Barry Koltnow, "The Face of Humor to Come?" *Orange County Register*, June 8, 1993, "Show" section, 4.
30. Hicks to John Lahr, October 9, 1993.
31. Hicks on *Capzeyze*, ACTV (Austin), October 30, 1993.
32. Quoted in Lahr, "Goat Boy," 115.
33. Quoted in Jeff Rubio, "Bill Hicks: A Comic of Ideas," *Orange County Register*, November 7, 1993, 4.
34. Quoted in Lahr, "Goat Boy," 115.
35. Hicks to Lahr, October 9, 1993.
36. Ibid.
37. Hicks at the Comedy Corner, West Palm Beach, Florida, October 5, 1993. Broadcast on *The Texas Radio Program*, KUT (Austin), March 11, 1994.

38. Hicks recorded his version of the banned set in his letter to John Lahr of October 9, 1993, which formed the basis of Lahr's *New Yorker* exposé. This letter is virtually identical to an unpublished essay written by Hicks the same month, entitled "Bill Hicks on Television . . . Sometimes." I am grateful to John Lahr and Colleen McGarr for providing me with copies of the letter and the essay, respectively, upon which my reconstruction is based.
39. Hicks, "Bill Hicks on Television," 1.
40. Ibid., 31.
41. Quoted in Auletta, "Late-Night Gamble," 46.
42. Ibid., 40.
43. Hicks on *Howard Stern Show*.
44. Hicks, "Bill Hicks on Television," 30.
45. "Bill Hicks: The Serious Side of Comedy," *Campus Activities Today*, January 1994, 46.
46. Hicks to Lahr, October 9, 1993.
47. *Texas Radio Program*.
48. Lahr, "Goat Boy," 121.
49. Sorenson, "In the Outlaw Area," 33.
50. "Bill Hicks: The Serious Side of Comedy," 36.
51. Hicks, "Bill Hicks on Television," 28.
52. Hicks on *The A List*, Comedy Central, repeated throughout 1992.
53. Quoted in Gerald Nachman, "Beware the Bark and Bite of Bill Hicks," *San Francisco Chronicle*, November 7, 1993, B7.
54. Quoted in Dennis McLellan, "Hard-Line Look at Humor," *Los Angeles Times*, June 10, 1993, 6.
55. Hicks on *Howard Stern Show*.
56. Quoted in Boulware, "Bill Hicks," 31.
57. Quoted in McLellan, "Hard-Line," 6.
58. Bill Hicks, *Relentless* (Video, Tiger Aspects, 1992). Hereafter cited as *RV*.
59. Quoted in Boulware, "Bill Hicks," 29.
60. ACTV Public Access video footage provided courtesy of Kevin Booth.
61. William Keough, *Punchlines: The Violence of American Humor* (New York: Paragon House, 1990), 194.
62. "Bill Hicks's Humor," *Bryan/College Station*, May 1992, 9.
63. "Bill Hicks: The Serious Side of Comedy," 37.
64. Bill Hicks, *Dangerous* (Invasion Records, 1990). Hereafter cited as *D*.
65. Quoted in Koltnow, "Face of Humor," 4.
66. Hicks on *Night After Night*, Comedy Central, repeated throughout 1992.
67. Bill Hicks, *Sane Man* (video, Sacred Cow/Bula Bula, 1989). Hereafter cited as *SM*.
68. Hicks, "Bill Hicks on Television," 29.

69. Bill Hicks, *One Night Stand*, HBO, January 15, 1991.
70. Hicks, "Bill Hicks on Television," 29–30.
71. Quoted on *Texas Radio Program*.
72. Albert Goldman, *Ladies and Gentlemen . . . Lenny Bruce!!* (New York: Random House, 1974), 269.
73. Hicks on *Capzeyze*.
74. Quoted in Lahr, "Goat Boy," 115.
75. Hicks to Lahr, November 1993 (date unspecified). Letter provided courtesy of John Lahr.
76. Hicks to Lahr, October 9, 1993.
77. Hicks on *Capzeyze*.
78. Quoted in Rubio, "Bill Hicks."
79. "Bill Hicks: The Serious Side of Comedy," 33.
80. Ibid.

Chapter Five

1. John Lahr, "The Goat-Boy Rises," *New Yorker*, November 1, 1993, 113, 121.
2. Kurt Vonnegut, *Fates Worse than Death* (London: Jonathan Cape, 1991), 183.
3. Kurt Vonnegut, *Hocus Pocus* (London: Vintage, 1991), 95.
4. Vonnegut, *Fates Worse than Death*, 183.
5. Kurt Vonnegut, "Opening Remarks," *The Unabridged Mark Twain*, ed. Lawrence Teacher (Philadelphia: Running Press, 1976), 1:xv.
6. Kurt Vonnegut, *Wampeters, Foma, and Granfalloons* (New York: Dell, 1979), xxi.
7. Robert Scholes, "Chasing a Lone Eagle," in *The Vonnegut Statement*, ed. Jerome Klinkowitz and John Somer (St. Albans: Panther, 1975), 53.
8. Kurt Vonnegut, *Cat's Cradle* (London: Penguin, 1965), 177. All further quotations are from this edition.
9. Kurt Vonnegut, *Mother Night* (London: Vintage, 1992), vii–viii, 116. All further quotations are from this edition.
10. Richard Todd, "The Masks of Kurt Vonnegut," *New York Times Magazine*, January 24, 1971, 26.
11. Vonnegut, *Palm Sunday*, 198.
12. Vonnegut, *Wampeters, Foma, and Granfalloons*, 163.
13. Vonnegut, *Palm Sunday*, 163.
14. Vonnegut, *Wampeters, Foma, and Granfalloons*, 238.
15. Ibid., 218.
16. Scholes, "A Talk With Kurt Vonnegut, Jr.," in *Vonnegut Statement*, 110–11.

17. Vonnegut, *Palm Sunday*, 182.
18. Vonnegut, *Wampeters, Foma, and Granfalloons*, 256.
19. Kurt Vonnegut, *Slapstick* (London: Vintage, 1991), 1. All further quotations are from this edition.
20. Mark Twain, *The Adventures of Huckleberry Finn* (London: Penguin, 1985), 149.
21. Christopher Buckley, "Gotterdammerung-22," *New Yorker*, October 10, 1994, 105.
22. William Rodney Allen and Paul Smith, "An Interview with Kurt Vonnegut," in William Rodney Allen, ed., *Conversations with Kurt Vonnegut* (Jackson: University Press of Mississippi, 1988), 288.
23. Reprinted in Vonnegut, *Wampeters, Foma, and Granfalloons*, 281.
24. Kurt Vonnegut, *Breakfast of Champions* (London: Vintage, 1992), 4. All further quotations are from this edition.
25. Lawrence R. Broer, *Sanity Plea: Schizophrenia in the Novels of Kurt Vonnegut* (London: UMI Research Press, 1989), 12–13.
26. Ibid., 189.
27. Israel Shenker, "Kurt Vonnegut, Jr., Lights Comic Paths of Despair," in Allen, *Conversations with Kurt Vonnegut*, 22.
28. William Rodney Allen and Paul Smith, "An Interview with Kurt Vonnegut," in Allen, *Conversations with Kurt Vonnegut*, 265, 285.
29. Leonard Mustazza, *Forever Pursuing Genesis: The Myth of Eden in the Novels of Kurt Vonnegut* (Lewisburg, Pa.: Bucknell University Press, 1990), 77.
30. Tony Tanner, *City of Words* (New York: Harper and Row, 1971), 189.
31. Kurt Vonnegut, *God Bless You, Mr. Rosewater* (London: Vintage, 1992), 27, 165–66.
32. Kurt Vonnegut, *Slaughterhouse-Five* (London: Paladin, 1989), 27, 80.
33. Vonnegut, *God Bless You, Mr. Rosewater*, 13, 163.
34. Vonnegut, *Slaughterhouse-Five*, 13, 97, 157.
35. Vonnegut, *Wampeters, Foma, and Granfalloons*, 283; and *Palm Sunday*, 304.
36. Mustazza, *Forever Pursuing Genesis*, 129.
37. Michael Wood, "Vonnegut's Softer Focus," *New York Times Book Review*, September 9, 1979, 1, 22–24.
38. Kurt Vonnegut, *Galapagos* (London: Flamingo, 1994), 13. All further quotations are from this edition.
39. Mustazza, *Forever Pursuing Genesis*, 170, 178.
40. Kurt Vonnegut, *Jailbird* (London: Vintage, 1992), 129, 140, 191. All further quotations are from this edition.
41. Kurt Vonnegut, *Deadeye Dick* (London: Flamingo, 1992), 77. All further quotations are from this edition.
42. Kurt Vonnegut, *Bluebeard* (London: Flamingo, 1992), 5. All further quotations are from this edition.

Chapter Six

1. Grover Sales, "Dagos and Niggers and Kikes, Oh My," *Nation*, December 7, 1992, 2.
2. Garrison Keillor, *We Are Still Married* (London: Faber, 1993), xvi, xxi.
3. James M. Cox, *Mark Twain: The Fate of Humor* (Princeton: Princeton University Press, 1966), 3.
4. Ibid.
5. Justin Kaplan, *Mr. Clemens and Mark Twain* (London: Jonathan Cape, 1967), 112.
6. Cox, *Mark Twain*, 33.
7. *Mark Twain to Mrs. Fairbanks*, ed. Dixon Wecter (San Marino, Calif.: Huntington Library, 1949), 63.
8. Ibid., 67n.
9. *Mark Twain-Howells Letters*, ed. Henry Nash Smith and William Gibson (Cambridge: Harvard University Press, 1960), 1:49.
10. Albert Bigelow Paine, *Mark Twain: A Biography* (London: Harpers, 1912), 1:786.
11. Kaplan, *Mr. Clemens and Mark Twain*, 382.
12. Ibid.
13. *Mark Twain-Howells Letters*, 1:248–49.
14. Ibid., 1:91.
15. Kaplan, *Mr. Clemens and Mark Twain*, 206.
16. *The Autobiography of Mark Twain*, ed. Albert Bigelow Paine (London: Harpers, 1912), 212–13.
17. Cox, *Mark Twain*, 152.
18. *Mark Twain-Howells Letters*, 1:108.
19. Ibid., 1:107.
20. Ibid., 1:146
21. Kaplan, *Mr. Clemens and Mark Twain*, 210.
22. *Mark Twain-Howells Letters*, 1:212.
23. "The Babies," in Mark Twain, *Tales, Speeches, Essays, and Sketches*, ed. Tom Quirk (London: Penguin, 1994), 142–44.
24. Quoted in Kaplan, *Mr. Clemens and Mark Twain*, 226–27.
25. Ibid., 251.
26. *Mark Twain-Howells Letters*, 1:144.
27. Tony Tanner, "Reviews and Comment," *Critical Quarterly* 4 (1962): 381.
28. Mark Twain, *The Adventures of Huckleberry Finn*, ed. Peter Coveney (Harmondsworth: Penguin, 1981), 127. All further quotations are from this edition.
29. *Mark Twain's Notebooks and Journals*, ed. Robert P. Browning et al. (Berkeley: University of California Press, 1979), 3:606.
30. Henry Nash Smith, *Mark Twain: The Development of a Writer* (Cambridge: Harvard University Press, 1962), 137.
31. Quoted in Cox, *Mark Twain*, 171–72.
32. Ibid., 175.

33. Quoted in Smith, *Mark Twain*, 113–14.
34. *Mark Twain's Notebooks and Journals*, 3:78.
35. Ibid., 3:216.
36. *Unabridged Mark Twain*, 1:1035.
37. Ibid., 1:962.
38. Quoted in Kaplan, *Mr. Clemens and Mark Twain*, 268–69.
39. Ibid., 269.
40. Ibid., 307.
41. Mark Twain, *Pudd'nhead Wilson*, ed. Malcolm Bradbury (Harmondsworth: Penguin, 1981), 91. All further quotations are from this edition.
42. Quoted in Kaplan, *Mr. Clemens and Mark Twain*, 133.
43. Ibid.
44. *Mark Twain's Contributions to "The Galaxy,"* ed. Bruce McElderry (Gainesville, Fla.: Scholars' Reprints, 1961), 131.
45. Mark Twain, *Following the Equator* (Mineola, N.Y.: Dover, 1989),119.
46. Quoted in Kaplan, *Mr. Clemens and Mark Twain*, 388.
47. Quoted in Cox, *Mark Twain*, 245.
48. Ibid., 237.
49. George E. Toles, "Mark Twain and *Pudd'nhead Wilson*: A House Divided," *Novel* 16 (1982): 74.
50. *Mark Twain-Howells Letters*, 2:689.
51. Mark Twain, *What Is Man?*, ed. Paul Baender (Berkeley: University of California Press, 1973), 124.
52. Jesse Bier, *The Rise and Fall of American Humor* (New York: Holt, Rhinehart, and Winston, 1968), 154.
53. Lewis P. Simpson, untitled review of *What Is Man?*, *American Literature* 45 (1973–74): 618.
54. Mark Twain, *"The Mysterious Stranger" and Other Stories* (Mineola, N.Y.: Dover, 1992), 121.
55. Ibid., 117.

Chapter Seven

1. P. M. Zall, ed., *Ben Franklin Laughing* (Berkeley: University of California Press, 1980), 142.
2. Thomas Mann, *Confessions of Felix Krull, Confidence Man*, trans. Denver Lindley (London: Penguin, 1958), 21, 94. All further quotations are from this edition.
3. John E. Seery, *Political Returns: Irony in Politics and Theory from Plato to the Antinuclear Movement* (Boulder: Westview Press, 1990), 10.
4. Thomas Mann, *Reflections of a Nonpolitical Man*, trans. Walter D. Morris (New York: Frederick Ungar, 1983), 3. All further quotations are from this edition.

5. Daniel W. Conway and John E. Seery, eds., *The Politics of Irony: Essays in Self-Betrayal* (New York: St. Martin's Press, 1992), 1–2.
6. Quoted in Zall, *Ben Franklin Laughing*, 153.
7. Ronald W. Clark, *Benjamin Franklin: A Biography* (London: Weidenfeld and Nicolson, 1983), 181, 304.
8. Quoted in Joseph Brennan, *Thomas Mann's World* (New York: Russell and Russell, 1962), 160.
9. Seery, *Political Returns*, 196–97. Unless otherwise noted, further quotations will be cited in parentheses.
10. Richard Rorty, *Contingency, Irony, and Solidarity* (Cambridge: Cambridge University Press, 1989), xv, 73.
11. Ibid., 79, 83.
12. Ibid., 73–74.
13. Seery, *Political Returns*, 261–62.
14. M. Bérubé and G. Graff, "Regulations for Literary Criticism in the 1990s," quoted in Linda Hutcheon, *Irony's Edge: The Theory and Politics of Irony* (London: Routledge, 1994), 7.
15. Alex Callinicos, *Against Postmodernism* (Cambridge: Polity Press, 1989), ix.
16. D. J. Enright, *The Alluring Problem: An Essay on Irony* (Oxford: Oxford University Press, 1986), 110.
17. Linda Hutcheon, *Irony's Edge: The Theory and Politics of Irony* (London: Routledge, 1994), 44.
18. Ibid., 27.
19. Quoted in Enright, *Alluring Problem*, 6.
20. Conway and Seery, *Politics of Irony*, 4.
21. Quoted in Enright, *Alluring Problem*, 20.
22. Quoted in William Keough, *Punchlines: The Violence of American Humor* (New York: Paragon House, 1990), xvi.
23. D. C. Muecke, *Irony* (London: Methuen, 1970), 20–21.

List of Sources

The A List. Comedy Central, 1992.

Allen, William Rodney, ed. *Conversations with Kurt Vonnegut.* Jackson: University Press of Mississippi, 1988.

Armstrong, A. Mac C. "The Idea of the Comic." *British Journal of Aesthetics* 25 (Summer 1985): 232–38.

Auletta, Ken. "Late-Night Gamble." *New Yorker,* February 1, 1993, 38–46.

Bakhtin, Mikhail. *The Dialogic Imagination.* Austin: University of Texas Press, 1981.

_____. *Rabelais and His World.* Bloomington: Indiana University Press, 1984.

Barnes, Clive. "Lenny: The Fine Art of Obscenity." *Times,* (London), June 5, 1971, 7.

Beidler, Philip D. "The 'Author' of Franklin's *Autobiography.*" *Early American Literature* 16 (Winter 1981–82): 257–69.

Berger, Phil. *The Last Laugh: The World of Standup Comics.* New York: Limelight Editions, 1985.

Bermant, Chaim. *What's the Joke: A Study of Jewish Humor through the Ages.* London: Weidenfeld and Nicolson, 1986.

Bier, Jesse. *The Rise and Fall of American Humor.* New York: Holt, Rinehart and Winston, 1968.

"Bill Hicks: The Serious Side of Comedy." *Campus Activities Today,* January 1994, 31–46.

"Bill Hicks's Humor." *Bryan/College Station,* May 1992, 9.

Blair, Walter. *Native American Humor.* San Francisco: Chandler, 1960.

Blair, Walter, and Hamlin Hill. *America's Humor: From Poor Richard to Doonesbury.* New York: Oxford University Press, 1978.

Booth, Wayne C. *The Rhetoric of Irony.* Chicago: University of Chicago Press, 1974.

Boulware, Jack. "Bill Hicks: High Plains Jester." *Nose,* March, 1993, 28–31.

Brennan, Joseph. *Thomas Mann's World.* New York: Russell and Russell, 1962.

Broer, Lawrence R. *Sanity Plea: Schizophrenia in the Novels of Kurt Vonnegut.* London: UMI Research Press, 1989.

Brooks, Van Wyck. *The Ordeal of Mark Twain.* New York: Meridian, 1955.

Bruce, Lenny, *The Berkeley Concert.* Bizarre/Reprise Records 6329.

_____. *The Essential Lenny Bruce,* ed. John Cohen. St. Albans: Panther, 1981.

_____. *The Essential Lenny Bruce: Politics.* Douglas Records 788.

_____. *How to Talk Dirty and Influence People.* St. Albans: Panther, 1981.

_____. *How to Talk Dirty and Influence People.* New York: Fireside, 1992.

————. *I Am Not a Nut, Elect Me!* Fantasy Records 7007.

————. *Lenny Bruce, American.* Fantasy Records 7011.

————. *Lenny Bruce Is Out Again.* Phillies Records 4010.

————. *The Midnight Concert.* United Artists Records 6794.

————. *The Sick Humor of Lenny Bruce.* Fantasy Records 7003.

————. *Thank You, Masked Man.* Fantasy Records 7017.

————. *What I Was Arrested For.* Douglas Records 2.

Buckley, Christopher. "Gotterdammerung-22." *New Yorker,* October 10, 1994, 104–9.

Buxbaum, Melvin H., ed. *Critical Essays on Benjamin Franklin.* Boston: G. K. Hall and Co., 1987.

Callinicos, Alex. *Against Postmodernism.* Cambridge: Polity Press, 1992.

Capzeyze. ACTV (Austin), 1993.

Carter, Bill. *The Late Shift: Letterman, Leno, and the Network Battle for the Night.* New York: Hyperion, 1995.

————. "Lots of Political Humor, and No Morton Kondracke." *New York Times,* February 27, 1994, 4–5.

Carr, Roy, et al. *The Hip: Hipsters, Jazz and the Beat Generation.* London: Faber, 1986.

Clark, Ronald W. *Benjamin Franklin: A Biography.* London: Weidenfeld and Nicolson, 1983.

Cohen, Sarah Blacher, ed. *Jewish Wry: Essays on Jewish Humor.* Bloomington: Indiana University Press, 1987.

Colfer, Patrick W. "The Spirit of Irony and the Problem of Negativity." Ph.D. diss., University of Edinburgh, 1981.

Conway, Daniel W., and John E. Seery, eds. *The Politics of Irony: Essays in Self-Betrayal.* New York: St. Martin's Press, 1992.

Cox, James M. *Mark Twain: The Fate of Humor.* Princeton: Princeton University Press, 1966.

Davies, Ioan. "Lenny Bruce: Hyperrealism and the Death of Jewish Tragic Humor." *Social Text* 22 (Spring 1989): 92–114.

DeMott, Benjamin. "The New Irony: Sickniks and Others." *American Scholar* 3 (Winter 1961–62): 108–19.

The Dennis Miller Show. Syndicated, 1992.

Desert Island Discs. BBC Radio 4, 1995.

"Dick Gregory Is Back." *New York Times,* June 6, 1993, B1.

Douglas, Mary. *Implicit Meanings: Essays in Anthropology.* London: Routledge and Kegan Paul, 1978.

Dudden, Arthur P., ed. *American Humor.* New York: Oxford University Press, 1987.

Duncan, Hugh Dalziel. *Communication and Social Order.* New York: Oxford University Press, 1962.

Eastman, Max. *Enjoyment of Laughter.* London: Johnson Reprint Co., 1970.

Eco, Umberto. *Travels in Hyper Reality.* London: Picador, 1987.

Edsall, Thomas Byrne. "America's Sweetheart." *New York Review of Books,* October 6, 1994, 6–10.

Edwards, Mark. "The Grin Reality." *Sunday Times*, (London), May 21, 1995, 4–5.

Ellison, Ralph. *Invisible Man*. London: Penguin, 1965.

———. *Shadow and Act*. London: Secker and Warburg, 1967.

Enright, D. J. *The Alluring Problem: An Essay on Irony*. Oxford: Oxford University Press, 1986.

Fisher, Seymour, and Rhoda Fisher. *Pretend the World Is Funny and Forever: A Psychological Analysis of Comedians, Clowns and Actors*. Hillsdale, N.J.: Erlbaum, 1981.

48 Hours. CBS-TV, 1991.

Franklin, Benjamin. *The Autobiography and Other Writings*. Edited by Kenneth Silverman. Harmondsworth: Penguin, 1986.

———. *Ben Franklin Laughing*. Edited by P. M. Zall. Berkeley: University of California Press, 1980.

———. *Franklin's Wit and Folly: The Bagatelles*. Edited by Richard E. Amacher. New Brunswick: Rutgers University Press, 1953.

———. *The Papers of Benjamin Franklin*, vol. 1. Edited by Leonard W. Labaree and Whitfield J. Bell. New Haven: Yale University Press, 1960.

———. *The Writings of Benjamin Franklin*. 10 vols. Edited by Albert Henry Smyth. New York: Macmillan, 1906.

Freud, Sigmund. *Jokes and Their Relation to the Unconscious*. Translated by James Strachey with Anna Freud. New York: Norton, 1960.

Gillman, Susan. *Dark Twins: Imposture and Identity in Mark Twain's America*. Chicago: University of Chicago Press, 1989.

Gillman, Susan, and Forrest Robinson, eds. *Mark Twain's "Pudd'nhead Wilson": Race, Conflict and Culture*. Durham: Duke University Press, 1990.

Gleason, Ralph. "The Trials of Lenny Bruce." *Guardian*, (London) April 27, 1965, 9.

Goldberg, Carey. "Welcome to New York, Capital of Profanities." *New York Times*, June 19, 1995, B2–B3.

Goldman, Albert. "The Comedy of Lenny Bruce." *London Magazine* 3 (January 1964): 68–75.

———. *Freakshow*. New York: Atheneum, 1971.

———. *Ladies and Gentlemen . . . Lenny Bruce!!* New York: Random House, 1974.

Good, Edwin M. *Irony in the Old Testament*. Philadelphia: Westminster Press, 1965.

Hall, Max. *Benjamin Franklin and Polly Baker: The History of a Literary Deception*. Pittsburgh: University of Pittsburgh Press, 1990.

Hauck, Richard B. *A Cheerful Nihilism: Confidence and the Absurd in American Humorous Fiction*. Bloomington: Indiana University Press, 1971.

Heller, Erich. *The Ironic German: A Study of Thomas Mann*. Boston: Little, Brown and Co., 1958.

Hicks, Bill. "Bill Hicks on Television . . . Sometimes." Unpublished, 1993. Courtesy of the Estate of Bill Hicks.

_____. *Dangerous*. Invasion Records, 1990.

_____. *Relentless*. Invasion Records, 1992.

_____. *Relentless* (video). Tiger Aspects, 1992.

_____. *Sane Man* (video). Sacred Cow/Bula Bula, 1989.

_____. *Totally Bill Hicks* (video). Tiger Aspects/Channel 4, 1994.

Hoffman, Daniel G. *Form and Fable in American Fiction*. New York: Oxford University Press, 1961.

The Howard Stern Show. WXRK (New York), 1993.

Huizinga, Johan. *Homo Ludens: A Study of the Play Element in Culture*. London: Routledge and Kegan Paul, 1949.

Hutcheon, Linda. *Irony's Edge: The Theory and Politics of Irony*. London: Routledge, 1994.

"Innocence and Experience." *Times Literary Supplement*, August 12, 1960, 512.

Kaplan, Justin. *Mr. Clemens and Mark Twain*. London: Jonathan Cape, 1967.

Keepnews, Orrin. "Without Apology: The Existential Jazz Aura of Lenny Bruce." *Downbeat*, November 3, 1966, 42.

Keillor, Garrison. *Lake Wobegon Days*. London: Faber, 1989.

_____. *A Prairie Home Companion*. National Public Radio broadcasts (1980–81).

_____. *We Are Still Married*. London: Faber, 1993.

Keough, William. *Punchlines: The Violence of American Humor*. New York: Paragon House, 1990.

Kerouac, Jack. *On the Road*. London: Penguin, 1991.

Kershaw, Justine, and David Helton. "Dressing for Dinner." *Hunters in the Wild*. BBC Television, 1993.

Kierkegaard, Søren. *The Concept of Irony, with Constant Reference to Socrates*. Translated by Lee M. Capel. New York: Harper and Row, 1966.

Kline, Michael. "Narrative Strategies in Garrison Keillor's 'Lake Wobegon' Stories." *Studies in American Humor* 6 (1988): 129–40.

Klinkowitz, Jerome, and John Somer, eds. *The Vonnegut Statement*. St. Albans: Panther, 1975.

Kofsky, Frank. *Lenny Bruce: The Comedian as Social Critic and Secular Moralist*. New York: Monad Press, 1974.

Koltnow, Barry. "The Face of Humor to Come?" *Orange County Register*, June 8, 1993, 4 ("Show" section).

Koziski, Stephanie. "The Standup Comedian as Anthropologist." *Journal of Popular Culture* 18 (1984): 57–76.

Kuhlman, Susan. *Knave, Fool and Genius: The Confidence Man in Nineteenth-Century Literature*. Chapel Hill: University of North Carolina Press, 1973.

Lahr, John. "The Goat Boy Rises." *New Yorker*, November 1, 1993, 113–21.

Laroche, Jacques M., and Claude J. Fouillade. "A Socio-Cultural Reading of *Lake Wobegon Days*, or Can You Go Home Again to Mid-America?" *Revue Francaise d'Etudes Americaines* 14 (November 1989): 427–38.

Lawrence, D. H. *Studies in Classic American Literature*. London: Penguin, 1971.

_____. *The Symbolic Meaning*. New York: Centaur, 1962.

Leary, Denis. *No Cure for Cancer*. London: Picador, 1992.

_____. *No Cure for Cancer* (video). Full Circle Films, 1992.

Lee, Judith Yaross. *Garrison Keillor: A Voice of America*. Jackson: University Press of Mississippi, 1992.

Legman, Gershon. *No Laughing Matter: An Analysis of Sexual Humor*, 2 vols. Bloomington: Indiana University Press, 1982.

Lenz, William E. *Fast Talk and Flush Times: The Confidence Man as a Literary Convention*. Columbia: University of Missouri Press, 1985.

Levine, Jacob, and Fredrich Redlich. "Failure to Understand Humor." *Psychoanalytic Quarterly* 24 (1955): 560–72.

Lewis, Sinclair. *The Man from Main Street*, ed. Harry E. Maule and Melville H. Cane. London: Heinemann, 1954.

_____. *Main Street*. London: Penguin, 1991.

Lhamon, William T. *Deliberate Speed: The Origins of a Cultural Style in the American 1950s*. Washington, D.C.: Smithsonian Institution Press, 1990.

Lindberg, Gary. *The Confidence Man in American Literature*. New York: Oxford University Press, 1982.

Mailer, Norman. *Advertisements for Myself*. London: Corgi, 1961.

Mann, Thomas. *Confessions of Felix Krull, Confidence Man*. Translated by Denver Lindley. London: Penguin, 1958.

_____. *Reflections of a Nonpolitical Man*. Translated by Walter D. Morris. New York: Frederick Unger, 1983.

McLellan, Dennis. "Hard-Line Look at Humor." *Los Angeles Times*, June 10, 1993, 6–7.

Melville, Herman. *The Letters of Herman Melville*. Edited by Merrell R. Davis and William M. Gilman. New Haven: Yale University Press, 1960.

_____. *Mardi*. Evanston: Northwestern University Press, 1970.

_____. *Moby-Dick*. New York: W. W. Norton, 1967.

_____. *Pierre, Israel Potter, The Confidence-Man, Tales, and Billy Budd* (Library of America edition). New York: Literary Classics of the United States, Inc., 1984.

Michelson, Bruce. "Keillor and Rolvaag and the Art of Telling the Truth." *American Studies* 30 (Spring 1989): 21–34.

Miller, John E. "The Distance Between Gopher Prairie and Lake Wobegon: Sinclair Lewis and Garrison Keillor on the Small Town Experience." *Centennial Review* 31 (Fall 1987): 432–46.

Miller, Jonathan. "The Sick White Negro." *Partisan Review* (Spring 1963): 149–55.

Morse, Donald E. "Monkeys, Changelings, and Asses: Audience, Fantasy and Belief." In *Aspects of Fantasy*. Edited by William Coyle. Westport: Greenwood Press, 1986.

Muecke, D. C. *The Compass of Irony*. London: Methuen, 1969.
_____. *Irony*. London: Methuen, 1970.
_____. *Irony and the Ironic*. London: Methuen, 1982.
Muggeridge, Malcolm. "America Needs a *Punch*." *Esquire*, April 1958, 59–61.
_____. "Books." *Esquire*, November 1965, 65–66.
Mushabac, Jane. *Melville's Humor*. Hamden, Conn.: Archon, 1981.
Mustazza, Leonard. *Forever Pursuing Genesis: The Myth of Eden in the Novels of Kurt Vonnegut*. Lewisburg, Pa.: Bucknell University Press, 1990.
Nachman, Gerald. "Beware the Bark and Bite of Bill Hicks." *San Francisco Chronicle*, November 7, 1993, B3, B7.
Night After Night. Comedy Central, 1992.
Olderman, Raymond. *Beyond the Wasteland*. London: Yale University Press, 1972.
One Night Stand. HBO, 1991.
Paine, Albert Bigelow. *Mark Twain: A Biography*, 2 vols. London: Harpers, 1912.
Poe, Edgar Allan. *Comedies and Sketches*. Harmondsworth: Penguin, 1988.
Powell, Chris, and George E. C. Paton, eds. *Humor in Society: Resistance and Control*. London: Macmillan, 1988.
Purdie, Susan. *Comedy: The Mastery of Discourse*. London: Harvester Wheatsheaf, 1993.
Quirk, Tom. *Melville's Confidence–Man: From Knave to Knight*. Columbia: University of Missouri Press, 1982.
Rankin, H. D. "A Modest Proposal About the *Republic*." *Apeiron* 2 (1968): 20–22.
Rorty, Richard. *Contingency, Irony, and Solidarity*. Cambridge: Cambridge University Press, 1989.
Rosenberry, E. H. *Melville and the Comic Spirit*. Cambridge: Harvard University Press, 1955.
Ross, Andrew. *No Respect: Intellectuals and Popular Culture*. London: Routledge, 1989.
Rourke, Constance. *American Humor*. Garden City, N.Y.: Doubleday, 1931.
Rubio, Jeff. "Bill Hicks: A Comic of Ideas." *Orange County Register*, November 7, 1993, 4.
Safer, Elaine B. *The Contemporary American Comic Epic*. Detroit: Wayne State University Press, 1989.
Sager, Mike. "The Gospel According to Hicks." *GQ*, September 1992, 288–95.
Sales, Grover. "Dagos and Niggers and Kikes, Oh My." *Nation*, December 7, 1992, 2.
Sarko, Anita. "Bill Hicks Is the Missing Link American Comedy Has Been Looking For." *Ray Gun*, August 1993, 5.
Schreffler, Peter Hans. "Caught Between Two Worlds: The Spiritual Predicament and Rhetorical Ambivalence of Garrison Keillor." Ph.D diss., Bowling Green State University, 1990.

Schulz, Max. "The Unconfirmed Thesis." *Critique* 12 (1971): 5–28.

Seely, John D. *Melville: The Ironic Diagram*. Evanston: Northwestern University Press, 1970.

Seery, John C. *Political Returns: Irony in Politics and Theory from Plato to the Antinuclear Movement*. Boulder: Westview Press, 1990.

Simpson, Lewis P. Untitled review of *What Is Man?*. *American Literature* 45 (1973–74): 617–18.

Smith, Henry Nash. *Mark Twain: The Development of a Writer*. Cambridge: Harvard University Press, 1962.

Sorenson, Edith. "In the Outlaw Area." *Houston Press*, June 3, 1993, 21, 23.

Stern, Doug. "Profile: Bill Hicks." *Austin Comic News*, February 1993, 7.

Swearingen, C. Jan. *Rhetoric and Irony: Western Literacy and Western Lies*. New York: Oxford University Press, 1991.

Tanner, Tony. *City of Words*. New York: Harper and Row, 1971.

_____. "Reviews and Comment." *Critical Quarterly* 4 (1962): 381.

The Texas Radio Program. KUT (Austin), 1994.

Thomas, William Karl. *Lenny Bruce: The Making of a Prophet*. Hamden, Conn.: Archon Books, 1989.

Thurber, James. "The State of the Nation's Humor." *New York Times Magazine*, December 7, 1958, 26.

Todd, Richard. "The Masks of Kurt Vonnegut." *New York Times Magazine*, January 24, 1971, 16–27.

Toles, George E. "Mark Twain and *Pudd'nhead Wilson*: A House Divided." *Novel* 16 (1982): 55–75.

Twain, Mark. *The Adventures of Huckleberry Finn*. Harmondsworth: Penguin, 1981.

_____. *The Autobiography of Mark Twain*. Edited by Albert Bigelow Paine. London: Harpers, 1912.

_____. *The Autobiography of Mark Twain*. Edited by Charles Neider. London: Chatto and Windus, 1960.

_____. *The Complete Humorous Sketches and Tales of Mark Twain*. Edited by Charles Neider. Garden City, N.Y.: Doubleday, 1961.

_____. *The Devil's Race-Track: Mark Twain's Great Dark Writings*. Edited by John S. Tuckey. Berkeley: University of California Press, 1980.

_____. *Following the Equator*. Mineola, N.Y.: Dover, 1989.

_____. *Letters from the Earth*. Edited by Bernard DeVoto. New York: Harper and Row, 1974.

_____. *Mark Twain to Mrs. Fairbanks*. Edited by Dixon Wecter. San Marino, Calif.: Huntington Library, 1949.

_____. *Mark Twain's Contributions to "The Galaxy."* Edited by Bruce McElderry. Gainesville, Fla.: Scholars' Reprints, 1961.

_____. *Mark Twain's Notebooks and Journals*, 3 vols. Edited by Robert P. Browning et al. Berkeley: University of California Press, 1979.

_____. *"The Mysterious Stranger" and Other Stories*. New York: Dover, 1992.

_____. *Pudd'nhead Wilson*. Harmondsworth: Penguin, 1981.

_____. *Tales, Speeches, Essays, and Sketches.* Edited by Tom Quirk. Harmondsworth: Penguin, 1994.

_____. *The Unabridged Mark Twain*, 2 vols. Edited by Lawrence Teacher. Philadelphia: Running Press, 1976.

_____. *What Is Man?* Edited by Paul Baender. Berkeley: University of California Press, 1973.

Twain, Mark, and William Dean Howells. *Mark Twain-Howells Letters*, 2 vols. Edited by Henry Nash Smith and William M. Gibson. Cambridge: Harvard University Press, 1960.

Vonnegut, Kurt. *Bluebeard.* London: Flamingo, 1992.

_____. *Breakfast of Champions.* London: Vintage, 1992.

_____. *Cat's Cradle.* London: Penguin, 1965.

_____. *Deadeye Dick.* London: Flamingo, 1992.

_____. *Fates Worse than Death.* London: Jonathan Cape, 1991.

_____. *Galapagos.* London: Flamingo, 1994.

_____. *God Bless You, Mr. Rosewater.* London: Vintage, 1992.

_____. *Hocus Pocus.* London: Vintage, 1991.

_____. *Jailbird.* London: Vintage, 1992.

_____. *Mother Night.* London: Vintage, 1992.

_____. *Palm Sunday.* London: Jonathan Cape, 1991.

_____. *Slapstick.* London: Vintage, 1991.

_____. *Slaughterhouse-Five.* London: Paladin, 1989.

_____. *Wampeters, Foma, and Granfalloons.* New York: Dell, 1979.

Wadlington, Warwick. *The Confidence Game in American Literature.* Princeton: Princeton University Press, 1975.

Wilbers, Stephen. "Lake Wobegon: Mythical Place and the American Imagination." *American Studies* 30 (Spring 1989): 5–20.

Wister, Owen. *The Virginian.* New York: Penguin, 1988.

Wolcott, James. "The Dennis Menace." *New Yorker*, June 6, 1994, 87–89.

_____. "Radical Cheek." *New Yorker*, September 5, 1994, 108–10.

Wood, Michael. "Vonnegut's Softer Focus." *New York Times Book Review*, September 9, 1979, 1, 22–24.

Wright, Andrew H. "Irony and Fiction." *Journal of Aesthetics and Art Criticism* 12 (September 1953): 111–18.

Index

Alcott, Louisa May, 220
Allen, Steve, 75, 87

Bakhtin, Mikhail, 101, 240
Balzac, Honoré de, 43
Barnum, P. T., 52
Barthes, Roland, 240
Bateson, Gregory, 13
Bellow, Saul, 89
Belzer, Len, 119
Belzer, Richard, 119, 142
Benny, Jack, 72, 87, 89
Berle, Milton, 72, 84, 85, 87
Bernhard, Sarah, 118
Bierce, Ambrose, 115
Bishop, Joey, 87
Bogosian, Eric, 110, 111, 118, 119, 132
Brice, Fanny, 89
Bruce, Lenny, 16, 38, 59, 70–112, 142, 147, 148, 187, 229; and Catholicism, 94–97; charges of obscenity, 98–104; convictions, 111, 112; and drugs, 74, 81–82, 107; compared with Bill Hicks, 115, 118, 119, 125, 135, 143, 144, 146; as hipster, 74–76, 86; ironic identity, 107, 112; and irony fatigue, 16; and jazz, 74–77; Jewishness, 86–94; and language taboos, 100–103; as martyr, 110–11; and rules, 103–4; on satire, 236; and sexuality, 83–84; as "sick comic," 84–85, 105–6; as spoil-sport, 16, 71, 86, 97–98, 107, 112; and truth telling, 78, 97–98, 107; as "White Negro," 86, 87

Buckley, Lord, 77
Buffoonery, 37, 62. *See also* Twain, Mark
Butler, Brett, 118, 121–22, 134, 140

Cable, George Washington, 193
Caesar, Sid, 87
Callinicos, Alex, 240
Camus, Albert, 237
Carlin, George, 114, 122
Castro, Fidel, 80
Chase, Chevy, 134
Chomsky, Noam, 114, 144
Clay, Andrew Dice, 118
Clemens, Samuel. *See* Twain, Mark
Comedian: as anthropologist, 106–7; as confidence man, 14, 15, 20, 57, 58–69, 147, 149, 150, 154, 167, 168, 170, 171, 174, 216, 219; as social critic, 11, 12, 36, 38, 40, 45, 240–41; as spoil-sport, 63, 64. *See also* Buffoonery, Fool, Spoilsport
Comedy, as drug, 178–79
Confidence men, 51–53, 65, 208
Conway, Daniel, 13, 39, 234, 236
Cooper, Gary, 14, 20, 242
Cosby, Bill, 118, 134
Crosby, Bing, 72

Davis, Sammy, Jr., 110
Defoe, Daniel, 38
Derrida, Jacques, 240
Diller, Phyllis, 87
Dumas, Charles, 44
Durst, Will, 118

Eastman, Max, 13, 14, 20, 60, 189
Eco, Umberto, 13, 20, 103, 189

Eisenhower, Dwight, 78, 79
Ellison, Ralph, 61–62, 73
Emerson, Ralph Waldo, 68, 197

Fairbanks, Mary, 193, 196
Fool, 60
Foxx, Redd, 122
Franklin, Benjamin, 15, 16, 17, 41–
    51, 232, 241; as confidence
    man, 15, 41–45, 51; critics of,
    45–51; hoaxes by, 41–45;
    ironic identity, 35, 45–47; as
    politician, 37, 235, 236–37; in
    Israel Potter (Melville), 15, 53,
    55–58; *Autobiography,* 15, 45,
    46, 47–51

Gaillard, Slim, 75, 76
Gallagher, Jack, 145–46
Goldberg, Whoopi, 134
Gould, Jay, 52
Grant, Ulysses S., 197–98
Greene, Graham, 40
Gregory, Dick, 78, 187
Grizzard, Lewis, 114
Gysin, Brion, 73

Hall, Arsenio, 131
Hawthorne, Nathaniel, 47, 53
Heller, Joseph, 166
Herblock (Herbert Block), 40, 237
Hicks, Bill, 16–17, 38, 113–46, 147,
    187; and advertising, 135,
    140–42; compared with Lenny
    Bruce, 115, 118, 119, 125, 135,
    143, 144, 146; and Gulf War,
    131–33; and irony, 115–17,
    130, 142, 144, 145; ironic iden-
    tity, 144; and *Letterman Show,*
    120–30; and truth telling, 115,
    118, 135, 144–45; and War on
    Drugs, 135–40; "The Cen-
    sored Seven Minutes," 125–29
Hipness, 74; "Hepcat Dictionaries,"
    75; linguistic hipness, 74–76
Holmes, Oliver Wendell, 197, 222

Hope, Bob, 72
Howells, William Dean, 194, 196
Hughes, Sean, 119
Huizinga, Johan, 12, 13, 14, 20–21,
    50, 97, 189, 233. *See also*
    Spoilsport
Hutcheon, Linda, 240, 241

Ironic identity, 12–16, 35–40, 45–46,
    107, 112, 147, 233, 235, 242.
    See also specific authors/co-
    medians
Irony, 12, 13, 35–40, 234–42; defini-
    tions of, 36–37; as political
    weapon, 233–39
Irony fatigue, 8, 12–18, 239–41

Jeni, Richard, 119, 122, 144
Jessel, George, 89
Jolson, Al, 89
Jones, John Paul, 44, 58

Keepnews, Orrin, 74
Keillor, Garrison, 15, 16, 26–35, 117,
    147, 148–49, 187, 241; and im-
    potence of comedy, 149; and
    irony fatigue, 15, 16. Works:
    Lake Wobegon Days, 32–35;
    Leaving Home, 29; *A Prairie
    Home Companion,* 29–31; *We
    Are Still Married,* 35
Kennedy, John F., 79
Kerouac, Jack, 73
Kierkegaard, Søren, 13, 117, 165
Kinison, Sam, 118

Lahr, John, 113, 116, 123, 125, 130,
    143, 144
Laine, Frankie, 110
Langdon, Olivia, 192, 196
Lawrence, D. H., 15, 47, 48, 49–50,
    55, 58
Leary, Denis, 118, 119
Leno, Jay, 113, 120, 122, 131, 134,
    142

Letterman, David, 113, 116, 134, 142; *Letterman Show*, 113, 115–16, 120–30
Lewis, Jerry, 84, 89
Lewis, Sinclair, 14–15, 16, 21–27, 187; ironic identity, 35. Works: *Babbit*, 27; *Main Street*, 14, 16, 21–26, 27, 28–29, 241
Liddy, Gordon, 117
Limbaugh, Rush, 114, 117, 118, 131, 145

Mailer, Norman, 72, 74, 75
Malamud, Bernard, 89
Mann, Thomas, 18, 232–37, 240. Works: *Confessions of Felix Krull, Confidence Man*, 18, 232–33, 236; "Mario and the Magician," 59; *Reflections of a Nonpolitical Man*, 18, 233–35, 237
McCarthyism, 72, 78, 90
Melville, Herman, 53–69, 70, 109, 121, 149, 150, 154, 185; as confidence man, 53; and Benjamin Franklin, 46–48, 53, 55–58; ironic identity, 35; and race, 61–63; and truth telling, 53–55, 241; and Mark Twain, 204, 217, 218, 228. Works: "Bartleby," 53, 54; "Benito Cereno," 54, 62; *The Confidence-Man*, 14, 15, 18, 57, 58, 59–69, 154, 170, 204, 217, 218, 224, 225, 228; *Israel Potter*, 15, 55–58, 170; *Mardi*, 54; *Moby-Dick*, 54, 176; *Omoo*, 54; *Pierre*, 54; *Typee*, 54
Miller, Dennis, 118, 120, 131
Miller, Jonathan, 74, 84, 105
Milosz, Czeslaw, 241
Molière, Jean Baptiste Poquelin de, 78
Morton, Robert, 121, 122, 123, 124
Muggeridge, Malcolm, 72, 107–8
Murphy, Eddie, 118

Newhart, Bob, 78

Osborne, John, 13

Plath, Sylvia, 73
Poe, Edgar Allan, 52
Pollock, Jackson, 168, 169, 182, 184

Rabelais, François, 89, 101
Rorty, Richard, 13, 239
Roseanne, 118, 134
Roth, Philip, 89
Ruby, Jack, 91
Rushdie, Salman, 21, 97

Sahl, Mort, 77, 78
Sales, Grover, 187
Satire, 37–40, 194, 236
Sartre, Jean-Paul, 239–40
Scallywag, 115
Seery, John, 13, 39, 233–39
Seinfeld, Jerry, 118, 134
Shaw, George Bernard, 11, 194
Skelton, Red, 72
Spoilsport, 12, 14, 21, 28–29, 63, 64, 71, 86, 112, 153, 188, 230–31; literary critic as, 240; social critic as, 21–26
Swift, Jonathan, 38, 115, 116–17, 142, 238

Television companies: CBS, 113, 121, 123, 124, 125, 129, 130; CNN, 132; Public Access TV, 133–34; NBC, 121, 123
Thompson, William ("The Confidence Man"), 52
Thoreau, Henry David, 68
Thurber, James, 72
Tucker, Sophie, 87, 89, 110
Twain, Mark, 12, 18, 20, 28, 47, 48, 51, 70–71, 148–49, 152, 187–231, 241; and alter ego, 12, 188, 195, 196, 223; as buffoon, 188, 193, 196, 220, 230; as comic/critic, 188, 191, 204,

215, 216–17, 223; and confidence games, 189, 216, 229, 231; creative blocks, 204; and Benjamin Franklin, 15, 48, 219; ironic identity, 69–70, 188, 216, 221; and Herman Melville, 204, 217, 218, 228; and *nom de plume*, 188–99, 223; rejection of comedy, 216, 217, 221, 231; and slavery, 224–25; as spoilsport, 188, 189, 230–31; and twins, 221–22. Works: *The Adventures of Huckleberry Finn*, 187, 189, 190, 192, 195–98, 199–217, 225; *The Adventures of Tom Sawyer*, 190, 194, 195, 199; "The Celebrated Jumping Frog of Calaveras County," 191; *A Connecticut Yankee in King Arthur's Court*, 190, 218–19; "The Facts Concerning the Recent Carnival of Crime in Connecticut," 195, 202; *The Gilded Age* (with Charles Dudley Warner), 194, 224; *The Innocents Abroad*, 191–92, 193; *Letters from the Earth*, 189; *Life on the Mississippi*, 190, 198; "Mark Twain's (Burlesque) Autobiography," 223; *The Mysterious Stranger*, 189, 203, 212, 230; "The Personal Habits of the Siamese Twins," 221; *The Personal Recollections of Joan of Arc*, 190; *The Prince and the Pauper*, 195–96, 220; "The Private History of a Campaign that Failed," 190; *Pudd'nhead Wilson*, 18, 189, 212, 217–29; *Roughing It*, 190; *Sketches, New and Old*, 196; "Those Extraordinary Twins," 221; "To the California Pioneers," 190; *What Is Man?* 189, 190, 203, 230

Tynan, Kenneth, 74

Ulysses (Joyce), 103

Vanderbilt, Cornelius, 52
Vidale, Thea, 121, 122
Vonnegut, Kurt, 17–18, 40, 42, 46–47, 59, 98, 101–2, 122, 147–86, 232, 233, 237–38; and abstract expressionism, 182–84; censorship of, 151–52; as comic/critic, 149–50, 152, 170, 175, 186; and confidence games, 11, 149, 155–56, 167–68, 174; as confidence man, 174; ironic identity, 151; and Herman Melville, 149–50, 154, 176, 185; and schizophrenia, 150, 151, 165–66, 167, 173, 241; and Mark Twain, 186, 187. Works: *Bluebeard*, 166, 177, 184; *Breakfast of Champions*, 11, 16, 166–67, 170–74; *Cat's Cradle*, 18, 149, 150, 151, 152, 154, 160–66, 168, 178; *Deadeye Dick*, 177–81, 184; *Fates Worse than Death*, 148, 166, 175; *Galapagos*, 175–76, 181; *God Bless You, Mr. Rosewater*, 168–69; *Hocus Pocus*, 103–4, 122, 147–48, 160, 166, 175, 177, 184–86; *Jailbird*, 176–77; *Mother Night*, 149, 150, 152, 154–60; *Slapstick*, 149, 150, 153–54, 175, 181; *Slaughterhouse-Five*, 169, 173

Walker, Alice, 73
Warner, Charles Dudley, 194, 224
Weber, Max, 47
Whittier, John Greenleaf, 197
Williams, William Carlos, 47

Youngman, Henny, 85